The Princeton Review

GMAT VERBAL workout

by Doug French

Random House, Inc.
New York

Princeton Review Publishing, L.L.C.
2315 Broadway
New York, NY   10024
E-mail: comments@review.com

ISBN: 0-375-75417-2

GMAT is a registered trademark of the Graduate Management Admission Council, which does not endorse this book.

Editor: Gretchen Feder
Production Editor: Kristen Azzara
Production Coordinator: Stephanie Martin

Manufactured in the United States of America on partially recycled paper.

9 8 7 6 5 4 3

First Edition

CONTENTS

ACKNOWLEDGMENTS

Gretchen Feder has edited three books' worth of my writing, and she has always been great to work with. Thanks for asking all the right questions and providing all the right answers. And thanks to Stephanie Martin, who made it all look good.

I'm especially indebted to Jack Schieffer and Rob Tallia, the directors who have supervised almost all of the GMAT course development work that I've done for The Princeton Review. Thanks for the work, boys.

Thanks as well to the many hundreds of GMAT students I've helped over the years, all of whom have helped me become a better instructor. My most challenging and satisfying teaching experience was the three-month course I taught at Samsung in South Korea, where my students were gluttons for homework. Much of this book derives from my experiences during that course; thanks for teaching me that the best weapons against the GMAT are diligence and patience.

And lastly, I owe a lot to the GMAT itself. I met my wife, Magda, while we were working on one of The Princeton Review's course revision projects. If the computer-adaptive test had not been implemented back in 1996, I probably wouldn't be the happily married slob I am today.

INTRODUCTION

THE IMPORTANCE OF BEING VERBAL

Welcome to The Princeton Review's *GMAT Verbal Workout*. If you've just purchased this book (or you're just casually browsing while you throw back your third cup of overpriced coffee), you probably fall into one of the following three categories:

(1) You're about the take the GMAT and you feel okay about the math section, but you need to brush up on your verbal skills so that you can get the best score possible;

(2) You're about the take the GMAT, you're petrified that you'll bomb it, and you've made it your goal to get the best test prep guide to ensure that you will avoid utter humiliation;

(3) You have no plans to take the GMAT, but you're just one of those people who digs books about grammar and wants to learn to read more efficiently.

If your circumstances match any of those above, you've found the right book. Sure, there are many prep guides for taking the GMAT (and as the GMAT increases in importance, these guides are sure to multiply), but this one is especially designed to concentrate *only on your verbal skills*. If you want to follow a test prep book that reviews all aspects of the GMAT, check out The Princeton Review's *Cracking the GMAT*. For further, specific review of the math section of the GMAT, The Princeton Review's *GMAT Math Workout* is an excellent resource.

Having strong verbal skills extends beyond increasing your appreciation of proper grammar and learning how to deconstruct arguments. Applying to business school is a decidedly verbal process, during which you will be judged by how well you assimilate information and how well you express yourself. If you doubt this, just look at all of the essays on Harvard's business school application. Most applicants don't get into b-school because they know the Pythagorean theorem or can calculate π to the 1,000th decimal place. Most students gain admission because their essays eloquently tell admissions committees about themselves and indicate how well they can share ideas with others.

This book's purpose is twofold. First and foremost, the goal of this book is to teach you how to improve your score on the GMAT's verbal section. But we're also going to look at the bigger picture; by learning to read aggressively and write expressively, you'll build skills that will serve you long after you gleefully descend some podium clutching your M.B.A. diploma.

Granted, our goal is not to turn you into James Joyce (especially since he's dead and all). It's just that in the business world, verbal skills are too often overlooked. If you can master the skills discussed herein, applying to business school and succeeding once you are there will be a lot easier.

A LITTLE HISTORY LESSON

The problems on the GMAT haven't changed much since Education Testing Service (ETS) first created it. In fact, most of the changes to the GMAT have been structural, and they've happened within the past decade.

At the beginning of the 1990s, the GMAT consisted of seven 30-minute sections: three verbal, three math, and one experimental. The three verbal sections were Sentence Correction (25 questions), Critical Reasoning (also known as Arguments, 20 questions), and Reading Comprehension (three passages, 25 questions). In sum, students spent 90 minutes to answer 70 questions; which figures to about 1 minute 17 seconds per question.

Then, in October 1994, the Analytical Writing Assessment (AWA) came along. The AWA consisted (and still does) of two essays—Analysis of an Issue and Analysis of an Argument—that students were given 30 minutes to write. To make room for this extra hour of work, ETS shortened each of the seven sections by five minutes. With these changes there were 22 Sentence Correction questions, 16 Arguments, and 18 Reading Comp questions (total: 56 questions) to analyze in 75 minutes. Average time per question: 1 minute 20 seconds. Not that three seconds is a colossal difference, but an improvement nonetheless.

We would then see the end of the paper-and-pencil (P&P) version of the GMAT.

Along Came the CAT

With the advent of the Computer-Adaptive Test (CAT) in October 1996, the sections have now been merged into one big 75-minute verbal behemoth. The types of questions (even the experimental ones) are all mingled together, so you'll probably see a Sentence Correction question, then a Reading Comp passage with four questions, then an Argument.

How the CAT Works

When a section begins, the first question you'll see will be in the medium difficulty range. If you get it right, you'll see a question that's a little harder; if you get it wrong, your next question will be easier. It's kind of like going on a job interview: you want to make a good impression right away; otherwise you have to try to make up ground later on. On the CAT, if you get a lot of questions wrong on the outset, the computer will send you easier questions because it will think you can't handle the hard ones. Even if you answer all the rest correctly, the CAT won't be impressed.

That's why it's important to take a lot of time on the early questions while the computer is still finding out about you. As the section progresses, a right or wrong question has less of an impact on your overall score. In fact, the computer has a pretty good idea what your verbal score will be when the section is about half over.

THE STRUCTURE OF THE TEST

When you take the GMAT, you'll spend about four hours in front of a computer screen. Your experience will go something like this:

- ◆ **Check-In:** You show your ID, fill out some paperwork, and wait for a computer to become available. Depending on the efficiency of your test site, this could take a long time. Use the waiting period to relax. Review a few problems if you want, or just read the paper and get your mind off the exam.

- ◆ **Tutorial:** ETS can't assume that you have all the computer skills necessary to work the CAT (even though you probably do), so the first thing you see when you reach your seat is an untimed tutorial about how to use a mouse, how to cut and paste, and how to enter answer choices—all basic stuff.

- ◆ **Essays:** The AWA consists of two essays: Analysis of an Issue and Analysis of an Argument. Each takes 30 minutes and is scored on a scale of one to six, and then the two scores are averaged. This score is *not* factored into your three-digit GMAT score. You get a separate essay score when you receive your official score report from ETS.

- ◆ **Five-Minute Break I:** Chug a soda, do some jumping jacks, whatever makes you happy and keeps you alert, but be prompt. The break is timed on your computer, and it will start the next section with or without you.

- ◆ **Math Section:** You get 75 minutes to answer 37 multiple-choice questions (including 9 that are experimental). If you're looking for insight on this section, you've got the wrong book—The Princeton Review's *GMAT Math Workout* is for you.

- ◆ **Five-Minute Break II**

- ◆ **Verbal Section:** You get 75 minutes to answer 41 multiple-choice questions (11 of which are experimental). The three types of questions—Sentence Correction, Arguments, and Reading Comprehension—are interspersed throughout the section.

- ◆ **Scores Delivered:** Before you leave, a site worker will hand you a folded piece of paper with your unofficial scores on it (excluding essays, which are graded separately). The written confirmation will arrive two to three weeks later in the mail.

How to Register

You can take the test during the first three weeks of every month, and it will cost you 150 smackers. The easiest way to register is through your computer; if you check out ETS' GMAT web site (www.gmat.org), you can find information on all sorts of topics, including:

- the latest GMAT information, including upcoming M.B.A. forums
- sample test questions
- AWA essay topics
- testing sites (and phone numbers)
- links to 500 business schools
- financial aid information

You can also e-mail ETS at www.gmat@ets.org and someone will get back to you.

If you're still doing things the old-fashioned way, give 'em a call at (609) 771-7330 (note that those cheapos do *not* have an 800 number) and ask them to send you a registration form.

DEPRESSION . . . AND CATHARSIS

At first, many students reacted negatively to the computer format, because different types of questions arrive in rapid-fire order. Plus, using the mouse to click on an answer can seem disconcerting when you're trying to eliminate wrong answers, because you can't cross 'em out.

When you think about it, though, there really isn't much to be upset about. Like any change, the new computer format has good points and bad points. Let's get the brief rundown out of the way now.

Depression . . .

- You can't skip any questions; you must answer every one.
- You can't cross off answer choices on the page or take notes in the margins of the exam like you could on the P&P.
- You'd better learn to type, because you have to type your essays.
- The test costs about three times as much as it used to.

. . . Catharsis!

- There are a lot fewer verbal questions on the CAT (41) than on the old P&P (56).
- The questions themselves haven't changed that much, so the techniques that The Princeton Review has been teaching for years (most of which are outlined in this book) still work.

- Since the time limit is the same but there are fewer questions, you have a lot more time (almost 30 seconds) per question.

- No need to worry about bubbling your responses on the answer sheet at the last minute.

- You get your scores as you leave the test center (you can choose whether to look at them right then or to wait until later).

When you consider all the pros and cons, you end up just about breaking even.

THE GMAT AND B-SCHOOL ADMISSIONS

Many students think too much about the importance of GMAT scores. Sure, they're required (even by Harvard Business School, which didn't start accepting GMAT scores until 1995), but there are many more factors involved. These include the following:

- your grade point average (GPA) in college

- the school at which you earned your GPA

- how long you've been out of college

- what you've done since college

- what your superiors think of what you've done since college (which will be expressed in their recommendations)

- your application essays

- your interview, if you have one

Admissions officers look at your GMAT verbal score as a (very) broad indicator of your verbal skills. It's not the best indicator of your abilities, but it's the best they've got. More importantly, though, business schools want to discern two important things from the vast quantity of verbal work you submit to them: They want to know that your command of English is sufficient to keep up with the lectures in class, and they prefer applicants who can illustrate that they can communicate ideas eloquently.

These two considerations are especially important if you're a foreign student hoping to attend business school in the United States. The number of b-school applicants from overseas has ballooned greatly over the past decade (almost one-third of all applicants are from beyond American borders), and entrance into the top programs has become much more competitive. If you are a foreign student, be sure to ask the programs in which you are interested about their requirements for the Test of English as a Foreign Language (TOEFL).

The AWA is also especially important if you're applying from abroad. Business schools added the AWA to the GMAT because they were skeptical that the application essays they received were actually written by the applicants. Thus, b-schools can compare AWAs to application essays and nail the slobs who pay native English speakers to write their essays.

As we'll discuss in the first chapter, Test-Taking Tips, it's never a good idea to get all wigged out about how the GMAT factors into your application. You have to take it, so just take it and do the best you can. You can't control what happens after that.

HOW TO USE THIS BOOK

As you might expect, there is one chapter dedicated to each of the three verbal question types—Sentence Correction, Arguments, and Reading Comprehension. There's a chapter on how to take standardized tests better, and there are also two chapters on overall skills: Be a Better Reader and Be a Better Writer. Use these to learn about developing a more basic appreciation for your verbal skills. Efficient reading is essential to improving your scores on Arguments and Reading Comp, and better writing will improve the quality of all the essays you're about to write.

Avoid the Decoys

As we'll discuss in chapter 1, one of the most useful skills you'll develop is the ability to determine why an answer choice is wrong. When ETS writers create GMAT questions, there are several cagey tricks they use to get you to pick the wrong answer. Each section will outline several decoys ETS uses to distract you, so you'll learn to recognize and eliminate them.

Note: The answer choices on the actual GMAT don't have letters assigned to them. Instead, you select your response by clicking on an adjacent oval. For the sake of clarity and brevity (and as a salute to the good old P&P format), we'll refer to the five answer choices as (A), (B), (C), (D), and (E).

Practice, Practice, Practice!

There are also many drills and questions to help you remember what you read, and there's a sample GMAT verbal section complete with answers and explanations. As you do the work, look for patterns in the questions you answer correctly and those you keep getting wrong. This will help you pinpoint your strengths and weaknesses and guide you to the areas in which you need more practice.

Most importantly, you're about to learn a bunch of techniques that will seem new and different to you. When you try the practice problems, *be sure to use the new techniques*. If you read up about all these cool new ways to beat down the GMAT but use the same old ways you're used to using when it's time to do the practice problems, you won't learn anything except how to further bad habits.

Keep practicing and stay focused. And good luck!

1 | TEST-TAKING TIPS

HAVE NO FEAR

Do you consider yourself a good test-taker? Or does the thought of all this rigidly timed mayhem reduce you to heart palpitations and night sweats?

The big bad GMAT can seem like a very intimidating impediment to your acceptance to business school. After all, the GMAT doesn't exist to help you get into school; it's mostly used as an excuse to keep you out. But the experience doesn't have to be as intimidating as you might make it out to be. This chapter is devoted to helping you get over whatever neuroses about the exam you might be harboring deep down in your soul, and it will also reveal a few basic elements of test-taking that will help you increase your score.

Pace Yourself!

Keeping your brain revved up to full power for four hours is a strenuous undertaking. Therefore, it's probably helpful for you to know that you don't have to stay in fifth gear during the entire exam. Working at a steady pace that's comfortable for you is actually better than racing through the entire section. Time is your most valuable asset on the GMAT, so learn to use it wisely.

As we discussed in the introduction, the CAT reacts to how well you're doing so far. In the early part of each section, the CAT is still getting a feel for how good you are, so it's best to make a good first impression. For this reason, it's best to linger on the early questions and take your time to ensure your best effort. Once you've answered twenty questions or so, the computer has made up its mind about you for the most part.

Thus, it makes sense to take extra time to answer the early questions, because they have a much greater impact on your score than the later ones do. In fact, if the verbal section gives you a lot of trouble, you would be better off spending the first hour on half of the questions and answering the rest with some preordained answer choice of the day, like C.

Guidelines

Even though you have to answer every question in each section (otherwise the test penalizes you), you don't have to give every question your maximum effort. Pace yourself with these guidelines in mind:

◆   Work slowly and deliberately on the first twenty questions of each section.

◆   Speed up gradually, keeping yourself aware of the time remaining.

◆   When there's five minutes left, just click through all the remaining questions, guessing shrewdly when possible or using that preordained letter.

◆   Don't linger on questions if you think they're just plain impossible. Staring at a question rarely creates the divine inspiration you're hoping for. Make an educated guess (as we'll show you in upcoming chapters) and move on.

WHY ETS HATES ANSWER CHOICES

Throughout our scholastic lives, we have been conditioned to provide our own responses to test questions. There's a reason why most exams do not have answer choices from which to choose—answer choices make the questions much easier!

Case in point: In 1994 ETS introduced the "student-produced response" to one math section of the SAT. (Yep. They called it that, too. But don't worry: The CAT's computer format prohibits ETS from putting these boxes on the GMAT.) There are ten such questions with no answer choices, and each question corresponds to a box on the answer sheet that looks like this:

Once a student finds the answer to one of these questions, he has to enter it into the answer box. Of course, it isn't that simple. If the answer is three-fourths, for example, then any of these student-produced responses would have to be credited:

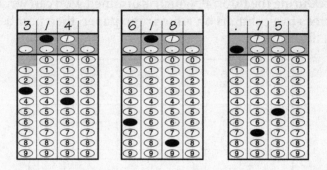

The grading computer has to be programmed to accept any of these as a correct response. ETS spent more than two years (and who knows how many millions of dollars) to develop this box just so that ten questions (about one-sixth of the math questions on the SAT) would not have answer choices.

ETS hates the unavoidable fact that standardized tests are multiple-choice. They know that among the incorrect answers, the right answer is staring right back at you. They also know that test takers easily learn to play the answer choices off each other to reveal the correct one. In the classroom, there is no greater joy for a GMAT teacher than when a student says, "I got this question right, but I don't know why." What does that statement mean? It means that the student has made ETS think that she knows something she really doesn't and thus artificially inflated her overall score.

How did she do it? By finding the correct answer after crossing off all the other choices.

POE Shall Set You Free

Process of Elimination (POE) is a beautiful thing, and POE will come up a lot in this book (or any other test-prep book that's worth the recycled paper it's printed on). POE is like shooting beer cans off a fence. Once you shoot down four of them, there's one left standing.

> If you've narrowed your choices down to two, don't look for reasons why one is better than the other. Instead, find reasons why one is *worse* than the other.

In many circumstances, you don't have to know why the correct answer is correct. All you have to realize is that the other four are definitely wrong. The only answer choice left is correct by default. Each chapter will discuss what makes wrong answers wrong in greater detail. For now, just recognize that POE is one of the biggest weapons in your arsenal.

Use Your Scratch Paper

Now that the CAT is in town, you can't cross off answer choices on a test paper anymore. But you can still use POE on your scratch paper, which the test center will provide for you. One side of each piece of paper is unlined, and the other side is graph paper. During the tutorial, which is untimed, you can write the letters (A) through (E) across five columns on your graph paper, then number the questions down the side like this:

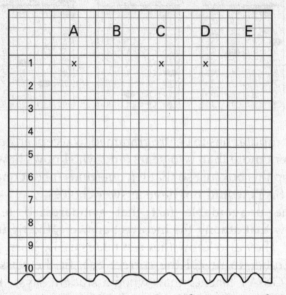

Using this technique, you can keep track of the answer choices you've eliminated more easily. With all that's going through your head during the exam, it pays to keep things as simple and direct as possible.

A LITTLE ZEN

Speaking of making things easier, here's a point that few test-prep guides bring up. Scoring well on standardized tests requires two very important and very different skills. Of course, you need to prepare for the exam by practicing techniques on sample material so that you know how to match up subjects and verbs and how to calculate percentages. But the second skill, which is just as important as the first, is the ability to be a better test-taker. Your eloquence and facility with the English language might put Churchill to shame, but if you stress out when the proctor says "Begin," you won't get very far.

Test stress occurs when you think too much about the consequences of the exam you're taking. Few would argue that taking a standardized test is a pleasant, stress-free experience. In truth, most find it a real pain. You're stuck in a room with a computer terminal staring at you mockingly. You know you need a good GMAT score to get into the top-echelon program of your choice.

Many students who have planned to attend business school for a long time become obsessed with the subtleties of the application process. They preoccupy themselves with questions such as "How important is the GMAT to my overall application?" and "What if my GPA is too low?"

All of these are valid questions, but you have no way of ascertaining their answers. We would all like to think that we know what admission folks want, but in truth, we don't. The process by which applications are considered is too subjective and too unpredictable to obsess over. So don't.

Stay Focused on the Task at Hand

The best way to approach a standardized exam is to live in the present. Don't think about your application, your interview, or the impact that your GMAT score will have on your chances for admission. Just accept the idea that you will give it your best shot and see if the admissions gurus think you would be a good fit for their program.

The same is true for the test itself. When you're working on a problem, try concentrating on that problem and nothing else. You can't skip it, so you might as well do your best and make your best guess. Whether you think you're doing well or poorly, don't dwell on it. The past is gone, and fortunes can change rapidly.

You can't change any of the responses you've already given, and you can't possibly predict the questions that lie ahead. Don't worry about things over which you have no control. Just give each question the best of your attention and see what happens.

If you can't help but concentrate on the long-term significance of this test, remember this: To be a doctor, you have to attend medical school and you must take the MCAT. To be a lawyer, you have to attend law school and take the LSAT. To pursue any other postgraduate degree, you have to attend graduate school and take the GRE. But the GMAT is the only exam you take as an option to enter the world of business—it's not a necessity to have your M.B.A.

Think about it. There are lots of incredibly successful businesspeople who have never attended business school. It's true, of course, that an M.B.A. carries a lot of weight in the business world, but it is *not* essential to your success. Remember that. If the absolute worst circumstance is that you end up not getting your M.B.A., it will not be the end of the world. Once you face down the fear of failure and realize that your world won't end if you don't do well, it won't gnaw at you as much and you'll be able to concentrate on the test at hand.

Patience, Grasshopper

Finally, there is the value of patience. A few of these techniques will seem strange at first. You're probably not accustomed to working backward using the answer choices the test provides. You also probably haven't worked much on your grammar, logic, or reading skills in a while.

Learning these techniques is like learning to ski for the first time. When you first clamp on those skis and head out of the lodge, your friends might encourage you to head to the top of a triple black diamond and work out the kinks on the way down. As many people who now walk with a limp will attest, this technique doesn't work. Let yourself learn GMAT skills without a time limit at first—that is, head for the bunny slope and learn such mundane skills as turning and stopping. As you get better, the speed will come naturally, and you'll be able to handle the moguls and the ice and those slow bratty kids who cut you off as they snowplow into the shrubbery.

Of course, the real stuff you're looking for in this book is the best way to ace the GMAT, shoot off to business school, and get on with the rest of your life. So let's get to it.

2 | SENTENCE CORRECTION

If you love someone, set them free. —Gordon "Sting" Sumner

Aha. Pronoun trouble. —Daffy Duck

You're about to find out the degree to which most Americans butcher the English language—especially in songs. Case in point: the lyrics above. Sting may have mastered the art of Tantric sex, but he's got some work ahead before he gets into Wharton. The grammar is off because the noun *someone*, which is singular, doesn't agree with the pronoun *them*, which is plural. The proper sentence could be rewritten correctly two ways:

> If you love someone, set **him or her** free.

> **OR**

> If you love **more than one person**, set them free.

Of course, had Sting bothered to achieve grammatical perfection, he would have messed up the meter of the song. Picture his backup singers chanting:

> Free, free. Set him or her free.

> Free, free. Set him or her free.

The supreme irony in all this is that before his musical career took off with The Police in the early 1980s, Sting worked as a primary school English teacher near Newcastle, England.

But enough of this banter.

WHY GRAMMAR?

You may be wondering why one-third of the verbal questions you'll see on the GMAT involve proper sentence construction, or why grammar could have the slightest impact on your business school education. You have a valid point; the odds are heavily against the possibility that your finance professor will ask you to conjugate a list of verbs for homework. For the sake of the GMAT, however, it is absolutely essential that you develop a grasp of what ETS considers proper grammar.

Learning ETS' grammar rules often provides students with the easiest way to improve their verbal scores, because the grammar questions don't rely as much on reading comprehension skills, which are often more difficult (but not impossible) to improve. To do well on the Sentence Correction section, you don't have to learn to read faster and with greater comprehension (which we'll discuss at length in later chapters); all you have to do is familiarize yourself with basic core of grammar rules that most Sentence Correction questions incorporate.

Don't be intimidated by the sentences that the GMAT throws at you. The questions might seem complicated, but the rules can be as basic as making sure the subject agrees with the verb. In this chapter we'll outline most of the basic grammar errors you should be able to recognize, and you'll have the chance to practice on many questions both here and in the sample verbal section in chapter 9.

THE DIRECTIONS

When you see your first Sentence Correction question, directions that look something like this will pop up:

> Directions: Part or all of each sentence that follows has been underlined. If you think the sentence is correct as written, pick the first answer choice, which simply repeats the underlined portion exactly. If you think there is something wrong with the sentence as written, choose the answer choice that best replaces the underlined portion of the sentence.
>
> Sentence Correction questions are designed to measure your correct use of grammar, your ability to form clear and effective sentences, and your capacity to choose the most appropriate words. Pick the answer that best states what was meant in the original sentence, avoiding constructions that are awkward, are unclear, or unnecessarily repeat themselves.

Once you're through with this chapter, you won't need to waste valuable time on the actual test reading these directions. It suffices to say that you want to find the answer choice that employs the best use of GMAT grammar.

Don't Look for Perfection

It's very, very important to make the distinction between the "best" answer and what you might perceive to be the "correct" answer. If you consider yourself someone who has a rather strong grasp of English usage, your quest for the perfect sentence may be stymied. Not all correct answers (which ETS likes to call "credited responses") employ perfect English; they use GMAT English, and the two don't always coincide. In fact, it is often the case that ETS defends a correct answer just because all the others are worse.

> Choosing your response to a question can be akin to voting for an elected official; you select the one that stinks the least.

This leads us to the importance of Process of Elimination. As we'll emphasize later in this chapter and throughout the book, the best way to improve your Sentence Correction skills is to differentiate the grammar ETS likes from the grammar it doesn't like. Many times you'll end up choosing the right answer by default.

Use Your Scratch Paper

Your test center will provide you with as much scratch paper as you'll need; one side of each sheet is plain, and the other has graph paper on it. You might think that the graph paper side is only good for math. Au contraire, mon frére. As we mentioned in chapter 1, set apart the first five columns of the graph paper and label them (A) through (E). Then you can write the question numbers along the left side. (Remember that little diagram that you saw in the first chapter on Test-Taking Tips?)

You can keep track of the answer choices you've eliminated by putting an X in their corresponding boxes. Given the stress of the exam, it's important to make POE as idiotproof and jitterproof as possible so that you can focus your concentration on the questions.

Don't Get Hung Up on "Difficulty"

Since the GMAT CAT sends you questions based on its perception of how well you're doing, you might be compelled to look at a question and ask yourself, "Is this a hard one?" Of the three types of questions in the verbal section, Sentence Corrections are the toughest to gauge in terms of difficulty. A grammatical construction that seems impossible to you might be a piece of cake for someone else. So if you find yourself trying to assess the difficulty of a Sentence Correction question, don't bother; it's just misdirected energy.

> If a question seems difficult to you, it's difficult. If it ain't, it ain't. Don't waste your time worrying about it.

Of course, there is an upside to working on a difficult question. If you've done a lot of preparation for the GMAT, then questions that seem difficult to you will also be deemed difficult by ETS. If you see a difficult question, then one of two things is true. Either:

- the CAT thinks that you're doing very well so far, and it's giving you more difficult questions to work on, or

- the question is experimental, and it doesn't count.

WHAT THE QUESTIONS LOOK LIKE

Each Sentence Correction question consists of one sentence, and part or all of that sentence is underlined:

<u>To attempt at curbing the water hyacinth, an ornamental plant which was infesting Lake Victoria and was native of</u> the Brazilian rain forest, ecologists are introducing weevils and fungi into the lake's ecosystem.

- ○ To attempt at curbing the water hyacinth, an ornamental plant which was infesting Lake Victoria and was native of
- ○ The attempt at curbing the infesting of Lake Victoria of the water hyacinth, an ornamental plant which is a native to
- ○ In an attempt to curb the water hyacinth, an ornamental plant which had been infesting Lake Victoria and had been native to
- ○ In an attempt to curb the infestation of Lake Victoria by the water hyacinth, an ornamental plant native to
- ○ By attempting to curb Lake Victoria's infestation of the water hyacinth, an ornamental plant native in

If you think the sentence is correct as it is written, choose answer choice (A), which always repeats the underlined portion word for word. If you can detect a flaw in the sentence, you can eliminate (A) and concern yourself with the other four answer choices, which provide alternative ways to write the sentence.

THE FIVE STEPS TO SENTENCE SUPREMACY

Consider, though, that the best answer in your mind might not match the best answer on the page. This brings us to the first of our five guidelines for grammatical glory:

1. **Whatever you do, DO NOT rewrite the sentence in your head and look for a match among the choices.**

This will grow to be a very common first impulse for you—especially if you feel as though your grammar chops are strong. If you've practiced sentence correction for a while, you might start to think that you can anticipate what the correct answer should look like. This might sound cool at first, but it's actually not very productive (as you'll see in subsequent examples). If you visualize the correct answer and then fail to find it among the answers (a situation that tends to happen more often than not), you're likely to get rattled and lose your equilibrium.

If you detect a flaw in the original sentence, there are myriad ways to fix it. Your universe, however, is restricted to the four other choices you've been given. The key to success, as always, is Process of Elimination. You'll have much more success if you learn to recognize the incorrect stuff and cross it off.

2. Train yourself to find grammatical mistakes.

Overall, it's more important (and a lot easier) to recognize rotten grammar than to defend proper grammar. Dedicate yourself to scrutinizing each answer choice and looking for problems. The moment you find one, give the answer choice the thumbs-down and move on.

Let's take another look at that sentence about the hyacinth:

> To attempt at curbing the water hyacinth, an ornamental plant which was infesting Lake Victoria and was native of the Brazilian rain forest, ecologists are introducing weevils and fungi into the lake's ecosystem.

If you're not positive the sentence is written incorrectly, assume that choice (A) is correct for the time being and move on to the other four answer choices. (Think of making an answer choices in terms of dating; you keep the one you like until something better comes along.) With lots of practice (and a little bit of luck), you'll start to recognize grammatical flaws right away. They'll stand out like this:

> To attempt at curbing the water hyacinth, an ornamental plant which was infesting Lake Victoria and was native of the Brazilian rain forest, ecologists are introducing weevils and fungi into the lake's ecosystem.

"Hey!" you'll say to yourself. "Those two words—*attempt* and *at*—don't go together! That's wrong! I'm gonna cross it out!" (We emphasize again that you should keep these epiphanies to yourself. Yelling out loud like that during the GMAT will elicit some choice dirty words from your test-taking brethren and sistren).

You found something wrong with the sentence, and you've crossed off answer choice (A). Now what?

3. Get rid of the choices that have the same grammatical flaw as the original sentence.

Put yourself in the test-writer's wingtips for a second. Anyone who has written thousands of these questions can tell you that it's relatively easy to write a grammatically correct sentence. The tough part is creating four decoy answer choices that are attractive enough to trick someone into choosing one of them, yet are defensively incorrect. One of the ways ETS creates wrong choices is by repeating an error that appears in the original sentence and changing another part of the underlined portion. This is somewhat akin to taking your car in for an oil change and getting it back with new shock absorbers instead.

Here are the answer choices for the hyacinth question again:

- ○ To attempt at curbing the water hyacinth, an ornamental plant which was infesting Lake Victoria and was native of
- ○ The attempt at curbing the infesting of Lake Victoria of the water hyacinth, an ornamental plant which is a native to
- ○ In an attempt to curb the water hyacinth, an ornamental plant which had been infesting Lake Victoria and had been native to
- ○ In an attempt to curb the infestation of Lake Victoria by the water hyacinth, an ornamental plant native to
- ○ By attempting to curb Lake Victoria's infestation of the water hyacinth, an ornamental plant native in

True to form, answer choice (B) has the same problem, so you can cross it off as well. The other three choices use the correct idiom *attempt to*. Before you know it, your chances of choosing the correct answer have jumped from one in five to one in three.

Lather, Rinse, Repeat

Try this process again and look for any new mistakes among the remaining choices. There are three choices left. What's wrong with any of the remainders?

- ○ In an attempt to curb the water hyacinth, an ornamental plant which had been infesting Lake Victoria and had been native to
- ○ In an attempt to curb the infestation of Lake Victoria by the water hyacinth, an ornamental plant native to
- ○ By attempting to curb Lake Victoria's infestation of the water hyacinth, an ornamental plant native in

Aha! Another gaffe! There are two ways to use the word *native*:

The gibbon is *native to* southeastern Asia.

John Cleese is *a native of* England.

Native in is not idiomatic, so you can kill choice (E). (If you didn't know this idiom before, check out the Idiom List appendix on page 211.) Now you have two choices left—and your odds are improving.

4. **Use Process of Elimination to play the answer choices off each other.**

Suppose you read the sentence and you can't find a mistake. (Hey, it happens.) You're not out of options. The right answer is right there in front of you, hidden among the five choices. Compare them to each other and see where they differ.

Look for a Two/Three Split

Poker fans recognize a "full house" as a five-card hand in which you have three of one type of card and two of another. Many Sentence Correction questions are created in a similar fashion.

> If you look at the five answer choices and three choices phrase the answer one way and the other two phrase it a different way, one of those two ways has to be right. Determine which is correct, then eliminate the wrong ones.

Never assume that the majority rules. You can't determine that one option is better than the other just because it appears more times in the answer choices. If you see a two/three split, be sure to judge each possibility on its own merit, not by its superior numbers. One grammar usage can appear in three choices and be wrong each time.

If you didn't see the faulty idiom in the sentence above, you could have compared the answer choices like this:

- ◯ To attempt *at* curbing the water hyacinth, an ornamental plant which was infesting Lake Victoria and was native of
- ◯ The attempt *at* curbing the infesting of Lake Victoria of the water hyacinth, an ornamental plant which is a native to
- ◯ In an attempt *to* curb the water hyacinth, an ornamental plant which had been infesting Lake Victoria and had been native to
- ◯ In an attempt *to* curb the infestation of Lake Victoria by the water hyacinth, an ornamental plant native to
- ◯ By attempting *to* curb Lake Victoria's infestation of the water hyacinth, an ornamental plant native in

See the two/three split? Two choices say *at*, and the other three say *to*; it has to be one or the other. At this point, you consult your mental idiom Rolodex, realize that the proper idiom is *attempt to*, and eliminate (A) and (B).

You would be surprised to see how common two/three splits are among the answer choices of Sentence Correction questions. (Take a look at a bunch of questions in *The Official Guide for GMAT Review* if you're not convinced. You can find this book in any bookstore or through ETS' GMAT web site at www.gmat.org.)

5. If you're down to two choices, find the flaw in the wrong one.

Now comes the final showdown. If you're like most people, eliminating the first three choices is a lot easier than knocking off the fourth. How many times have you narrowed down your choices to two and then picked the wrong one?

Let's revisit the hyacinth question and the two remaining answer choices:

To attempt at curbing the water hyacinth, an ornamental
plant which was infesting Lake Victoria and was native of the
Brazilian rain forest, ecologists are introducing weevils and
fungi into the lake's ecosystem.

- In an attempt to curb the water hyacinth, an ornamental plant which had been infesting Lake Victoria and
  had been native to
- In an attempt to curb the infestation of Lake Victoria by
  the water hyacinth, an ornamental plant native to

Both choices pass the idiom tests and seem plausibly correct. Ask yourself this: How are they different? The top choice uses the past perfect verb tense (*had been infesting* and *had been native*), and the other choice is in the present tense. Which do you use?

Look at the sentence's main clause, which is not underlined (and thus must be grammatically correct): *ecologists **are introducing** weevils and fungi into the lake's ecosystem*. This is written in the present tense, and the verb tense of the underlined portion should match. Therefore, answer choice (C) doesn't match, and the best answer is (D).

That's the best process to follow. Succinctly put, it's easier to point out why an answer choice is wrong than to defend why an answer choice is right. So make things easier for yourself and learn to spot the flaws.

Note: If any of those grammar terms flew over your head (like "main clause" or "past perfect verb tense"), don't sweat it. Refer to the Grammar Review section below, and check out the Grammar Glossary appendix on page 207.

GRAMMAR REVIEW

First things first: This book is not a comprehensive English grammar textbook. If you want to learn how a gerund differs from a present participle, go have a cup of tea with your fifth-grade English teacher (you know, the one who made you diagram all those complex sentences). Or you can scan the grammar textbook section of one of those famous tremendous bookstore web sites. With few exceptions, this book details only the basic grammar principles that ETS bothers to test. We'll start out with basic sentence construction from its most simple to the rather complex. Other rules will reveal themselves as we discuss ETS' favorite mistakes later in the chapter.

The Simple Sentence

If you hitch any *noun* (for anyone who's never seen *Schoolhouse Rock*, a noun is a person, place, or thing) to any *verb* (which denotes action), you get a simple sentence:

Noun	Verb
Bill	ate.
Pittsburg	rocks.
Speed	kills.

The subject noun commits the action in a sentence, and you can add another noun—the object noun—to receive action.

> Fuad kicked **the ball**.
>
> Mandy married **Max**.

Types of Modifiers

As far as proper sentence structure is concerned, the rest is all fluff and modifiers. The key is making sure that none of the modifying stuff compromises the sentence structure:

> After a long courtship, Mandy, a brilliant brain surgeon, married her boyfriend, Max, in a small church on the property of a huge farming combine in Michigan.

Notice that even though you know a lot more about Mandy and Max, the original simple sentence remains intact. The three main types of modifiers are:

- **Adjectives:** An adjective is a descriptive word placed next to the noun it describes. What kind of courtship was it? A *long* courtship. What kind of brain surgeon was she? A *brilliant* brain surgeon. You get the idea.

- **Appositives:** Appositives are descriptive phrases set off from the main sentence by commas. They can appear at either end of a sentence (*After a long courtship,* . . .) or smack-dab in the middle (. . . , *a brilliant brain surgeon,* . . .).

- **Prepositional Phrases:** You can make a prepositional phrase by combining a preposition with a noun. Here's another look at that sample sentence with all the prepositional phrases bracketed:

> After a long courtship, Mandy, a brilliant brain surgeon, married her boyfriend, Max, [in a small church] [on the property] [of a huge farming combine] [in Michigan].

Note again that each of these modifiers is there only to add description. They act as the flesh that makes the skeleton of the basic sentence more interesting and informative. As you analyze the various sentences, make sure that the modifiers don't screw up the grammar.

Why Is It Wrong?

Now is an important moment in your GMAT-prep career. As of this moment, it is no longer adequate to cross off an answer choice because "it looks kinda strange." Every so often, ETS likes to use grammatical formats that are perfectly legal yet are seldom used in conversational English. That's how they get you. Unless you can find a tangible problem with a possible answer (such as when the subject and verb don't agree), leave the choice alone at first. It may end up to be the right choice if you find errors in the other four options.

Referring back to the sample question, answer choice (A), which was a repetition of the underlined text, has just as much of a chance of being the correct answer as the rest of the answer choices, so don't be afraid to pick it. Before you do, though, it pays to consider the other answer choices and make sure that none of them are better.

ETS's FAVORITE MISTAKES

Sure, it's important to recognize grammatical mistakes. But the thought of memorizing every grammar rule leaves you queasy, doesn't it? You don't have to do that. Luckily, most of the errors that ETS conjures up in its Sentence Corrections section fall into several clear categories. Here are the seven most common goofs that ETS sets up for you to detect. If you can spot these, you'll be in great shape.

#1 Common ETS Goof: Using Misplaced Modifiers

There is one basic rule about words that modify, or describe, other words:

> When one word modifies another word, the two should be next to each other.

The most common example of this occurs when a sentence has an opening phrase (or appositive) followed by a comma, as in this example:

Unwilling to threaten the revenue generated by the city's two airports, <u>the plan to build a third airport outside the city limits was opposed by the mayor.</u>

- ◯ the plan to build a third airport outside the city limits was opposed by the mayor
- ◯ the mayor opposed the plan to build a third airport outside the city limits
- ◯ opposition to the plan to build a third airport outside the city limits was expressed by the mayor
- ◯ it was opposed by the mayor that a third airport was planned to be built outside the city limits
- ◯ the third airport that had been planned to be built outside the city limits was opposed by the mayor

The opening phrase *Unwilling to threaten the revenue generated by the city's two airports* is not underlined. Therefore, the first noun that appears after the comma has to be the subject that the opening phrase modifies. The way the question is written, it looks as though *the plan* was unwilling to threaten the revenue. That's obviously wrong, so you can get rid of it.

Whom does the phrase modify? The mayor! Once you realize that, this question is rather easy. The only answer choice that begins with *the mayor* is (B). Attention you skeptics out there: Some Sentence Corrections questions are this easy!

Exercises

Which of these sentences are correctly written, and which need to be fixed? If you find an incorrect sentence, how would you correct it? The answers are in chapter 8.

1. Crazed with hunger, the park ranger finally subdued the stray coyote.

2. Based on several manuscripts that date back to the Middle Ages, historians believe that Charlemagne first rose to power as a mere teenager.

3. First published at the turn of the nineteenth century, *The Literary Quarterly Review* has provided its readership with examples of the era's finest fiction.

4. Unlike executive skills, which most people can learn at any qualified business school, a person usually derives a sense of leadership from social relationships.

5. Though usually a calm person, Arthur's patience was tried more than once by his son's destructive behavior.

6. Although Bill had not driven the car in weeks, his father had no trouble starting the engine.

Another Way to Fix the Problem

Most misplaced modifiers come down to making sure that the opening phrase, followed by a comma, modifies the subject of the sentence. There is a possible solution to other problems, however, that don't occur very often on the GMAT. As the Grammar Glossary will tell you, there is a fundamental difference between a phrase and a clause: A clause contains a subject and a verb, and a phrase lacks either a subject or a verb.

> **Clause:** Although he looked for his glasses for hours,

> **Phrase:** Having looked for his glasses for hours,

See the difference? If you take away *Although* from the clause, you have a complete sentence: *He looked for his glasses for hours*. The phrase, however, has no chance to stand by itself as a complete sentence. The misplaced modifier rule applies to phrases, but *not* to clauses. Therefore:

> You can change a misplaced modifier into a legal sentence by changing a phrase into a clause.

Here's an example:

> **Wrong:** While leaving the bank, Evelyn's purse was stolen.

> **Right:** As she was leaving the bank, Evelyn's purse was stolen.

The opening phrase is now a clause (with the subject *she* and the verb *was*), so it's okay.

#2 Common ETS Goof: Using Improper Pronouns

We owe pronouns a great debt. Without them, we would all have to talk like this:

> "When Janet brought Janet's car to the mechanic, the mechanic told Janet that the mechanic would call Janet after the mechanic looked at Janet's car in the mechanic's garage."

In return for all this linguistic convenience, pronouns ask only that we observe two conditions. The first one is this:

> **Pronoun Rule 1:** Each pronoun must agree with the nouns they replace.

Whoa, there. If you spotted the error in the gray box, don't assume The Princeton Review is filled with a bunch of idiots. We made the error on purpose to see if you were on your toes. Subject-verb agreement is an easy error to miss. Because *pronoun* is a singular word and *they* is a plural pronoun, the sentence is incorrect. You need to rewrite the sentence in one of two ways:

> **Each pronoun** must agree with the noun **it** replaces.

> **OR**

> **All pronouns** must agree with the nouns **they** replace.

If you have a singular noun, be sure to replace it with a singular pronoun. If the antecedent is plural, its pronoun must be plural.

> **Pronoun Rule 2:** Each pronoun must refer directly and unambiguously to the noun it replaces.

Assume nothing. When you're considering whether all the pronouns refer directly to the nouns they've replaced, there's no such thing as "probably." You have to be certain. Take a look at this example:

After Victor Hugo referred to the newly crowned Emperor Napoleon as a "crayfish," **he** tried to have **him** arrested.

Upon reading this, you might assume that *he* refers to Napoleon (since he was the guy in power) and *him* refers to Hugo. It might make common sense to make this assumption, but it does not make grammatical sense. (After all, it is possible that Hugo tried to have Napoleon arrested.) Therefore, in the eyes of the GMAT grammar gurus, that sentence is incorrectly constructed.

Exercises

Which of these sentences are correctly written, and which need to be fixed? If you find an incorrect sentence, how would you correct it? The answers are in chapter 8.

1. As the melon farmers drove their crops to market, they were dismayed to find that they were infested with fruit flies.

2. The Commerce Department, which usually doesn't make any fiscal announcements until after the budget is ratified, announced that their accounting practices would be overhauled next year.

3. Enrico and Simone have absolutely no idea how valuable their father's antique desk is.

4. There is a psychological difference between people who do their taxes as soon as they receive all the forms and those who wait until the very last minute.

5. Neither Alice nor Beatrix could figure out why they failed the math exam.

6. Every employee brought their softball mitt to the game.

For additional information about specific pronouns, as well as a few tips on making sure the subject pronouns agree with the object pronouns, be sure to consult the Grammar Odds and Ends appendix.

#3 Common ETS Goof: Changing the Verb Tense Unnecessarily

Situations when you have to change the verb tense of a sentence are pretty rare. Therefore, the tense of the verbs in a sentence usually stay the same. When in doubt, keep it as simple and consistent as possible.

> The verb tense of a sentence should remain consistent. If the tense is established somewhere in the sentence, there's rarely a need to change it.

The best way to determine the proper verb tense is to look at the portion that is not underlined, because it sets the tone for the rest of the sentence.

Every time Martin goes to the beach, <u>he will get a really bad sunburn</u>.

The first part of the sentence isn't underlined, so it isn't subject to change. Therefore, it must be correct. *Martin goes* is in the present tense, so there's no need to move into the future tense (*he will get*). The correct sentence is:

Every time Martin goes to the beach, <u>**he gets** a really bad sunburn</u>.

The Basic Tenses

Sentence Correction questions seldom stray from the three basic tenses that we use every day in ordinary conversation.

- The *past tense* indicates that something has already happened:

    Wayne **attended** the Bueller School of Business.

- The *present tense* indicates that something is currently happening:

    Wayne **is attending** the Bueller School of Business.

- The *future tense* indicates that something will happen later:

    Wayne **will attend** the Bueller School of Business.

The Complex Tenses

There are also three more complicated tenses that you should know how and when to use. Don't worry about their official names; just learn to recognize when they're needed.

- The *past perfect tense* indicates that two things have happened in the past, and you have to show which one happened first. For this, you use the word *had*:

    Wayne **had attended** business school for over a year when he got married.

In this example, we now know that Wayne attended school *before* he got married. The important thing to remember is that you should never use *had* unless you explicitly have to. If only one thing has happened in the past, then the use of *had* is wrong.

- The *present perfect tense* indicates that something has been going on for a while and is still occurring. For this, you use the word *has*:

    Wayne **has been attending** (or **has attended**) business school since last October.

Now we know that Wayne started school in the past, and he is still there. The best clue that you need to use the present perfect is the word *since*.

♦ The *future perfect tense* indicates that something will have finished happening at a certain date in the future. Here, you use the words *will have*:

> When Wayne gets married, he **will have been attending** (or **will have attended**) business school for over a year.

At some future date, Wayne's schooling will be half over (assuming he's in a two-year business program). The future perfect is extremely rare on the GMAT, so don't get too worked up over it.

Exercises
Which of these sentences are correctly written, and which need to be fixed? If you find an incorrect sentence, how would you correct it? The answers are in chapter 8.

1. Before the new library was built, children are playing around in the vacant lot.

2. A recent study has found that within the past decade, many lawyers not considered for partnership had chosen to quit rather than wait until the following year.

3. John is jealous of Judy because she has a nicer briefcase.

4. Fire alarms will sometimes fail to detect a fire if they haven't been cleaned recently.

5. Never before had my parents been more surprised as they had been when my sister brought home her new fiancé.

6. The old gymnasium was abandoned until a real estate consortium bought the facility and renovated it.

Note: The only other verb tense that is worth studying for the GMAT is the subjunctive tense, and we discuss that in Grammar Odds and Ends.

#4 Common ETS Goof: Constructing Sentences That Aren't Parallel

In the same way that verb tenses should be consistent within a correctly written sentence, parallelism is also a structural necessity on the GMAT. It ties in with the need for the consistency of word forms when you're making a list as well as of the tenses of all the verbs.

See how that last sentence is parallel? It sets up a nice, consistent structure by using the preposition *of* twice:

It ties in with the need for the consistency **of** word forms when you're making a list

as well as **of** the tenses of all the verbs.

When in doubt, be consistent.

The need for parallelism exists in its most basic form when a sentence features a list:

> The CEO attributed her company's increased revenue to higher-than-expected sales of its new product line, the expanded budget for research and development, and demand was increasing in emerging markets.

The CEO cites three factors—*sales, budget,* and *demand*—so each should appear as the same part of speech. In this case, the list is inconsistent because the third factor is not expressed in the same form as the previous two. For the sentence to be correct, the underlined portion must also be expressed as a simple noun:

> The CEO attributed her company's increased revenue to higher-than-expected sales of its new product line, the expanded budget for research and development, and <u>increased demand</u> in emerging markets.

This works the same way with verbs. As long as each verb is in the same format, the sentence is perfectly legal:

> The Alaskan sea otter spends the majority of its time <u>sunning</u> itself on offshore rock formations, <u>foraging</u> for small shellfish along the ocean floor, and <u>swimming</u> playfully with its companions.

When ETS gets a little frisky, it likes to factor a red herring into the sentence, and you might think that this red herring is part of the list when it actually is not. Can you spot the distractor in this sentence?

> In order to change the company's image, the marketing director suggested <u>a modified strategy targeted at younger consumers, new market research for designing the new company logo, and searching</u> for well-known actors to appear in its TV commercials.

ETS wants you to think that all the items in the list should be *-ing* words, but that's wrong. ETS put *designing* in the second part of the list, and it wanted to trick you into thinking that *searching* is parallel with *designing*. In fact, the items in the list should all be nouns, and the corrected sentence looks something like this:

In order to change the company's image, the marketing director suggested <u>a modified **strategy** (noun 1) targeted at younger consumers, new market **research** (noun 2) for designing the new company logo, and **a search** (noun 3)</u> for well-known actors to appear in its TV commercials.

Comparing the answer choices to one another is especially useful here, because you can keep the answer choices that exhibit parallel construction and dump the ones that don't.

Exercises

Which of these sentences are correctly written, and which need to be fixed? If you find an incorrect sentence, how would you correct it? The answers are in chapter 8.

1. Doctors agree that their patients should take medication within a strictly monitored regimen instead of at random times during the day.

2. When he reached the age of sixty-one, my father chose to retire over searching for another job.

3. To evaluate Internet stocks using antiquated valuation models is like competing in the Indianapolis 500 with a horse and buggy.

4. Even the most experienced teen counselor can find it difficult to distinguish attention deficit disorder, which results when a student is chemically unable to process information, from being bored.

5. Members of ant colonies have skills as diverse as protecting the queen against predators, gathering food from the surrounding area, and maintaining the fragile infrastructure of the anthill's many chambers.

6. The first task to accomplish when writing an application essay is formulating an outline that lists all the things you want to say.

#5 Common ETS Goof: Comparing Apples and Oranges

Once again, the need for consistency looms overhead. (Do you see a pattern emerging here?) The concept of "apples and oranges" relates to the consistency of anything that is compared with something else.

> Whenever you make a comparison in a sentence, you have to make sure the things you compare are, in fact, comparable.

Whenever an answer choice does not make a comparison in a consistent manner (or there's any ambiguity as to the validity of a comparison), it's incorrect:

> A recent market research study revealed that the back of Michael Jordan's shaved head is more recognized than Bill Clinton, Newt Gingrich, or Jesus Christ.

This sentence is unclear, because we don't know if the author is comparing Jordan's head to the heads of the other men or to the other men themselves. If you see a sentence like this one, scan the answer choices for one that clarifies the situation like this:

> A recent market research study revealed that the back of Michael Jordan's shaved head is more recognized than **the back of the shaved head of** Bill Clinton, Newt Gingrich, or Jesus Christ.

You can also use a pronoun in the second half of the comparison. Learn to recognize the proper use of a pronoun in these situations, because ETS almost always prefers to use a pronoun rather than sound redundant or verbose:

> A recent market research study revealed that the back of Michael Jordan's shaved head is more recognized than **that of** Bill Clinton, Newt Gingrich, or Jesus Christ.

Another rare occurrence is the comparison of actions instead of nouns.

> French wines taste better than Australian wines.

Although this sentence might seem perfectly fine in conversation, it's incorrect in ETS' beady little eyes. The wines aren't being compared; the way the wines *taste* is being compared. So a verb needs to appear in both the front and the back of the sentence, in any of these forms:

- French wines taste better than Australian wines **taste**.
- French wines taste better than Australian wines **do**.
- French wines taste better than **do** Australian wines.

Exercises

Which of these sentences are correctly written, and which need to be fixed? If you find an incorrect sentence, how would you correct it? The answers are in chapter 8.

1. The population of Asian Americans in California is almost twice as big as Missouri.

2. Ordinary people have much more trouble solving the Sunday crossword puzzle than does the average member of MENSA.

3. In New Zealand, the average sheep eats almost ten more pounds of grass annually than that of its Australian counterpart.

4. Edouard Manet's struggle for acceptance among the European art community was not unlike that of Pablo Picasso, who went on to enjoy enormous success before he died.

5. My uncle Rupert grows tomatoes that are bigger than a baby's head.

6. The New York Public Library's main branch, located on the southwest corner of Fifth Avenue and 42nd Street, is larger than any branch in Manhattan.

#6 Common ETS Goof: Making the Subject and Verb Disagree

In its typical fashion, ETS likes deception. When an ETS writer constructs a long sentence, he or she likes to put the subject at the beginning, the verb near the end, and a bunch of modifiers and other junk in between to distract you.

> Once you determine the subject and verb of each question, decide if they agree.

Take a look at this exaggerated example of how the simple subject-verb connection can be lost among the muddling modifiers:

> The cross-eyed Burmese white panther, a species indigenous to the deepest jungles of Southeast Asia and sought as a trophy by wildlife poachers who hunt the massive, myopic beasts using 12-gauge shotguns and assault rifles, are rapidly nearing extinction.

See the nasty trick? The verb of the sentence is *are,* and the noun nearest to that verb is *rifles,* which is plural. "Rifles are" makes grammatical sense, but *rifles* isn't the subject of the sentence. When determining the subject of a sentence, ask yourself: "Who or what is this sentence about?" Answer: the panther.

> The cross-eyed Burmese white **panther**, [a species indigenous] [to the deepest jungles] [of Southeast Asia] and sought [as a trophy] [by wildlife poachers] who hunt the massive, myopic beasts [using 12-gauge shotguns and assault rifles,] **are** rapidly nearing extinction.

After you bracket off all of the prepositional phrases and appositives, you can see that this sentence is written incorrectly. The corrected sentence looks like this:

> The cross-eyed Burmese white panther, a species indigenous to the deepest jungles of Southeast Asia and sought as a trophy by wildlife poachers who hunt the massive, myopic beasts using 12-gauge shotguns and assault rifles, **is** rapidly nearing extinction.

Remember what we said at the beginning of the Grammar Review: Properly constructed sentences on the GMAT need a subject and a verb; the rest is all filler.

Exercises

Which of these sentences are correctly written, and which need to be fixed? For each of these examples, put brackets around the parts of the sentence that are not crucial to its structure and identify the subject and the verb. Then show how you would correct it. The answers are in chapter 8.

1. Neither my pet monkey nor my sister's pet rabbit is able to drive a car.

2. All of the major food groups, including proteins, fruits and vegetables, and carbohydrates, is crucial for optimal health.

3. Of all its sea-faring relatives, the California gray seal stands out because of its winsome demeanor and shiny coat.

4. A small number of buildings that were damaged in the Great Fire of 1909 are finally about to be rebuilt with the cash of an anonymous benefactor.

5. Each of Liz Taylor's husbands—including actor Burt Lancaster, Virginia senator John Warner, and construction worker Larry Fortensky—have described her as a rare beauty both in body and in mind.

6. A secret cache of personal journals that were the property of Finnbar Brenneisen, the renowned and reclusive billionaire known as much for his eccentric behavior as for his extraordinary philanthropy, are about to be published.

Note: There's a bit of information in the Grammar Odds and Ends appendix that addresses singular pronouns, such as *either* and *every*, that have shown up on the GMAT. Be sure to make a note of them. And while you're there, check out the words that have weird plurals.

#7 Common ETS Goof: Using Incorrect Idioms

Idioms are examples of proper usage of the English language. Certain words just go together. For example, you wouldn't say "I'm *applying at* the Darden School of Business," because *at* doesn't go with *apply*. The correct expression is "I'm *applying to* the Darden School of Business."

> Idioms don't have rules. They just are. Make a list of idioms and learn to recognize them.

Most idioms will just sound correct to your ear because you've been using them since you first learned to speak. If you're a student whose first language is not English, you probably have a lot of studying to do, because like many things in the English language these can be tricky, and the Idiom List appendix at the back of this book is a terrific way to get started. Take note of proper idiomatic writing as you read. If you come across an idiom that you haven't seen before, add it to the list.

> Elizabeth Taylor's passion for life is most evident in the list of her husbands, who range from wealthy and influential men such as actor Burt Lancaster and Virginia senator John Warner and ordinary construction worker Larry Fortensky.

This sentence is incorrect, because *range from . . . and* is unidiomatic. The correct way to write this one is to replace *and* with *to*:

> Elizabeth Taylor's passion for life is most evident in the list of her husbands, who **range from** wealthy and influential men such as actor Burt Lancaster and Virginia senator John Warner **to** ordinary construction worker Larry Fortensky.

There are no exercises here, because six little exercises about idioms wouldn't begin to scratch the surface. Consult the Idiom List and work as many problems as you can, both in this book and in *The Official Guide for GMAT Review*.

Make Note of the Miscellaneous

Unfortunately, an exhaustive chronicling of every error that ETS has included in every GMAT over the years won't fit in this chapter, or this whole book, for that matter. The goal of this chapter is to acquaint you with the mistakes that ETS uses most often, and more than 95 percent of all Sentence Correction questions will incorporate one or more of the above in some way. Try as many questions as you can to determine as thorough a list as you desire. Once you do enough practice questions, the mistakes will start to leap out at you.

SAMPLE QUESTIONS

Put the collective knowledge of this behemoth chapter together and try these sample Sentence Correction questions. The answers and explanations are in chapter 8.

1. Equestrian enthusiasts predict that the alleged abuse of anabolic steroids among horse trainers <u>would subside as long as the testing of the animals is more random and</u> more rigorously enforced.

    ○ would subside as long as the testing of the animals is more random and
    ○ would subside if the testing of the random animals were
    ○ will have subsided when testing of the animals is more random and
    ○ will subside if random testing of the animals were
    ○ will subside if the random testing of the animals is

2. A representative of the Internal Revenue Service usually finds <u>most people are willing to cooperate during an audit, yet they become agitated, defensive, and suspect</u> computer error.

- ○ most people are willing to cooperate during an audit, yet they become agitated, defensive, and suspect
- ○ most people to be willingly cooperative during an audit, and they are also agitated, defensive, and they suspect
- ○ that most people are willing to cooperate during an audit, yet they become agitated, defensive, and suspicious of
- ○ that people are mostly willing to cooperate during an audit, and they become agitated, defensive, and suspicious of
- ○ that most people are willingly cooperative during an audit, yet they are becoming agitated, defensive, and suspect

3. The Center for Public Integrity has discovered that drug companies obtain people's health records through the Internet either to contact them individually and suggest alternative forms of treating various illnesses or <u>the estimation of</u> the market of each new drug they produce.

- ○ the estimation of
- ○ to estimate
- ○ for estimating
- ○ they want to estimate
- ○ it wants to estimate

4. Gianlorenzo Bernini should <u>be judged not by the degree to which his sculptures and architecture are admired throughout the world, but by</u> his Bacchanalian lifestyle, his notorious temper, and his scathing jealousy of his counterparts.

- ○ be judged not by the degree to which his sculptures and architecture are admired throughout the world, but by
- ○ not be judged by the degree of admiration the world has for his sculptures and architecture, and instead by
- ○ be judged to the degree that his sculptures and architecture are admired throughout the world, and not by
- ○ not be judged by the degree to which the world admires his sculptures and architecture, but instead
- ○ be judged to the degree of admiration which the world has for his sculptures and architecture, not by

5. The three largest American airlines stunned the financial world by announcing a full-scale merger of their <u>business, which created an alliance controlling</u> over 60 percent of all domestic air traffic.

   ○ business, which created an alliance controlling
   ○ businesses, creating an alliance that would control
   ○ businesses that created a controlling alliance of
   ○ business, and this alliance controlled
   ○ business that created an alliance that would control

6. The Johns Hopkins Center for Gun Policy and Research revealed that half of all American men keep a gun in the house, and that on any given day, <u>one out of every fifty adults carry</u> a handgun away from home.

   ○ one out of every fifty adults carry
   ○ every one out of fifty adults carry
   ○ out of every fifty adults, one carries
   ○ each adult among fifty carries
   ○ one adult in fifty carries

7. The price of a bushel of corn has fallen so drastically that some farmers <u>have found it to be more cost-effective to destroy their crops as to make</u> the effort to get them to market.

   ○ have found it to be more cost-effective to destroy their crops as to make
   ○ found that the destruction of their crops is more cost-effective than making
   ○ find the destruction of their crops as more cost-effective than making
   ○ find it more cost-effective to destroy their crops than to make
   ○ are finding that the destruction of their crops is more cost-effective than the making of

8. In 1985, the California Supreme Court lifted a ban on fortune tellers, <u>which likened them as</u> economic prognosticators and investment counselors who also make predictions for profit.

   ○ which likened them as
   ○ who have been likened as
   ○ who are likened to be
   ○ likening them to
   ○ which were likened to be

9. Otto Wichterle, the Czech inventor who created the first soft contact lens, was not like most successful inventors due to his making a fortune from human vanity instead of being inspired by necessity.

   ○ Otto Wichterle, the Czech inventor who created the first soft contact lens, was not like most successful inventors due to his making a fortune from human vanity instead of being inspired by necessity.
   ○ The Czech inventor Otto Wichterle, who was not like other inventors' developments that were inspired by necessity, made his fortune from human vanity instead by creating the first soft contact lens.
   ○ Unlike most successful inventors, whose developments were inspired by necessity, Otto Wichterle, the Czech inventor who created the first soft contact lens, made a fortune from human vanity.
   ○ The first soft contact lens, which was created by Czech inventor Otto Wichterle, who made a fortune from human vanity, was unlike most successful inventors whose developments were inspired by necessity.
   ○ The developments of most successful inventors, which had been inspired by necessity, were unlike the first soft contact lens that was created by Czech inventor Otto Wichterle, who made a fortune from human vanity.

10. Any political figure who is intending on running for president will not succeed without a large quantity of campaign money contributed by wealthy benefactors.

    ○ who is intending on running
    ○ who has the intention of running
    ○ who is intent to run
    ○ intending on running
    ○ intent on running

11. The government's attempts to store chemical weapons in a rural community in Oregon, a state with a decidedly environmentalist history, have encountered massive political resistance from Oregon's state legislature.

    ○ have encountered massive political resistance
    ○ has encountered massive resistance politically
    ○ have politically encountered massive resistance
    ○ has encountered massive political resistance
    ○ had encountered politically massive resistance

12. The most prominent result of Professor Winick's archaeo-
logical research has been discovering that a pharaoh who
had ruled in the last days of Egypt was buried with fewer
artifacts than their earlier counterparts.

- ⬭ discovering that a pharaoh who had ruled in the last
days of Egypt was buried with fewer artifacts than
their
- ⬭ the discovery that pharaohs who had ruled in the last
days of Egypt were not buried with as many artifacts as their
- ⬭ to discover that pharaohs, which ruled in the last days
of Egypt, was buried with fewer artifacts than their
- ⬭ the discovery that pharaohs who ruled in the last days
of Egypt were buried with fewer artifacts than were
their
- ⬭ to discover that a pharaoh who ruled in the last days of
Egypt was buried with fewer artifacts than were his

13. Due to his temperament being fueled by distrusting technology, Stanley Kubrick did his best to insulate himself from
what he termed "the pains of modern living."

- ⬭ Due to his temperament being fueled by distrusting
- ⬭ Because his temperament was being fueled by a
distrust of
- ⬭ His temperament fueled by a distrust of
- ⬭ Due to the fact that his temperament had been fueled
by a distrust in
- ⬭ Having had his temperament fueled by his lack of trust
in

14. Unlike smaller apartment buildings, which have fewer than
four residential units in them, each room within any residential complex must be equipped with a sprinkler system.

- ⬭ Unlike smaller apartment buildings, which have fewer
than four residential units in them
- ⬭ Apart from those apartments that are in buildings that
contain fewer than four residential units
- ⬭ In contrast to smaller apartment buildings that contain
fewer than four residential units
- ⬭ Unless the apartment building contains fewer than four
residential units
- ⬭ Excluding those apartment buildings that have fewer
than four residential units in them

15. Goethe's talents as a poet, painter, and dramatist were <u>so diverse they inspired</u> his many fans to refer to him as the "giant of Weimar."

- ◯ so diverse they inspired
- ◯ so diverse as to inspire
- ◯ as diverse as those which inspired
- ◯ diverse enough so as to inspire
- ◯ as diverse as to inspire

16. Since 1994, when voters in several American cities rejected plans <u>for the using of public money in building of new sports stadiums, voters in San Diego, Pittsburgh, and Denver</u> changed their minds.

- ◯ for the using of public money in building of new sports stadiums, voters in San Diego, Pittsburgh, and Denver
- ◯ to use public money to build new sports stadiums, voters in San Diego, Pittsburgh, and Denver have
- ◯ for using public money for the building of new sports stadiums, voters in San Diego, Pittsburgh, and also in Denver
- ◯ for the public use of money to build new sports stadiums, voters in San Diego, Pittsburgh, and Denver have
- ◯ to use public money to build new sports stadiums in San Diego, Pittsburgh, and Denver

17. Any real estate professional will tell you that the value of a parcel of land is most directly affected by <u>the extent of its development</u> and how close it is to a major business center.

- ◯ the extent of its development
- ◯ whether it has been developed extensively
- ◯ how extensively it has developed
- ◯ the extent to which it has developed
- ◯ how extensively it has been developed

18. Baseball, the only major professional sport during the Great Depression, was <u>as present as the weather, and as much discussed</u>.

- ◯ as present as the weather, and as much discussed
- ◯ present like the weather was, and it was also discussed as much
- ◯ as present and was discussed as the weather was
- ◯ so present as to be discussed like the weather
- ◯ present and discussed as often as the weather was

19. Never again will sports fans suffer <u>collective grief as much as they had</u> the day that Joe DiMaggio died.

   ○ collective grief as much as they had
   ○ so much collective grief as
   ○ so much grief collectively than
   ○ as much collective grief as they did
   ○ as much grief collectively than

20. <u>Proponents of affirmative action, including most university presidents, need only cite declining minority enrollment in universities in California and Texas, the two most populous states, to support their cause.</u>

   ○ Proponents of affirmative action, including most university presidents, need only cite declining minority enrollment in universities in California and Texas, the two most populous states, to support their cause.
   ○ Most university presidents who are proponents of affirmative action need to support their cause by only citing that declining minorities are enrolling in universities in the two most populous states of California and Texas.
   ○ In order for proponents of affirmative action, which include most university presidents, to support its cause, they need only to cite the decline in minority enrollment in universities in California and Texas, the two most populous states.
   ○ Minority enrollment in universities in California and Texas, the two most populous states, are declining, and proponents of affirmative action, including most university presidents, only need to cite this fact to support their cause.
   ○ University presidents, including those in California and Texas, the two most populous states where declining minorities are enrolling in universities, should cite these facts and support their cause as proponents of affirmative action.

21. <u>As did</u> many other newer American cities, Atlanta doubled in size in only its first ten years of existence.

   ○ As did
   ○ As have
   ○ Like
   ○ Just like
   ○ As with

22. Accredited travel agents <u>were not required to provide advice pertaining to hotels and entertainment when they were organizing travel packages, but many do so</u> anyway in an attempt to secure repeat business.

○ were not required to provide advice pertaining to hotels and entertainment when they were organizing travel packages, but many do so

○ are not required to provide advice pertaining to hotels and entertainment when they organize travel packages, but many do so

○ were not required for providing hotel and entertainment advice when they organized travel packages, but many do it

○ were not required that they provide advice pertaining to hotels and entertainment when they organized travel packages, but many had been doing so

○ had not had the requirement for them to provide advice pertaining to hotels and entertainment when they organize travel packages, but many do it

3 | BE A BETTER READER

Everyone who hates reading comprehension questions please raise your hand and shout, "Yes! Yes! Reading comprehension is a colossal pain in my [insert body part here]!" Okay. Enough with the primal scream therapy. Now sit down and compose yourself.

When you consider the diversity of the major standardized tests, or the Big Six (PSAT, SAT, GMAT, GRE, LSAT, and MCAT), it's interesting to note that the only question type they all share is Reading Comprehension. If you're an average test-taker, you're either intimidated by the prospect of having to sponge up so much dense material in such a small amount of time or annoyed because ETS seems to value speed-reading so highly.

Now is the time to conquer whatever emotions you have and realize that fearing or hating Reading Comp questions will not make them go away. You can develop proficiency on them just as you would in any activity: by practicing. The first step is to learn to absorb information as efficiently as you can by reading aggressively.

THE ART OF INFORMATION GATHERING

Everyone reads something at some point in his or her day, even if it's just a stop sign at the crosswalk. Very few of us, though, are required to read aggressively as part of our daily lives. In fact, reading for adults usually falls into two categories: (1) reading for work, which usually involves skimming newspapers, trade publications, specialized magazines, and internal correspondence (e-mails, memos, etc.), and (2) reading for pleasure, when you read something that is interesting to you at your ideal pace. Neither of these practices is adequate training for the Reading Comp section of the GMAT.

Improving your skill on Reading Comp questions begins with these two words—minimize rereading. We all spend too much time reading paragraphs again and again, mainly because it's hard to concentrate on the subject matter when you're under such time pressure. No one expects you to eliminate rereading altogether, but if you can train yourself to understand what you've read the first time you read it, you'll be amazed at how much easier the Reading Comp questions will become.

Reading Paragraph by Paragraph

Have you noticed that reading is a lot easier when the text is broken up into a lot of paragraphs? That's why the average paragraph in a newspaper story is usually no longer than seven or eight lines of text. (That's also why your AWA essays should have many paragraphs, so that the readers have an easier time reading them—but more on that later.) Rather than regarding the Reading Comp passage as a large, imposing hulk of material to read, look at it as the sum of several smaller parts. If you assimilate little bits of information at a time, you will have read (and understood) the whole thing before you know it.

The Three C's

Test your ability to summarize any written paragraph using the three Cs. Pick a paragraph anywhere in this book, read it once, then close the book and ask yourself, "What did I just read?" The summary you come up with should be clear, concise, and conversational:

- ◆ **Clear:** Any person older than ten should be able to understand it thoroughly. That means no ultra-big words. If you see the words "infatuated with" on the page, think "crazy about" in your head.

- ◆ **Concise:** Keep the thoughts as brief as possible and avoid redundancy. Once you've got the basic idea, move on.

- ◆ **Conversational:** Rethink what you read as if you're explaining it to a close friend, your spouse, your kids, or anyone else to whom you speak informally and casually.

Let's try an example. Suppose you were visiting an art museum with your ten-year-old niece and you read this on the wall next to a particular painting:

> In 1949, Erno Blenckmann established a highly reductive compositional format: the vertical alignment of expansive, soft-edged, rectangular forms suspended within a monochromatic field.

At this point, the kid is scratching her head quizzically (and frankly, you might be too). If you were to translate this sentence into kid-speak, it might sound something like this:

> Blenckmann painted some fuzzy boxy shapes stacked on top of each other.

See? You've turned twenty-three words of dense babble into something anyone could grasp at first sight. If you can develop a talent for this, you'll be able to remember the content of Arguments and Reading Comp passages a lot more readily.

START PRACTICING NOW

Just as your first driving lesson shouldn't take place among the Indy cars at Le Mans, your first attempts to read aggressively shouldn't be on Reading Comprehension passages. Start out with your favorite magazine or newspaper, because odds are that (1) you'll find the subject matter at least remotely interesting and (2) the text will be divided into small, easy-to-digest paragraphs.

Let's look at the first few paragraphs from a sample article in the newspaper:

Turkish Foreign Policy Still Vibrant Despite Domestic Strife

by Gordon Hobbie

ISTANBUL, Turkey—Though Turkey has lurched forward without a functioning government for over six weeks since its prime minister, Mesut Yilmaz, lost a confidence vote in Parliament, its foreign policy has remained assertive. Turkish leaders have learned to exploit its Eurasian position and burgeoning economy to achieve its policy goals.

Translation: Turkey's government is a mess right now, but it still has some money and some international clout.

See? When you explain something to a ten-year-old kid, you can't use highfalutin words like *assertive* and *burgeoning*. Boiling passages down to simple English makes it easier to absorb right away.

Here's the next paragraph:

Despite stern warnings of economic sanctions and military intervention, Turkey has benefited from a growing power vacuum in the Middle East, which for decades has been dominated by Russia, Iran, Iraq, and former satellites of the now-defunct Soviet Union. In recent months, a series of foreign policy successes has emboldened the Turks to flex their muscles and build their influence in this chaotic region.

Translation: Other countries are weaker, so the Turks are taking the opportunity to act tough, and they've had some success lately.

Given the content of the last sentence, can you predict what the next paragraph will discuss? It will probably give details of the "successes" to which the article refers.

Turkey's most recent foreign policy came on the tense island of Cyprus, where the Greek-backed government had planned to test antiaircraft missiles recently acquired from Russia. When Turkey threatened to bomb the Greek side of the island, the Cypriots acceded to Istanbul's demands.

<u>Translation</u> (as predicted): For example, Turkey just bullied the Greeks on Cyprus into not shooting off their new Russian rockets.

> Though NATO was instrumental in helping the Turks resolve the Cypriot standoff, Turkey has also won some important battles strictly on its own. Last October, Syria agreed to release the Kurdish rebel leader Abdullah Ocalan after Turkey amassed troops along the Syrian border in a tacit threat of invasion.

<u>Translation</u>: Sometimes they need help to get what they want, but sometimes they do it all by themselves—like when they bossed Syria around and got that guy Ocalan released.

You get the idea. Now, build a summary of the summaries, and you have a basic grasp of the material that has been presented so far:

> The Turks haven't got a prime minister, but they're looking a lot tougher to their neighbors because they've bossed some people around and absorbed some of the power that other traditional powers in the area have lost.

Keep It Short and Sweet

When you first try this exercise, don't be surprised if your summaries become longer than the text itself. This happens a lot, because most students are not comfortable leaving out any details. That's fine at first, but as you practice you should concentrate on making your synopses more concise.

Whatever you do, resist the temptation to cheat by looking back at the page. That's no help at all. Make yourself remember what you read without refreshing your memory. If you struggle at first, don't take any sneak peeks. Start again from scratch. It will get easier as you practice.

If you lack the discipline to keep from looking back at the text (and you're not alone if you do), try working with a friend.

If You Can Explain It, You Know It

If you can train yourself to paraphrase the stuff you read as you read it (and you can take notes at first, if you have to), you'll be in great shape to improve your overall verbal score. And the best part about this whole exercise is that you haven't yet forced yourself to do the hardcore reading for content yet. There are two reasons for this:

- ◆ Since reading for content is difficult, why not put it off as long as you have to?
- ◆ Since the questions only pertain to a portion of the passage, why read the whole thing when you'll end up responsible for only part of it?

Exercises

Here are some more paragraphs containing text you might see on the GMAT. The first two have been "translated" for you; use the blank lines provided to write your own summaries for the other ten. Try to boil them down to their most basic meaning, and don't forget the three Cs.

Sample 1:

> Reasons for the big movie studios' disappointing holiday film season extend far beyond the fact that Christmas fell on a Friday, which cut short the most profitable week of the season. Throughout the six weeks between Thanksgiving and New Year's Day, blockbusters were few, and those rare films that received both critical acclaim and modest financial success were released by smaller art houses.

Translation:

There are many reasons why the big studios didn't make a lot of cash between Thanksgiving and New Year's, and most of their big movies lost out to smaller films.

Sample 2:

> Sir Walter Scott's memoirs revealed his fierce Scottish patriotism during the last seven years of his life. The breadth of his political influence suggests that he had become an uncrowned monarch upon whom most Scots relied for inspiration and leadership.

Translation:

Walter Scott's book about himself shows that many people in Scotland listened to him and looked up to him as if he was king (even though he wasn't).

Although there are no correct answers for these exercises, turn to chapter 8 for approximations of the length of your synopses and the type of language you should use.

1. Among academic historians, a rift of sorts has arisen between social historians, who pinpoint their studies on the suffering of victims of prejudice, and traditional historians, who prefer to emphasize wars, diplomacy, and the great personalities involved.

Translation:

_____

_____

2. Botanists have recently undertaken to recreate the natural diversity among species of trees in Hong Kong's forests. Massive deforestation before World War II denuded thousands of acres of land, and the consequent soil erosion that the southern coastline has endured is endangering several indigenous animals and plants.

Translation:

_____

_____

3. Two prominent Japanese investment banks, Nikko and Nomura, are endeavoring to pattern themselves after American counterparts. Rather than charge high fixed commissions, these two financial powers have shifted some of their emphasis to building wealth for individual investors.

Translation:

_____

_____

4. Tchaikovsky received financial support for nearly fourteen years from his patron, Nadezhda von Neck, the widow of a wealthy German railroad magnate. It has been rumored that Tchaikovsky resisted meeting her because he was too paralyzed with self-doubt to convey his love for her.

Translation:

_____

_____

5. The clearest advantage that the new Ferro-Electric Random-Access Memory (FeRAM) chip has over its predecessor, the dynamic RAM chip, is FeRAM's ability to retain and reproduce information with far greater security and at much greater speed. It will be at least a decade, though, before FeRAM is inexpensive enough for mass production.

Translation:

_____

_____

6. Given the recent rise of unemployment and a rapid drop in the prices of Korean stocks, a rapidly increasing number of Korean parents have found themselves unable to send their children to the same elite American and European private schools that they themselves attended many years ago.

Translation:

_____

_____

7. A new group of investment advisors has started a new web site designed to disabuse average citizens of the complexity of personal investing. In order to encourage repeat visits to the web site, the group will begin a real-money portfolio and encourage investors to follow it day by day.

Translation:

_____

_____

8. Throughout the Midwest, the number of visitors that come to state fairs has tripled within the last decade. These fairs offer tens of thousands of attendees the opportunity to sample local agricultural products, enter various contests, and attend political rallies conducted by candidates for local office.

Translation:

_____

_____

9. The International Monetary Fund (IMF) has declared that before it will green-light any further funding, the country's new leaders will have to commit themselves to creating a functional market economy and not succumb to populist resistance to change. The new government is convinced that it can live up to the IMF's demands and repay all loans within five years.

Translation:

_____

_____

10. Due to a peculiar phenomenon known as orbital decay, satellites gradually accumulate vast quantities of atmospheric particles that cling to the external navigation mechanisms. Burdened with this debris, the satellites lose an average of 10 percent of their altitude within twelve months after launch.

Translation:

_____

_____

ANTICIPATING WHAT'S NEXT

Of course, it shouldn't be ALL work. There are a few ways to guess what's coming without actually having to read it.

If you've ever consulted someone who has already taken the GMAT about Reading Comp passages, he or she might have advised you to circle words like *but*, *however*, *therefore*, etc. That was a good idea on the paper-and-pencil test, but it's no longer an option (unless you have one of those cool telestrators that announcers use at televised football games). However, those words are still good ones to notice; they help show you if a supporting point (or a contrary point) is being made.

Take the second sentence of that last paragraph, for example:

That was a good idea on the paper-and-pencil test, **but** it's no longer an option.

The first part was a good point, and the *but* changed the direction and made a contrary point. Then came the word *However*; just by reading that one word, you knew that the remainder of that sentence would revert back to good reasons for circling the words.

Call 'em whatever you want—indicators, signposts, clues, trigger words, etc. These words can keep the passage flowing in the same direction, or they can change the direction by signaling a contrasting thought. Either way, recognizing them can help speed the reading process a lot.

Words that suggest a *supporting or continuing point* come in several categories:

♦ Additional points (furthermore, in addition, also, too)

♦ Additional examples (similarly, likewise, for example)

♦ Structure (secondly, thirdly)

♦ Conclusions (thus, therefore, in conclusion)

Many of ETS's passages explore both sides of an issue, and often the first paragraphs express one position and are followed by the other side's viewpoint. For example, if a sentence begins with *Although*, you can expect two contradictory thoughts to appear in it:

> *Although* cigarettes make you look really cool [good point], it has also been hypothesized that they can give you cancer and kill you [not-so-good point].

Each of these words lets you know that a *contrary point* is on the near horizon:

> although, though, even though
>
> but
>
> despite, in spite of
>
> except
>
> however
>
> nevertheless
>
> unless
>
> while

Check out how anticipation works on this paragraph:

> Scientists have posited for centuries that there is intelligent life living somewhere in the universe. In fact, most experts speculate that, somewhere in the outer regions of the universe, there are other carbon-based life forms that draw oxygen and expel carbon dioxide in order to survive. **However,** these musings are utterly without merit. There is now concrete, irrefutable proof that outer space is a bitterly cold, lifeless void.

From the first sentence and the word *However*, you can probably guess how this paragraph will play out without reading the rest of the text. Here's the rest of the paragraph:

> Scientists have posited for centuries that there is intelligent life living somewhere in the universe. In fact, most experts speculate that, somewhere in the outer regions of the universe, there are other carbon-based life forms that draw oxygen and expel carbon dioxide in order to survive. However, these musings are utterly without merit. There is now concrete, irrefutable proof that outer space is a bitterly cold, lifeless void.

Did you anticipate correctly? You'll find that many GMAT passages work this way, and it's a great way to assimilate information as quickly as possible. Here's another example:

> The Iridium satellite-telephone network had been so named because the network was reported to contain seventy-seven satellites (and there are seventy-seven electrons in an iridium atom). Subsequent research has concluded, though, that there are only sixty-six satellites in the network. Thus, it should be renamed as the Dysprosium network.

There's your opening thought; what do you think the rest of the sentence will say, and how do you know?

> The Iridium satellite-telephone network had been so
> named because the network was reported to contain
> seventy-seven satellites (and there are seventy-seven
> electrons in an iridium atom). Subsequent research has
> concluded, though, that there are only sixty-six satellites
> in the network. Thus, it should be renamed as the
> Dysprosium network.

The key words *had been so named* tell you that something new has happened, and that the network probably has a new name by now. We call these indicators dead giveaways, because the first part of the sentence helps you predict what the second half will say.

Dead Giveaways

As we'll discuss in chapter 6, using proper sentence structure is crucial to good writing. Anticipating structure is also helpful for better reading. If you see a sentence in the introduction that says *Toaster pastries will bring about the end of Western civilization for the following four reasons*, you can comfortably assume that those four reasons are forthcoming.

There are several common ways that ETS uses to express contrasting thoughts within its Reading Comprehension passages. In each of the following examples, indicate what you think the next sentence will be and circle the dead giveaways. Turn to chapter 8 for the answers.

1. Most large corporations in the United States were once run by individual stockholders who owned most of the company shares and dominated the board of directors.

2. Normally, possums are timid nocturnal creatures who rarely venture from their nests.

3. At first glance, Shays's rebellion of 1787 appeared to be the ineffectual revolt of a few destitute farmers.

4. Traditionally, stocks have been valued mostly by their price-to-earnings ratio.

5. Until the end of the eighteenth century, the fledgling American government had been dominated by the Federalist party.

Reading Arguments More Efficiently

This strategy works well on Critical Reasoning questions as well. Most GMAT students admit that they spend even more time rereading Arguments than they do rereading Reading Comp passages. This stands to reason, because the wording of Arguments can be a lot more subtle; once you've eliminated a few answer choices (and you probably have more than one left), you usually have to reread to determine which of the remaining choices fall by the wayside and which one is left standing.

Still, getting the gist of an Argument the first time can create a lot more time to ruminate on the answers. Follow the math: There are about fifteen Arguments on the GMAT. If you can save thirty seconds per question, that's more than seven minutes of extra time to spend playing the answer choices off each other.

Below are some Arguments for you to translate into your own words to make them easier to understand. When you are finished, turn to chapter 8 to compare your translations to the ones we came up with. Remember there are no absolutely correct answers here.

1. It is unwise to dismiss rural homeowners as a key advertising demographic for luxury items. Because the cost of living is much greater in urban and suburban areas, the disposable income of the average rural homeowner is a greater percentage of his or her overall income.

Translation:

_____

_____

2. Due to the city's crumbling transport infrastructure, the comptroller has suggested that several renewal projects be privatized in order to ease the residents' tax burden. Objectors to this plan cite London's newly privatized commuter railroad, which has endured countless delays and breakdowns since the government sold it off.

Translation:

_____

_____

3. Ratings made by large investment banks on certain bellwether stocks are not the most reliable benchmark for investment. Many of these banks maintain large mutual funds, and it is possible for a bank to invest in a company and then assign a favorable rating to its stock in order for their own portfolio to increase.

Translation:

_____

_____

4. Buying advertising space during the Super Bowl is no longer cost-effective. None of the teams with the largest fan bases is likely to reach the game anytime soon, so it doesn't make fiscal sense to spend excessive amounts of the marketing budget on production of a one-day advertisement that fewer viewers are likely to see.

Translation:

_____

_____

5. Many institutions of higher learning enjoy increased enrollments during periods of strong economic growth. Graduate programs, however, suffer declines in applications because there is greater incentive to stay in the workforce and make the money that has become available.

Translation:

_____

_____

6. Sales of Internet networking systems have increased dramatically over the past decade. In order to reap the benefit of this burgeoning medium, York Associates plans to expand production of its dial-up products, which have accounted for more than half of the company's profits since 1993.

Translation:

_____

_____

7. The dramatic increase of the use of antibiotics has put excessive strain on pharmaceutical companies. Several viruses have developed resistance to the drugs that are currently being administered, and drug companies must expand research to create newer products that are more effective against superbugs.

Translation:

_____

_____

8. When people neglect to pay the income tax they rightfully owe, they end up costing themselves more money. Tax evasion results in insufficient government funds and forces lawmakers to raise income tax rates to make up the difference. Higher rates encourage tax evaders to maintain their illicit practices until they are eventually caught and fined rigorously.

Translation:

_____

_____

9. Many people assert that aggressive advertising on billboards and in magazines should be curbed because it encourages teenagers to experiment with alcohol and thus break applicable laws pertaining to underage drinking. But in France, where alcohol-related advertising is commonplace, rates of teenage crime and disease in which alcohol is involved are half those in the United States.

Translation:

_____

_____

10. Waylon Phipps, a collector known throughout New Orleans as the consummate connoisseur of antique writing desks, has publicly asserted that a cache of hidden furniture recently found in the basement of the Palace at Versailles is a blatant forgery. None of the tables bears the trademark of Louis XVI on its underside, nor do the top drawers feature the burled mahogany struts of which the king had been quite fond.

Translation:

_____

_____

EXPAND YOUR VOCABULARY

Suppose you and your spouse learn that you're expecting a new baby. You buy one of those baby care books, and you read the following sentence in the introduction:

> Opinions of parenthood vary from couple to couple, but most parents agree that raising children can be an enervating experience.

If you don't know what *enervating* means (and let's face it—it isn't a word that you come across often), are you likely to look up the word? Or will you just assume that you can figure out the word's meaning using the context of the sentence?

If you fall into the latter category, you might come to the conclusion that *enervating* means "exhilarating" or "life-affirming." And you would be incorrect: *enervate* means to "lessen the vitality or strength" of something!

Fall Back in Love with the Written Word!

One of the most powerful ways to improve your verbal skills is to redevelop an appreciation for the English language. We see written words all the time, so we tend to take them for granted. If you sit back and think about the many ways we weave them together to make prose, you'll see how versatile they are. And you'll also see how awful it is that we confine ourselves to the same small fraction of the verbal spectrum in our daily dialogue.

You were probably first told to learn new words when you started scribbling the meanings of big words on index cards as you prepared for the SAT. Right now, you're probably thinking to yourself, "Exactly. That's what kids do." As it happens, you're never too old to expand your lexicon, especially since you're going to spend the next several months writing essays both on the GMAT and for your b-school applications.

So don't be so contumacious. Avoid recalcitrance and nescience. As you're reading whatever you're reading, take note of any words you haven't seen before. Don't just get a feeling for the word using the context of the sentence. Instead, follow these simple instructions:

- Get up.

- Go find a dictionary (every GMAT student should have one) and blow the dust off it.

- Look the word up. It's very simple. For your convenience, all the words in the dictionary are in alphabetical order.

We'll talk more about the importance of increasing your vocabulary in chapter 6. In the meantime, get in the habit of learning at least ten new words a week. You'll be surprised how fast your appreciation for language improves.

All right. Now that we've covered some good practice techniques, it's time to concentrate on applying them to Arguments and Reading Comprehension.

4 | ARGUMENTS

Let's get ready to argue!

If you're a naturally contentious person, Critical Reasoning questions (also known as Arguments) might be your favorites. (And you might want to consider putting this book down and buying an LSAT manual instead, because almost half of the LSAT questions are Arguments.) Or you might be one of the many students who narrow the answer choices down to two and always seem to pick the wrong one. With practice, you'll better understand the standard logic patterns that ETS uses, and you'll learn how to differentiate relevant answer choices from irrelevant ones.

Note: If you haven't yet read the previous chapter about reading faster and more efficiently, go back and do that first. You should train yourself to read the arguments more efficiently before you start working on the actual questions.

THE NUTS AND BOLTS

Roughly one-third of the forty-one verbal questions on your GMAT CAT will be Critical Reasoning questions. (That still works out to three or four fewer Arguments than there were on the P&P GMAT.) Each question starts with a terse little nugget of information that's about three to four sentences long, followed by a question about the passage and five answer choices:

> Scientists estimate the cost of a transatlantic flight for an aerosonde, an unmanned airplane designed to collect atmospheric data, to be $20,000. An ordinary weather balloon, by contrast, can collect virtually the same information for about $200. Therefore, weather balloons are clearly the more cost-efficient method for gathering information.

Which of the following, if true, calls the above conclusion into question?

- ◯ Aerosondes are less costly than piloted planes and also do not put human life at risk.
- ◯ Politicians who have lobbied for federal funds to construct the aerosonde are astonished at its in-flight agility.
- ◯ Weather balloons are subject to violent weather changes that can blow them miles off course.
- ◯ Aerosondes can be used over and over again, but weather balloons, because of their frailty, can only be used once.
- ◯ In the time it takes to launch an aerosonde, it is possible to launch more than 100 weather balloons at once.

As we discussed in chapter 3, your first goal on every Argument is to understand what the statement is saying as quickly as possible with minimal rereading.

First Things First

Get ready for the next big revelation: When you see an Argument question, train yourself to read the question first.

Here's why: ETS knows that the average human likes to start reading at the top of the page; therefore, the question appears below the argument. If you read the argument first and then read the question, what do you usually end up having to do? Read the argument again, that's what. Save yourself a little time. Fifteen seconds might not seem like much for one question, but if you multiply that by fourteen questions, you stand to save almost four minutes of reading time that would otherwise be wasted.

Second, the questions that ETS uses on Argument questions fall into a few basic categories, and each question type involves slightly different techniques. If you read the question to each argument first, you can read the argument with your ultimate goal already stored in the back of your mind.

Don't Think So Much

Each argument is a self-contained bit of logic that doesn't require any outside information. As you consider the answer choices, you may be tempted to consider other thoughts of your own that, though valid, are immaterial to the argument. Don't do it.

> Everything you need to consider on an Argument question is right there in front of you.

As we'll discuss later, the vast majority of wrong answers to Argument questions are incorrect because they're irrelevant. Therefore, the best way to avoid picking irrelevant answer choices is to develop a sense of tunnel vision to help you ignore the stuff that doesn't matter. That's another difference between the GMAT and real life: On the GMAT, it's actually better to have a very narrow mind.

THE PARTS OF AN ARGUMENT

Most arguments are constructed using two basic building blocks: *premises* and *assumptions*. The author uses these ideas as supporting points for the argument's *conclusion*. Most arguments follow the conclusion-premise-assumption construct; we'll call it the CPA Model just to make you accountants feel at home. (Is it possible to be both a CPA and a model?)

The difference between the two types of supporting points is that premises are stated within the passage, and assumptions are not (they're assumed). Let's look at an example of how ETS builds arguments:

> I want to go the movies. My car broke down last week. There-
> fore, I need to buy a new car.

This seems like an overly simple example, but the logic doesn't get much more complicated. (It's just the complicated word usage they use that muddies the water.) From the use of the word *Therefore*, you can tell that the last sentence is the conclusion:

> **Therefore**, I need to buy a new car.

The author has concluded that he needs to buy a new car, based on two stated premises:

> **Premise 1:** I want to go the movies.

> **Premise 2:** My car broke down last week.

These are the premises, because they appear in black and white, right before your eyes. But arguments cannot stand on premises alone. There have to be other supporting points that are *assumed* to be true in order for the conclusion to work. What does the author assume?

> **Assumption 1:** The only way to get to the movies is by car.

The author has concluded that he needs a new car because he wants to go to the movies. The author assumes, then, that his automobile is the only mode of available transportation. If it were possible that he could take a bus or a subway to the movies, he wouldn't have to get a new car.

> **Assumption 2:** The car can't be repaired.

This is also a big assumption. If he could fix his car, then he would not need to buy a new one. In both cases, the assumptions have to be true in order for the conclusion to be valid. Keep this idea in mind, because we'll talk more about it in the weaken/strengthen portion of the chapter.

That's the basic construction of most GMAT arguments: a conclusion that rests upon a few supporting points (either explicit or assumed). The confusion sets in because the text of most arguments is deliberately hard to grasp right away.

PROCESS OF ELIMINATION

The CAT may have taken away your ability to skip around and do the questions out of order, but good old POE is still a quality technique.

Who Cares?

In fact, POE is especially useful because of this fact:

> Most of the wrong answers to Argument questions are incorrect because they're irrelevant.

After you read an answer choice, you're more than likely to ask yourself, "Who cares?" That's because the information in the choice won't have a direct bearing on the passage. Take a look at this example:

> [argument] Because of an unusually cold winter, Nebraska's annual corn output will be one-third of what it was last year. As a result, the price of corn is sure to rise, and moviegoers can expect to pay an extra dollar for a large serving of popcorn.
>
> [question] Which of the following, if true, most seriously weakens the argument above?

The argument states that popcorn prices are going to rise, and you have to weaken it. Thus, you're looking for answer choices that suggest that popcorn prices *won't* rise. Now look at some answer choices:

- ○ Meteorologists are predicting that next winter will be even colder than this past one.
- ○ This year, theaters are expected to spend upwards of $50 for a bushel of popcorn.
- ○ Several theaters that have offered their patrons the choice of regular or caramel-covered popcorn have enjoyed steadily rising popcorn sales in each of the past four years.
- ○ The cold winter did not have as detrimental an effect on Nebraska's barley output.
- ○ Studies show that movie ticket sales soar during periods of especially cold weather.

Which of these answer choices is relevant to the argument? Don't stare at them too long, because it's a trick question—they're all irrelevant! And when we say irrelevant, we mean *irrelevant to the argument*. Each answer choice contains subject matter that pertains to cold weather and/or the price of popcorn, but none of them addresses the validity of the argument that the cold Nebraska winter will ultimately force you and me to shell out more dough for a bucket of popcorn.

○ Meteorologists are predicting that next winter will be even colder than this past one.

Analysis: This might be true, and it might result in even higher prices in the future. But what about the present? We're concerned with the here and now, not the there and then.
Decision: Irrelevant.

○ This year, theaters are expected to spend upwards of $50 for a bushel of popcorn.

Analysis: Great. So we know how much popcorn costs. Big deal! Is this any proof that the price can't go higher? In fact, this choice is especially evil because it wants us to think that popcorn is already expensive. ("Fifty bucks? Wow, that's a lot. That's even more than this book costs.") But we have no other prices for comparison. Last year, the per-bushel price could have been $5 or $500, so we don't know if prices are rising or falling.
Decision: Irrelevant.

○ Several theaters that have offered their patrons the choice of regular or caramel-covered popcorn have enjoyed steadily rising popcorn sales in each of the past four years.

Analysis: This one wants to put a positive spin on the situation by stating that movie patrons are buying more popcorn. That doesn't mean the price won't rise, though.
Decision: Irrelevant.

○ The cold winter did not have as detrimental an effect on Nebraska's barley output.

Analysis: OK. Do they make popcorn out of barley kernels? If not, then we have no reason to consider this one any further.
Decision: Irrelevant.

○ Studies show that movie ticket sales soar during periods of especially cold weather.

Analysis: This one is especially nutty. It tries to appear relevant by linking two separate parts of the passage, but it omits a crucial point: What about *popcorn*? Do we know that all these moviegoers are buying popcorn at theaters?
Decision: Irrelevant.

The Relevant Choices

The argument says that prices will rise because supply will fall. Therefore, there are several very important assumptions in play here (and none of the previous five choices addressed them). Each of these, however, is much more likely to be a credited response:

○ Other corn-producing states enjoyed an unseasonably warm winter, and their corn production will be higher than usual.

Analysis: The choice pertains to the assumption that Nebraska is the only state in which corn is grown. If other states are also supplying corn that will make up for Nebraska's shortfall, then prices are unlikely to rise; thus the argument is weakened.

○ Most theaters have struck long-term deals with corn wholesalers to purchase popcorn kernels in bulk at a fixed price.

Analysis: The argument also assumes that supply and price are always directly related. In this instance, however, theater owners won't be affected by fluctuations in supply because their popcorn costs are fixed. Again, this weakens the argument.

○ The majority of Nebraska corn farmers anticipated the cold winter and stockpiled vast quantities of corn during the fall.

Analysis: The supply isn't so low after all, because corn farmers can compensate for this year's drop. Weakened again.

○ In response to their more health-conscious clientele, many theaters are replacing the popcorn they normally sell with miniature rice cakes.

Analysis: This choice attacks the assumption that demand among theater owners for popcorn will remain the same. If theaters aren't buying as much popcorn anymore, then the decreased demand will match the decreased supply and prices won't rise. This, too, weakens the argument.

○ The last time the price of popcorn was raised by a dollar, protest riots broke out all over the country causing many theaters to close for months for repairs.

Analysis: OK, this one is sort of goofy. But it's relevant to the argument because the argument assumes that theater owners always want to turn a profit at their concession stands. If this answer choice were true, theater owners might think twice about raising the price and instead just ride out the tough times until popcorn was plentiful again. This weakens the argument.

When you read an argument, don't sit and think of all the possible assumptions that could pertain to it. You'll lose lots of valuable time and still not find the one related to the correct answer. It's better to scan the answer choices and learn to recognize which ones involve the argument's assumptions and which do not. All of this relates to relevance to some degree, but there is also a quality technique that we'll talk about in the section about assumption questions later in the chapter.

THE PLAN OF ATTACK

Remember the five-step plan in chapter 2? Well, we're all really fond of step-by-step programs here at The Princeton Review, so here's the four-step plan for each Argument:

1. **Read the question first and identify what type of question it is.**

There are fewer than ten types of Critical Reasoning questions (as you'll see below), and each has its own considerations. Take a moment to read the question first and determine what exactly is being asked of you—especially if the question has a lot of double negatives that are meant to confuse you. Then move on to the argument.

2. **Read and paraphrase the passage.**

As we talked about in chapter 3, the paramount skill to have on the GMAT verbal section is the ability to read and understand what you read as quickly and completely as possible. So minimize your rereading as best you can and paraphrase each passage into conversational English that a ten-year-old would understand. You'll be better prepared to assess the answer choices that way.

3. **Consider the answer choices individually and get rid of irrelevant stuff.**

Once you know what's going on in the argument (and it's easier to read some of them than others), determine which choices have nothing to do with the argument's logic.

4. **Use POE on any remaining choices.**

If you're down to two or more choices and are having trouble deciding, find flaws in the wrong choices. If the CPA Model is relevant, breaking the argument down into its parts will help you find the choice that answers the question best.

THE QUESTION TYPES

Reading the question first is very useful, because you're only going to see about fourteen Arguments on your GMAT. These questions will all fall within the categories we're about to discuss.

> To answer these questions (especially if you're down to two choices), it will usually be useful for you to consult the CPA Model.

Weaken and Strengthen Questions

Probably half of the Arguments that you see on your GMAT will ask you to weaken or strengthen an argument. Depending on the difficulty of the question, ETS will also try to phrase the weaken question in several ways, varying from the straightforward to the convoluted:

- Which of the following, if true, would most seriously **weaken the conclusion**?

- Which of the following, if true, **is the best basis for a criticism** of profit-sharing among construction unions?

- Supporters of the plan to force all politicians to shave their heads would likely face the strongest opposition if which of the following were voiced?

> When answering a weaken question, look for an answer choice that undermines the conclusion and is relevant to the premises. The answers to weaken questions usually refute an assumption.

Weaken and strengthen questions rely heavily on the CPA Model, because they're closely related to an argument's assumptions. As you might imagine, strengthen questions are the reverse of weaken ones.

- Which of the following, if true, could **proponents** of the plan above most appropriately cite as evidence of the **soundness** of their plan?

- Which of the following, if true, taken together with the information above, best **supports** the conclusion that fire-eaters will pay more in insurance premiums?

> When answering a strengthen question, look for an answer choice that generally supports the conclusion and is relevant to the premises. The answers to strengthen questions usually state an assumption.

Let's look at an Argument and determine how assumptions factor into these types of questions.

A new interactive television company offering subscribers the ability to download movies off the Internet will have an easy time installing its new equipment in Hong Kong. Most of Hong Kong's residential buildings are easy to rewire and in close proximity to one of the company's central video servers. Thus, this new service is destined to succeed, despite the high cost to subscribe.

Which of the following, if true, casts the most doubt on the validity of this argument?

- ○ There are no plans to set up similar services in any other major Asian city in the next decade.
- ○ Surveys indicate that many of Hong Kong's residents would like the option of American movies that are subtitled rather than dubbed, and the new company cannot offer that yet.
- ○ The residents of Hong Kong who have the most wealth, and are thus most likely to subscribe to the service, live too far away from the city center to be connected.
- ○ The current cable-television provider in Hong Kong has lost money in each of the past four years.
- ○ Hong Kong's Bureau of Zoning has authorized the construction of more than twenty new movie theaters next year.

Each of these answer choices has something positive to say about the cable industry in Hong Kong. Your job is to determine which one is relevant to the premises that are given.

- ○ There are no plans to set up similar services in any other major Asian city in the next decade.

Analysis: Nice try, but we're looking at the problem in Hong Kong; the situation anywhere else is not necessarily comparable.
Decision: No.

- ○ Surveys indicate that many of Hong Kong's residents would like the option of American movies that are subtitled rather than dubbed, and the new company cannot offer that yet.

Analysis: This one serves to undermine the popularity of the service, but the key word is *yet*. It's possible that the new company will eventually find a way to give the people what they want.
Decision: So long.

- ○ The residents of Hong Kong who have the most wealth, and are thus most likely to subscribe to the service, live too far away from the city center to be connected.

Analysis: The argument says that the cost to subscribe is high, and the author assumes that everyone who lives close enough to get wired for the new service will want to buy it. The company won't succeed if the only people who can afford the service can't get it.
Decision: Yes!

○ The current cable-television provider in Hong Kong has lost money in each of the past four years.

Analysis: Again, we're making a comparison—this time between the current cable provider and the new interactive TV company. We can't assume that the two are comparable, because their products are probably very different. And the management teams could run their businesses in different ways.

Decision: Move on.

○ Hong Kong's Bureau of Zoning has authorized the construction of more than twenty new movie theaters next year.

Analysis: ETS would want us to think that these new movie theaters will threaten the home-viewing business. This may be true, but it's also possible that Hong Kongers would still prefer to stay home if the service were available to them.

Decision: Bye-bye. The answer is (C).

We've established that the assumption of this argument is that the people who live close enough to a central video server will be willing and able to afford the service. Therefore, there are several ways to strengthen the argument using this assumption:

○ As the required technology becomes more commonplace, subscription prices are sure to come down.

○ People would pay more to stay home and watch a movie whenever they want rather than be obligated to go out and adhere to a theater's projection schedule.

○ Surveys indicate that movies are by far the most common form of entertainment among Hong Kong's residents.

Each of these answer choices strengthens the argument, because each one is directly relevant to the assumptions that people will be able to afford the service and they will want to pay for it. It is important for you to distinguish relevant answer choices from irrelevant ones.

Indicate the Flaw Questions

Questions that want you to find the mistake are related to weaken questions, but they're not the same. They usually look something like this:

♦ Which of the following indicates **a flaw** in the reasoning above?

♦ The argument is **flawed** in that it ignores the possibility that . . .

In a weaken question, you have to determine which answer choice (which represents *new* information) would make the conclusion less plausible. In a flaw question, the mistake is already there, and you have to determine what it is.

There is some truth to the speculation that the Olympic boxing judge from Country M has been favoring athletes from his home country. Of all the boxing matches he has assessed that involved a boxer from Country M, he has judged his countrymen to be victorious 75 percent of the time.

Which of the following statements suggests that the above argument is flawed?

This argument is just plain sneaky, because it exploits our innate sense of numerical fairness. Since the judge has favored his countrymen more than half the time, he must be a crook, right?

○ The other judges who presided over the same Olympic fights as the judge from Country M judged that Country M's boxers should have won in more than 80 percent of the fights.

Even though Country M's judge supported his boxers 75 percent of the time, it's possible that Country M is a nation of superboxers who deserved to win even more than they did. The argument is flawed because it wants to assume that unfair equals more than half, when unfair actually equals more than *they should*. For that reason, answer choice (E) might also appear like this:

○ Though the judge from Country M favored his country-men more than half of the time, it is possible that Country M's boxers deserved to win even more than they actually did.

This should help you realize that no new information was added; the flaw in the logic was merely exposed.

Assumption Questions

In order for a conclusion to be valid, its premises and assumptions must be true. That's why the best way to weaken an argument is to prove that an assumption is false. Below are examples of assumption questions you are likely to see on the GMAT:

◆ The argument above **assumes** that . . .

◆ The conclusion above would be **more reasonably drawn** if which of the following were inserted into the argument as **an additional premise**?

◆ The conclusion drawn in the last sentence depends on which of the following **assumptions**?

> On assumption questions, find the conclusion and determine which answer choice needs to be true in order for the conclusion to be valid.

When using the Process of Elimination, get rid of all the answer choices that either don't support the conclusion or don't affect the conclusion's soundness.

> The World Trade Organization (WTO) has stepped up its scrutiny of the offshore production facilities owned by the world's top producer of athletic footwear. A recent labor probe in Country P found that each of the company's production plants violated several labor laws, and the WTO forced the company to double the minimum wage of each of its workers within that country. Therefore, the company's costs of producing athletic footwear will rise.
>
> The conclusion above is based on which of the following assumptions?
> - ○ The company has never been forced to raise the minimum wage of its workers in the past.
> - ○ Sales of the company's footwear in Country P will rise.
> - ○ Footwear that is produced in Country P is superior to that produced in any other country.
> - ○ The company will continue to produce its athletic footwear in Country P.
> - ○ The company's public display of compassion for its workers will ultimately translate into a better image among consumers.

This is an assumption question, and the loose translation of the passage goes something like this: The WTO forced a company to pay its workers more money in Country P, so the company's production costs will go up.

One of the best ways to determine whether an answer choice is the sought-after assumption is to negate each one and see if the conclusion survives. Once you realize that an answer choice is crucial to the conclusion's survival, you know you've hit paydirt.

> - ○ The company has never been forced to raise the minimum wage of its workers in the past.

Negation: The company *has* been forced to raise the minimum wage of its workers in the past.

Analysis: Whether or not this has happened in the past has no impact on what will happen in the future. And we still know nothing about costs.

Decision: Eliminate it.

○   Sales of the company's footwear in Country P will rise.

Negation: Sales of the company's footwear in Country P will *not* rise.

Analysis: ETS would like us to believe that the workers in Country P will enjoy their new wealth by buying the shoes they're making (which will increase the company's *profits*), but what they do with their money has no impact on the company's *costs*.

Decision: Nope.

○   Footwear that is produced in Country P is superior to that produced in any other country.

Negation: Footwear that is produced in Country P is *not* superior to that produced in any other country.

Analysis: It sounds logical to us that the company would choose to make its product with the best workers possible, but we don't know that for sure. And how does this impact costs?

Decision: Eliminate it.

○   The company will continue to produce its athletic footwear in Country P.

Negation: The company will *not* continue to produce its athletic footwear in Country P.

Analysis: Yes! The author of the argument concludes that the company's production costs will go up because of the wage increase. It must be assumed, therefore, that the company will stay in Country P. If it decides to shift its production to another country, it's possible that the labor laws are different and the company will keep its production costs down.

Decision: We have a winner.

○   The company's public display of compassion for its workers will ultimately translate into a better image among consumers.

Negation: The company's public display of compassion for its workers will *not* ultimately translate into a better image among consumers.

Analysis: Just another heartstrings issue. Of course, we care about the oppressed workers, but a greater public image still does not address the company's production costs.

Decision: Gone. The best answer is (D).

Try to use this negation technique to figure out which answer choices are invaluable and which are irrelevant.

Evaluate the Argument Questions

This type of question is related to relevance. A conclusion is asserted, and ETS wants to know which choice helps to determine whether the conclusion is valid. Below are two ideas of what evaluate the argument questions will be like:

- Which of the following determinations is most likely to yield significant information that would help to evaluate the researcher's hypothesis?

- Which of the following must be studied to assess the validity of the argument above?

On the AWA Argument essay, you're asked to provide any other information that would help you to determine whether the argument makes logical sense. These questions work in much the same way. Wrong answers to evaluate the argument questions are usually just not relevant to the debate.

> A growing number of urban school districts have embraced the practice of "social promotion," whereby a student is automatically promoted to the next highest grade regardless of whether he or she has passed or failed English class. This policy is flawed, because the only criterion that a student must fulfill in order to advance is to pass a state-wide standardized test.
>
> The answer to which of the following questions would be most useful in evaluating the validity of "social promotion"?
>
> ○ Do students have the option of taking a standardized test in a language other than English?
> ○ What is the rate of graduation from schools at which "social promotion" is commonly practiced?
> ○ How rigorous are the questions on these standardized tests that pertain to English skills?
> ○ How prevalent is "social promotion" among school districts in more suburban areas?
> ○ If a student fails a standardized test, is he or she given the chance to take it again before having to be kept back?

If you look at each of these separately, you'll see that all but (C) are irrelevant to the argument. If we knew more about the standardized test that the kids must pass, we would have a better idea of the English skills that the kids have. It might be that this test is a better judge of English skills than one's grades.

WHEN THE CPA MODEL DOESN'T APPLY

From here on, don't worry about the CPA Model. The question types below all have something quite different at stake.

Inference Questions

When you infer something, you determine that something is definitely true even though you weren't directly told so. If someone told you that she lived in a U.S. state directly south of Washington and directly north of California, you could correctly infer that she lived in Oregon. She didn't tell you directly; she *implied* it, and you *inferred* it. The questions will look something like this:

- If each of the statements above is true, which of the following must also be true?

- From the previous statements, it most directly follows that . . .

- Which of the following can be **correctly inferred** from the statements above?

Inference questions don't deal much with the CPA Model. If anything, the passage is a series of premises and the correct answer choice is the only conclusion that can be properly drawn.

> When you see an inference question, you have to ask yourself only one question: "Which of the answer choices absolutely, positively, must be true based on what I've read?"

If you can't find direct proof that the answer choice is true, then it's out. Period. For that reason, stay away from answer choices that are too strong in their assertions. The right answer is usually a small detail that seems too obvious to merit mention.

Beware of Your Heartstrings!

We are all human, and we all have feelings. Because of this, ETS likes to mine its answer choices with sentimental favorites that appeal to our sense of decency or fairness. It's a tough world out there, though, and logic derives from the head, not the heart. Here is an example:

> Health professionals have argued that too much butter in a person's diet can cause the dangerous overdevelopment in the bloodstream of high-density lipoproteins that can clog arteries and put that person at risk of a heart attack. In South Korea, however, where per-capita butter consumption is almost non-existent, the incidence of heart attacks is no less than that in countries where butter is commonly served at every meal.

Which of the following statements represents the most reliable conclusion that can be drawn from the information above?

- ○ Most people, if told of the potential risk of butter consumption, would willingly switch to margarine or some other butter substitute.
- ○ Despite arguments to the contrary, butter does not have a deleterious effect on the human heart.
- ○ Koreans avoid butter because they dislike the taste, not because of the health risk.
- ○ Butter consumption is probably not the only factor that can be linked to the incidence of heart attacks.
- ○ Other dairy products such as cheese and yogurt pose an equal threat to cardiovascular fitness.

Let's take a crack at the answer choices:

- ○ Most people, if told of the potential risk of butter consumption, would willingly switch to margarine or some other butter substitute.

Analysis: This is a heartstrings answer. We would like to think that the average person will give up something to preserve his health, but that's not necessarily the case. As much as we'd like to believe this, we don't know for a fact that it's true.
Decision: Eliminate it.

- ○ Despite arguments to the contrary, butter does not have a deleterious effect on the human heart.

Analysis: Here is a classic example of an answer choice that goes too far. We don't know that butter doesn't affect the heart; it could still be as dangerous as the health officials say.
Decision: Move on.

- ○ Koreans avoid butter because they dislike the taste, not because of the health risk.

Analysis: Please. Is there any clue about this anywhere in the passage? Not even a hint.
Decision: Get rid of it.

- ○ Butter consumption is probably not the only factor that can be linked to the incidence of heart attack.

Analysis: Aha. We can defend this one. Butter may be dangerous to your bloodstream, yet Koreans (who don't eat any butter) are also getting heart attacks. That means that something else must be causing heart trouble over there.
Decision: Bingo.

◯   Other dairy products such as cheese and yogurt pose an equal threat to cardiovascular fitness.

Analysis: Not even close. Here, ETS is trying to appeal to some shred of sense that might lead you to believe that all dairy products are bad for you just because butter might be. But you're not about to fall for that, are you?

Decision: Nope.

Paradox Questions

A paradox question asks you to explain a discrepancy or resolve two statements that don't seem to coexist well. Each paradox question contains two seemingly contradictory facts, and the question will read something like this:

◆   Which of the following, if true, contributes most to an explanation of how the department store's revenues tripled despite the closing of more than half its stores?

◆   Fact 1 would be most likely to contribute to an explanation of fact 2 if it were also true that . . .

◆   Which of the following statements, if true, would best explain the 1984 increase in paranoia?

Your job is to find the answer choice that shows that the facts aren't contradictory after all.

A month ago, the average price of a gallon of gasoline in Albemarle County rose 15 cents. Since then, however, each of the gas stations in Albemarle County has reported an increase of at least 20 percent in the aggregate number of gallons purchased.

Which of the following, if true, would best explain why so much more gasoline was purchased despite the steep price increase?

◯   In an effort to fund a second refining facility nearby, the oil refinery that serves the majority of the gas stations in Albemarle County raised its prices.

◯   A marketing strategy devised by a powerful environmentalist interest group has inspired many commuters who normally drive to work alone to organize car pools with coworkers.

◯   A statewide strike of all commercial and commuter railway workers has brought all rail traffic to a halt.

◯   Drivers are also purchasing more cans of heavy-grade oil, even though the price per can has remained virtually unchanged.

◯   Almost no one who lives within Albemarle County also works within Albemarle County.

Straightforward, right? No conclusions, no assumptions, none of that CPA stuff. Just a funny situation for you to reconcile: People are buying a lot more gas even though the price is higher. One of the answer choices explains this, and the rest don't.

○ In an effort to fund a second refining facility nearby, the oil refinery that serves the majority of the gas stations in Albemarle County raised its prices.

Analysis: This might explain why the price is higher, but why are people buying more of it?
Decision: Eliminate it.

○ A marketing strategy devised by a powerful environmentalist interest group has inspired many commuters who normally drive to work alone to organize car pools with coworkers.

Analysis: This one is no help whatsoever. If commuters have started car pooling, then it would follow logically that even less gasoline is being purchased. This choice is supposed to appeal to our heartstrings, because we all perceive environmentalists to be enlightened protectors of our diseased planet. Yeah, whatever.
Decision: Nope.

○ A statewide strike of all commercial and commuter railway workers has brought all rail traffic to a halt.

Analysis: It might seem irrelevant at first. After all, who cares about the railroads? But railroads function as an alternate form of transportation—especially commuter transportation. Therefore, it's feasible that commuters from Albemarle County are taking alternate gas-consuming forms of transport (such as cars or buses) to work.
Decision: Keep it.

○ Drivers are also purchasing more cans of heavy-grade oil, even though the price per can has remained virtually unchanged.

Analysis: So people are buying oil, too. Well, oil and gasoline are both petroleum products, but this answer choice's usefulness ends there. This doesn't address the higher cost of gasoline, or why the gas is flying into gas tanks.
Decision: No dice.

○ Almost no one who lives within Albemarle County also works within Albemarle County.

Analysis: This is supposed to suggest to us that it's possible for residents of Albemarle County to get their gas elsewhere. It still doesn't explain why more gas is being bought.
Decision: Forget it. The best answer is (C).

Identify the Reasoning Questions

Success with these questions derives from mapping out how an argument is structured and finding the answer choice that best describes the logic used. They're related to structure questions pertaining to Reading Comprehension passages.

The Montridge Town Council has just voted to increase the local tax rate on all new commercial businesses within the town's border. The council believes that if it acts to keep the town as residential as possible, the town will attract wealthier people who will gravitate toward the town's charm and will not complain about an increase in property taxes.

Which of the following best expresses the logical pattern underlying the Montridge Town Council's recent decision?

○ It rationalized that a drop in revenue from one source would ultimately be offset by an increase from another source.

○ It established its distaste for commercial activity within Montridge.

○ It questioned the assumption that all commercial businesses would react to the tax hike by leaving town.

○ It believes that in order to achieve goals, they must be prioritized.

○ It weighed several options and chose the one that it believed would result in the least collateral damage.

If you paraphrase the passage, you can see that the Montridge Town Council was willing to forgo corporate tax money in return for the residential tax money it would later collect from the rich folks who moved in. Therefore, (A) is the best choice.

OTHER POINTS TO CONSIDER

Keep these other points in mind as you develop your technique for analyzing Arguments. Find as many practice problems as you can, and take note of the number of times each of these topics surfaces.

Avoid Extremes

We humans are conditioned, for the most part, to think in extremes. If it's not black, it's white. GMAT arguments, however, have more of a gray area. If a question says *weaken*, the correct answer will make the argument less plausible. It won't necessarily render the argument absolutely useless. Similarly, the correct answer to a strengthen question doesn't necessarily make the argument airtight and perfect. It just increases the chance, however, slightly, that the argument is valid.

What Caused What?

The causal argument is very common on the GMAT because its makeup fits so neatly in the CPA Model: A conclusion is deemed to be true *because* of a few premises.

When an argument asserts that A causes B, there are two common assumptions involved:

- There was no other cause for B.
- B didn't cause A.

There are several dead giveaways for a causal argument, including phrases such as *because of*, *due to*, and *as a result*.

> Attendance at a local indoor health club has suffered in the last three months. One community leader believes that people have stayed away from the facility because it recently raised the price of a month-to-month membership by 35 percent.
>
> Which of the following, if true, would undermine the validity of the community leader's conclusion?

Each of the following two answer choices is a possible correct answer:

> ○ Due to a recent stretch of unseasonably warm weather, most people have taken to exercising outdoors.

This answer choice weakens the argument because it suggests an alternate reason why fewer people are going to the health club. Since it has been warm outside, it's possible that the weather (and not the higher membership prices) is keeping people away.

> ○ Committed to maintaining its profit margins, the health club decided to offset the decrease in the number of paying customers by increasing the price of membership to those who already belonged.

This one turns the causal relationship on its head. The community leader believes that the price increase caused the decrease in paying customers (A caused B) when, in fact, the decrease in customers caused the price increase (B caused A). Either of these is a valid way to undermine a causal relationship.

Statistics, Numbers, and Lies

Anyone who has ever had to crunch numbers knows that the shrewdest doctors can bend statistics to support any conclusion they want. There are two major points to know about when you're dealing with numbers. The first relates to conclusions that rely on some sort of survey or poll:

> When an argument is based on statistical evidence, the assumption is that the people polled are representative of the whole.

It's a rather simple strategy—so simple, in fact, that questions like the one below have become more scarce lately:

> Employees of Drubb Corporation seem to be very pleased with the work that the company's board of directors is doing. Just last week, the majority of the company's secretaries signed a letter of support for the company's decision to announce a two-for-one stock split.

The author of this argument thinks that every employee likes the directors' new decision because the secretaries have expressed their support. The way to weaken the argument is to disprove the assumption that secretaries are just like all the other employees.

> ○ As a result of a lawsuit that the board recently settled with the National Secretaries Union, each of the secretaries receives three times as many stock options as any other employee.

All this stuff about lawsuits might appear irrelevant, but it creates a reason why the secretaries are not representative of all employees (they're happier because they have more stock).

Math? In *This* Book?

The second statistical matter to learn about involves a little mathematical computation. Believe it or not, ETS likes to bring math into the equation every once in a while, because the numbers are likely to confuse you—especially if you're in the middle of a seventy-five-minute verbal section. Many math-related questions involve inferences.

> Country L used to import wheat from Country S because Country S's price per bale was the cheapest available. When Country S raised its price by 25 percent, however, Country L decided to transfer its business to Country D, which now boasted the best deal available.
>
> Which of the following, if true, would be best supported by the assertions above?
> ○ The cost to harvest a bale of wheat in Country S increased by 25 percent.
> ○ If Country S were to lower its price below Country D's price, then Country L would resume its import relationship with Country S.
> ○ If Country L could somehow reduce the cost of producing domestic wheat by 25 percent, it wouldn't need to rely on any wheat imports.
> ○ Country S and Country D do not import or export any wheat from each other.
> ○ If Country D were to increase its price per bale of wheat by 25 percent, then a bale of wheat from Country S would once again be less expensive.

ETS likes to fill your head with alphabet soup to distract you from the task at hand, and it usually works. If you've done any math review with The Princeton Review, you know that one of our marquis techniques is to plug in real numbers for any variables. That technique works here as well.

◯ The cost to harvest a bale of wheat in Country S
increased by 25 percent.

Analysis: We'd all like to think that Country S has no profit motive and thus increased its price by the exact percent that its costs rose. But we don't know if that's true.
Decision: Goodbye.

◯ If Country S were to lower its price below Country D's
price, then Country L would resume its import
relationship with Country S.

Analysis: This one looks tempting, because it's possible that Country S could be the cheapest again.
Decision: Keep it.

◯ If Country L could somehow reduce the cost of pro-
ducing domestic wheat by 25 percent, it wouldn't
need to rely on any wheat imports.

Analysis: It's too extreme (*rely on any wheat imports?*). Besides, we have no information about domestic wheat production.
Decision: Sayonara.

◯ Country S and Country D do not import or export any
wheat from each other.

Analysis: This one is barely worth looking at. We have no clue whether Country S and Country D do any business together.
Decision: Eliminate it.

◯ If Country D were to increase its price per bale of
wheat by 25 percent, then a bale of wheat from
Country S would once again be less expensive.

Analysis: Use numbers to bear this one out. Since we're dealing with percents, let's say that Country S's price was $100, and it shot up to $125. Since Country D didn't have the best deal available but it does now, Country D's price must be somewhere between $100 and $125. If you take any number in that range and increase it by 25 percent, the result will be greater.
Decision: (E) is the correct answer because the numbers back it up. But, you ask, what about (B)? Well, it's possible that Country S would be the cheapest again, but we've disallowed the possibility of a fourth country in the game. If Country S's price went from $100 to $125, and County D's price was $120, we can't assume that Country S would be the cheapest again if it lowered its price to $110. What if Country X sold wheat for $105? Thus (B) is dead, and the answer is (E).

Arguing by Analogy

How many of you out there can relate to this scenario?

> You: Mom, will you let me stay up until 11 o'clock?

> Mom: Why should I let you stay up until 11 o'clock?

> You: Because Derek's mother lets him stay up until 11 o'clock!

Most ten-year-olds first learn to back up their logical positions by arguing by analogy: Something should be true about your family because it's true in Derek's family. It makes sense on the surface, but how does your mom respond to effectively kill your argument and send you to your room devastated?

> Mom: Well, I'm not Derek's mother.

You tried to make an argument by analogy, and your mom shot you down by refuting your assumption that all families are alike.

> When an argument is based on an analogy between two separate things, the assumption is that the two things are very much the same.

If you're asked to weaken an argument by analogy, look for an answer choice that indicates that the two things are different.

> Last month, the Hungarian embassy had to be emptied because of a perceived threat of a bomb in the building. Therefore, anyone who targets the Nigerian embassy next door will create similar chaos.

> Which of the following, if true, would most weaken the conclusion above?

The author concludes that life at the Nigerian embassy will be disrupted by a bomb threat because it happened at the Hungarian embassy. The author assumes that the two embassies will be equally affected because they are equally prepared. Therefore, the correct answer might read something like this:

> ◯ In response to the trouble at the Hungarian embassy, each of the other embassies on the block tightened security by doubling the number of watchmen who patrol the border of the property.

This answer choice asserts that the two embassies are different, so the chance that the two will be affected equally by a bomb threat is weakened. The argument isn't ruined, of course (after all, all the new guards could be idiots or blind or something), but you still have to scratch your head as to whether the argument is defensible.

EXCEPT Questions

Most people think that EXCEPT questions are the most difficult ones to work with, but that doesn't necessarily have to be the case. In fact, they're remarkably similar to regular questions; instead of four wrong answers and one correct one, there are four correct answers and one wrong one. Either way, one answer choice is supposed to stand out from the others.

The only difference is that you have to remember that you're working with an EXCEPT question. Too many students forget this in the heat of battle; in fact, many students don't even see the EXCEPT sitting right in front of them, even though it's right there in capital letters.

To keep your focus, follow this technique:

  ◆   Write the letters (A) through (E) on your scratch paper.

  ◆   Work the problem as you always do.

  ◆   Write "Yes" next to answer choices that answer the question properly, and "No" next to the one that doesn't.

  ◆   Pick the choice with "No" next to it.

Let's say you're faced with a question like this, for example:

Each of the following is a state capital EXCEPT

  ○   Trenton
  ○   Sacramento
  ○   Tallahassee
  ○   Moscow
  ○   Columbus

Your scratch paper should look something like this:

A   Yes
B   Yes
C   Yes
D   No
E   Yes

Now you can pick (D).

PUTTING IT ALL TOGETHER

All right. We've covered just about everything you're likely to see and everything you'll need to know. Let's put the plan of attack into action as we analyze the sample Argument from the beginning of the chapter.

1. Read the question first and identify what type of question it is.

> Which of the following, if true, calls the above conclusion into question?

It's a weaken question. The CPA Model applies, so we should keep an eye out for the argument's conclusion.

2. Read and paraphrase the passage. Remember this argument from the beginning of the chapter? Let's see what you've learned.

> Scientists estimate the cost of a transatlantic flight for an aerosonde, an unmanned airplane designed to collect atmospheric data, to be $20,000. An ordinary weather balloon, by contrast, can collect virtually the same information for about $200. Therefore, weather balloons are clearly the more cost-efficient method for gathering information.

This argument has three sentences. The last one is the argument's conclusion (again, *Therefore* is a dead giveaway):

Therefore, weather balloons are clearly the more cost-efficient method for gathering information.

The author bases this conclusion on the two previous statements:

Premise 1: Scientists estimate the cost of a transatlantic flight for an aerosonde, an unmanned airplane designed to collect atmospheric data, to be $20,000.

Premise 2: An ordinary weather balloon, by contrast, can collect virtually the same information for about $200.

Loose translation: Weather balloons are a better deal than these new, high-tech weather planes because the balloons are much cheaper.

We're trying to weaken this argument, so our goal is to find an answer choice that suggests either that weather balloons are not a better deal or that the aerosondes are more cost-efficient than the passage portrays them to be.

3. Consider the answer choices individually.

> ◯ Aerosondes are less costly than piloted planes and also do not put human life at risk.

Analysis: This makes a good point about aerosondes, but *piloted planes* are not the issue. There's no direct contrast with weather balloons, either. (Besides, it's possible to say the same things about weather balloons.)

Decision: Kill it.

○ Politicians who have lobbied for federal funds to construct the aerosonde are astonished at its in-flight agility.

Analysis: Another answer choice that pulls at your heartstrings because it stresses one of the aerosonde's good qualities, but is *agility* related to *cost*? Nope. This one's out of the scope as well.
Decision: See ya.

○ Weather balloons are subject to violent weather changes than can blow them miles off course.

Analysis: Not even close. It tries to make itself attractive by taking a swipe at weather balloons, but it doesn't address the core issue of this argument: *cost*. Therefore, it's out of the scope.
Decision: Kill it.

○ Aerosondes can be used over and over again, but weather balloons, because of their frailty, can only be used once.

Analysis: Might seem irrelevant at first, but it does compare the aerosonde to the weather balloon directly—something that no other answer choice has managed to do yet.
Decision: Keep it.

○ In the time it takes to launch an aerosonde, it is possible to launch more than 100 weather balloons at once.

Analysis: Also an attractive choice, because the numbers seem to add up.
Decision: Let's say that you keep this one as well.

4. Use POE on any remaining choices.

You're left with (D) and (E). Check the argument's parts again: The weather balloons are more cost-effective because they are one-hundredth as expensive. Aha! Upon further reflection, however, you finally see the trouble with (E), which tries to lull you with numbers. The aerosonde costs 100 times as much as a weather balloon, and you might want to pick this if you're seized by a panic. But this doesn't weaken the argument at all. If anything, it *strengthens* the argument by adding that in addition to being far less expensive, weather balloons are also a lot easier to launch.

You found a flaw in each of the other answer choices, so (D) must be the best choice just by Process of Elimination. As it turns out, (D) does a good job of weakening the argument because it attacks a very important assumption: that *cost* equals *cost efficiency*. It's a subtle difference, but numbers like this are commonly confused. If the plane can be used over and over, as (D) asserts, then it might be true that the aerosonde will ultimately be less expensive to use.

Note: Here's a good point to recall the importance of not thinking in terms of extremes. If (D) is true, it must further be proved that the aerosonde can fly 101 missions before it is more cost-effective than the weather balloon. However, the argument is indeed weakened.

SAMPLE QUESTIONS

Take a stab at these Argument questions, and take special note of which ones pertain to the CPA Model and which do not. Also, don't forget to read the question before you read the argument, and try to read the argument just once and paraphrase it in your head before you start in on the answer choices. The answers and explanations are in chapter 8.

1. The Sports and Exhibition Authority has announced that the next election will feature a statewide referendum for the allotment of public funds to build a new football stadium in the state's capital city. Although the current facility is small and outdated, voters should reject this proposal because it stands to benefit only those who live in or near the capital at the expense of all of the state's taxpayers.

   Which of the following, if true, could supporters of the new stadium cite in response to the author's criticism?

   ○ A new facility will attract new retail businesses whose taxes will be used to fund statewide individual tax cuts.

   ○ The owner of the state's football franchise has threatened to move his team to another state across the country if a new stadium is not built.

   ○ During football season, the state's team plays only eight home games.

   ○ In each of the past five seasons, the football team has improved its record and increased its appeal among the state's football fans.

   ○ Five years ago, a neighboring state built a brand-new football stadium and successfully convinced an out-of-state team to relocate there.

2. A series of glitches within the satellite infrastructure of a cellular phone service company has resulted in service interruptions and several complaints from the company's clients. The company has responded by offering its clients free months of service and other rebates in order to keep its clients from changing to another service provider. Because of this new policy, the company's profits are destined to keep falling for years to come.

   Which of the following, if true, taken together with the information above, best supports the conclusion that the company's financial situation will only worsen as long as this new policy is in place?

   ○ Clients who experience technical difficulties with their cellular phones are unlikely to recommend the service to friends and business associates.
   ○ Since satellite technology and construction is still a relatively new industry, it's unwise to assume that every satellite will always work perfectly.
   ○ The money that the company passes on as rebates to its clients whose service has been interrupted had been previously budgeted to be spent on repairing the satellites.
   ○ In order to balance out the lost and forfeited revenue, the company will have to lay off at least 10 percent of its employees.
   ○ The company has no plans to launch any new satellites anytime soon.

3. Citing a year-long downward trend in global sales of personal computers, the CEO of Farmer Computer has announced that his company will shift much of its emphasis from PC production to corporate networking systems. Personal computers are now much more able to adapt to new networking software, but the software itself must be updated frequently.

   Which of the following, if true, casts the most serious doubt onto this new strategy?

   ○ The Farmer brand name is well respected in the computer industry, but few industry analysts believe that Farmer will have the same success with networking.
   ○ Sales of Farmer PCs have increased dramatically over each of the past six quarters, and they show no signs of slowing down.

○ A slew of new competitors in the PC production
   business will inevitably result in widespread cost
   cutting to preserve market share.

○ Sales of cellular phones and other mobile communica-
   tions are expanding at three times the rate of
   networking companies.

○ Two other companies have approached Farmer with
   the prospect of a three-way merger to form a
   dominant company that would own market share in
   the PC business.

4. Ms. S, an adoptive mother, recently read an article about a
   birth father who is suing the adoptive parents for custody of
   his child, who had been offered up for adoption without the
   birth father's permission. Ms. S adopted her child several
   years later through the same agency, but she should not be
   worried that her child's birth father will sue her for custody.

   Which of the following, if discovered to be true, would lend
   the most support to the conclusion above?

   ○ The birth mother of Ms. S's child never informed the
      birth father that she was pregnant, so the birth
      father does not know of the child's existence.

   ○ In the last twenty years in the state in which Ms. S
      lives, adoptive parents have won 90 percent of the
      cases in which birth parents have sued for custody
      of an adopted child.

   ○ The adoption in the article was completed two months
      before a policy was instituted by the agency requir-
      ing the signatures of both birth parents on the
      paperwork releasing the child for adoption.

   ○ The birth father in the case described in the article was
      over the age of eighteen at the time the adoption
      was completed.

   ○ Ms. S adopted one child through the agency men-
      tioned in the article and another child through a
      lawyer specializing in adoptions.

5. Monique: Whenever I get depressed about the direction in which my life is going, I seem to receive another bit of horrible news. It's almost as if someone up there waits until I am at my most emotionally vulnerable and decides to make things worse.

The flaw in Monique's reasoning is the possibility that
- ○ the phrase "emotionally vulnerable" is difficult to quantify.
- ○ Monique would feel better if she braced herself for bad news whenever she felt depressed.
- ○ people deal with bad news in many different ways because some people are more stable than others.
- ○ when Monique is emotionally vulnerable, the bad news she hears seems much more horrible than it actually is.
- ○ her feelings of depression might be treatable if she sought professional counseling.

6. A team of efficiency consultants conducted a study of Company X and found that 85 percent of its employees suffered a "midafternoon slump" between the hours of 2:00 p.m. and 4:00 p.m. During this slump, each employee's productivity went down an average of 30 percent. The consultants recommended, therefore, that management institute a policy encouraging employees to take their lunch breaks sometime between the hours of 2:00 p.m. and 4:00 p.m., since employees do not need to be productive as they eat lunch.

The consultants' conclusion relies on which of the following assumptions?
- ○ The consultants found no correlation between consumption of food and the feelings of lethargy experienced by the employees of Company X during the midafternoon slump.
- ○ Some of the employees of Company X do not eat breakfast until they arrive at the office at 9:00 a.m.
- ○ The consultants had seen the same slump phenomenon at Company P, and had made the same recommendation to change the lunch hour.
- ○ Most of the employees of Company X expressed a preference to eat lunch sometime between the hours of 1:00 p.m. and 3:00 p.m.
- ○ The consultants also suggested adjusting the work schedules of half of the employees of Company X so that they would come in early in the morning and leave by 2:00 p.m.

7. The occurrence of schizophrenia in the general population is 1 percent. If one parent is schizophrenic, however, the incidence rises to 12 percent, and a child with two schizophrenic parents has a 45 percent chance of also suffering from the disease.

 Which of the following can be most reasonably inferred from the passage above?

- ○ One's risk of developing schizophrenia is greater if one has a schizophrenic grandparent than if one has a grandparent with no diagnosed mental disease.
- ○ Early diagnosis of schizophrenia may reduce the severity of the impact of the disease on the patient's life.
- ○ One's risk of developing schizophrenia is higher if one has a full sibling with the disease.
- ○ Over the past forty years, psychiatrists have advanced significantly in their understanding of the causes and treatments of schizophrenia.
- ○ A person's risk of developing schizophrenia is at least partially determined by genetic factors.

8. A poll has revealed that 95 percent of the residents of Essex County believe that the way to reduce violent crime is to build larger maximum-security prisons. When a referendum for the construction of a maximum-security prison in Essex County was added to the ballot the following November, however, the proposal was voted down by a three-to-one margin.

Which of the following, if true, forms the best basis for at least a partial explanation of the apparent discrepancy described above?

- ○ The threat of a life sentence in a maximum-security prison has been shown to be an adequate deterrent of violent crime.
- ○ The prison would have been constructed by a private company, and it would have been impossible for the county government to oversee the company's finances.
- ○ Fewer than half of the registered voters in Essex County voted.
- ○ Much of the substantial cost of the prison could have been offset by increasing the tolls required to cross the bridge over nearby Lake Essex.
- ○ Maximum-security prisons are a boon to the overall well-being of the state, but they also pose a considerable risk in the areas in which they are located.

9. Most doctors dismiss male pattern baldness as a problem of heredity. A new theory, however, postulates that baldness can also result from any number of external factors, such as a stressful urban lifestyle. Supporters of this new theory point to the fact that the incidence of baldness is almost twice as common among males who live in large cities as it is among those who live elsewhere.

Which of the following, if true, most seriously weakens the new theory described above?

- ○ Scientists have developed several drugs that halt baldness in men and can be taken internally.
- ○ Census reports show that most men who are born in large cities live almost their entire lives within the city of their birth in order to be near their families.
- ○ Most men do not develop male pattern baldness until they reach the age of fifty-five, at which point their thoughts turn to pursuing a more restful lifestyle.
- ○ Men who have never lived in a large city are those least likely to develop male pattern baldness.
- ○ A fertility study determined that men who have developed male pattern baldness are less likely to marry and reproduce.

10. After several states negotiated a $195 billion settlement with the tobacco industry, State F used some of its money to create a youth-advocacy group whose antismoking advertising campaign was written entirely by high school-age students. The governor of State F has urged the state legislature to increase funding of this group because only teenagers know how to persuade other teenagers.

Which of the following, assuming that it could be carried out, would be most useful in order to evaluate the governor's desire to provide further funding to the youth-advocacy group?

- ○ comparing the short-term effects of State F's antismoking campaign to the project long-term success the campaign will probably enjoy
- ○ breaking down the statistics for the decline of teen smoking into a month-by-month analysis and determining which months saw the steepest decreases

○ comparing the decline in teen smoking in State F to the decline of teen smoking in other states that received money from the settlement and implemented advertising campaigns written by adults
○ requiring that more adults be hired to supervise the group's finances
○ comparing the aggregate number of smoking products bought the year before the group was set up to the number of smoking products bought during the year since the group was set up

11. Sport-utility vehicles have become extremely popular because of the robust and energetic image they project. Although these vehicles look sturdy, they are subject to only a small fraction of the safety standards the government imposes on ordinary passenger cars. Consequently, a high-impact collision involving both a passenger car and a sport-utility vehicle is much more likely to injure the latter and not the former.

Each of the following serves to strengthen the conclusion above EXCEPT

○ those who design vehicles are inclined to make them safe only if government rules dictate that they must
○ sport-utility vehicles have a higher center of gravity, which makes them more susceptible to turning over in a collision
○ the government rigorously enforces its standards for maximum roof strength and impact resistance in all passenger cars
○ sport-utility vehicles are less aerodynamic than passenger cars, and this extra bulk hinders their ability to accelerate
○ people who drive sport-utility vehicles are often instilled with a false sense of security and therefore neglect to wear their seatbelts

12. In 1984, almost 2 percent of humans who were admitted to hospital emergency rooms after suffering a scorpion bite in the southwestern United States died from the attack. Ten years later, this figure had jumped to 4 percent. Clearly, the venom of the scorpion has become much more toxic to humans.

    Which of the following statements, if true, most seriously weakens the above conclusion?

    ○ The scorpion population in the southwestern United States has remained steady since 1984.
    ○ There have been few innovations in the treatment of scorpion bites since 1984.
    ○ Most people who suffer scorpion bites are inexperienced hikers who are unaware of the best methods to avoid coming in contact with a scorpion.
    ○ Since 1984, people have learned that scorpion bites can be treated in the home as long as they are detected early.
    ○ People who survive one scorpion bite have a better than average chance of surviving a second bite.

13. At many universities in the United States, the average price of a used computer has risen dramatically. This rise has come about mostly because of increased demand from students entering college who need a computer but cannot afford to purchase a new one. In order to take advantage of this market, college seniors have been selling the computers that they have used throughout their college careers to incoming freshmen. This trend is sure to exert an upward pressure on the price of new computers as well.

    To support a conclusion that the average price of a new computer will rise, it would be most important to establish which of the following?

    ○ The proliferation of e-mail and the Internet has made buying and selling used merchandise much easier.
    ○ Since most students need a computer to perform only basic duties, used computers are usually just as useful as new ones.
    ○ Most students who sell their used computers are inclined to replace them with new computers.
    ○ College seniors are more likely to wait until they secure employment before making any expensive purchases.
    ○ The majority of students who purchase new computers before entering college purchase another one before they graduate.

14. In order to help the most famine-stricken areas of the world, genetic engineers have proposed injecting certain animals with the growth hormone lipazine, which increases the animals' ratio of meat to body fat. Those who oppose this plan are concerned that the hormone could cause health problems in the humans who eat the meat. A physician has defended the proposal, however, by asserting that humans can ingest as much as fifteen milligrams of lipazine daily, and no animals would ever receive a dosage higher than ten milligrams.

Which of the following statements, if true, would be of the most use to the plan's critics in response to the physician's claim?

○ Lipazine occurs naturally in many animals that are farmed for human consumption.

○ Each package of meat that had been treated with lipazine would bear a label warning consumers of that fact.

○ Lipazine is widely used among weight lifters who desire to build muscle mass in a brief period of time.

○ Some religions that are prevalent in famine-stricken countries have deemed that consumption of meat is sinful.

○ Lipazine has been shown to cause sterility in certain animals.

15. In 1994, the most common eye-related disease from which Americans suffered was conjunctivitis, and glaucoma was a distant second.

Glaucoma is much more common among patients who are more than fifty years old than it is among those who are fifty or younger, but the incidence rate for conjunctivitis is the same for people of all ages.

The average age of all Americans is expected to exceed fifty by the year 2010.

Which of the following conclusions can be most properly drawn about eye-related diseases from the information given?

○ Conjunctivitis will remain the most common eye-related disease among Americans in 2010.

○ By the year 2010, glaucoma will overtake conjunctivitis as the most common eye-related disease.

○ More people will suffer from conjunctivitis in 2010 than did in 1994.

○ Most Americans will encounter either conjunctivitis or glaucoma by 2010.

○ The average age of Americans suffering from conjunctivitis will increase between 1994 and 2010.

16. Scientists previously believed that human cells could divide an infinite number of times, as long as the tissue harboring those cells remained perfectly healthy. However, human spleen cells grown in an artificial, yet healthy, environment were shown to divide exactly twenty-four times before they died off.

The bold phrases play which of the following roles in the argument?

○ The first phrase is the author's conclusion, and the second phrase provides an additional premise for that conclusion.

○ The first phrase states a theory, and the second phrase weakens that theory by providing a counterexample.

○ The second phrase clarifies an ambiguity that the first phrase neglects to address.

○ The first phrase asserts a possible phenomenon, and the second phrase offers a condition for that phenomenon to take place.

○ The second phrase provides evidence that the theory presented in the first phrase is incomplete.

17. Malcolm: I refuse to feel any contrition about failing to report all of my income on my income tax return last year. I have discussed this topic extensively with many friends, family members, and business associates, and it is clear to me that most Americans have bent the truth on their income tax returns at one time or another.

Luka: It is improper for you to rationalize your actions that way. Regardless of how often it occurs, an illegal deed is still illegal and should be punished.

Which of the following statements summarizes Luka's reasoning in response to Malcolm's admission?

○ She questions the credibility of the sources whom Malcolm has consulted.

○ She offers evidence that Malcolm's actions were much more severe than he perceived them to be.

○ She demonstrates that Malcolm's rationalizations are based on insufficient evidence.

○ She asserts that the frequency of a crime does not lessen its severity.

○ She introduces the possibility that the moral convictions of different people can differ greatly.

18. At a certain investment bank that specializes in mergers and acquisitions, the highest percentage of potential deals that are never completed are those in which the bank's senior partner was the lead negotiator. Each of the senior partner's colleagues, however, states unequivocally that she is the most adept negotiator at the bank.

Which one of the following, if true, goes furthest toward showing that these two statements could both be correct?

- ○ The current senior partner has a better record of success than her immediate predecessor did.
- ○ Many of the junior partners were trained by the senior partner when they first joined the firm.
- ○ The senior partner works only on potential deals that have the least chance of coming to fruition.
- ○ The number of mergers in which the investment bank has been involved has declined slightly in each of the past three years.
- ○ The senior partner was chosen by the board of directors of the bank's parent company, a large publishing conglomerate.

5 | READING COMPREHENSION

If you skipped right to this chapter without reading chapter 3, Be a Better Reader, please go back and read that chapter first. There are some techniques you can use to score higher on Reading Comprehension questions, but here's one point you can't escape:

> Better scores on Reading Comp rely heavily on gathering information more efficiently.

There are no easy answers or shortcuts. In order to get better, you have to practice. After all, this book is called the *GMAT Verbal Workout*, not the *GMAT Verbal Casual Stroll*. Workouts require a little exertion.

All right. Enough with the sermon, already. Now let's take a closer look at the Reading Comprehension passages and questions.

THE STRUCTURE

On the verbal portion of the exam, you'll encounter four Reading Comp passages, and you'll have to answer three to four questions about each one. That makes for a total of fourteen or so questions out of the forty-one in the section. (This is fewer than the eighteen to twenty questions that appeared on the old P&P GMAT.) Reading Comp is not as imposing on the CAT, because the passages are spaced out within the verbal section. You no longer have to answer twenty questions in a row, as you did on the P&P.

The passages appear in a large, clear font, average six to seven words to a line, and vary in length from thirty to seventy lines. For the most part, the passages contain somewhere between 200 and 400 words.

ETS can write passages that are short and rather simple, and it can churn out huge ones full of esoteric terminology. The difficulty of the passage you get depends on how the computer thinks you're doing so far (the better you're doing, the harder the passages become), but the questions themselves don't adapt to your ability. Everybody who reads a certain passage gets the same questions in the same order.

The Types of Passages

The subject matter of the passages seldom strays from these three categories:

- **Business:** You might read about financial or economic theory, the ins and outs of investing, or the way that certain financial institutions operate. Pretty dull stuff.

- **Social Science:** These passages are the most diverse, because they can range from history (especially American) to a brief biography of a famous person or group of people.

- **Science:** These are usually the most straightforward in the way they discuss scientific facts, but you're also likely to encounter a lot of intimidating jargon like *lymphocytes* and *geosynchronous orbit*.

As different as the topics can be, though, there is one quality that almost all passages share: tedium. Few people walk away from a Reading Comp passage thinking, "Wow! I learned something today!" In fact, more people think, "Wow! I think my brain has turned to liquid!"

What Your Screen Will Look Like

When it's time for Reading Comp, a passage will appear on the left side of the screen, and the first question pertaining to that passage will appear on the right, like this:

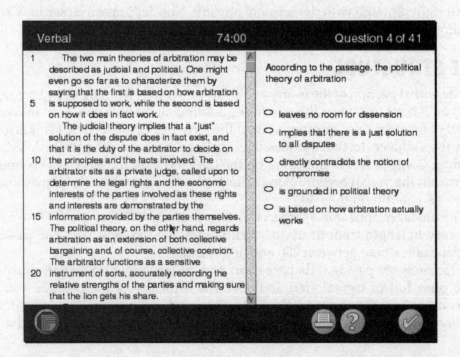

The entire passage will rarely fit in that box on the left; you'll usually have to use the scroll bar, which is that long, slender, vertical rectangle on the right side of the passage. Odds are that you're familiar with how scroll bars work—and how annoying they can be. If you're not, don't worry. The computer tutorial at the beginning of the exam will teach you everything you need to know.

If you've been blessed with a photographic memory and can read an entire passage while retaining most of the material, Reading Comp won't pose that much of a threat to you. In fact, there's not much of a reason to read this chapter. Please put this book down and go play outside.

If you're among the majority of GMAT takers who need to read something at least twice to absorb what's written, read on.

DON'T DO WHAT ETS WANTS

There's a reason why the passage is on the left side of the screen. ETS knows that we read left to right and top to bottom, so when we first see a page with printed matter on it, our eyes invariably gravitate to the upper-left-hand corner. (Smart folks, aren't they?)

ETS also knows that the average test-taker sees a Reading Comprehension passage and just dives right in. Do you do that? If so, what usually happens? You spend about five to ten minutes reading the whole thing, look up, and say to yourself, "What the heck did I just read?" Net result: ten wasted minutes.

Get Your Goodies and Go

We're all conditioned to read the whole thing first; we've been doing it since we delivered our first book reports in grammar school. This process on the GMAT differs greatly from preparing a book report. For one thing, the questions pertain only to a small portion of the passage, so you don't have to analyze the whole thing. You only have to find the answers to a few questions and move on as quickly as possible. Ultimately you need to decide for yourself whether you are more comfortable skimming the passage or reading the whole thing carefully— but skimming is usually sufficient.

There's a prevalent view out there that reading comprehension is neither reading nor comprehension. (Discuss.) You're not so much a researcher as you are a burglar who gets in, finds what she wants, and gets out as quickly as possible. If you've had any experience as a professional thief (or you're thinking of attending Thief College in case the whole M.B.A. thing doesn't work out), you know that the first thing a burglar does is case the joint.

Map Out Your Grocery Store

Ultimately, your goal is to make a mental map of where things are discussed within the passage. It's a bit like moving to a new neighborhood and entering the local grocery store for the first time. As you walk around, you take note of where to find milk, eggs, veggies, Cheez Wiz, and so forth. When you return to the store the next time with a specific item in mind to buy, you'll know where to find it.

The same is true for Reading Comp passages. If you know how the passage is structured, you can read a question and figure out the best place to look for the answer.

Take Notes

If you're having trouble keeping track of the structure of the passage, use the scrap paper you've been given.

Sample Passage A

Here is a rather long passage with which we'll be working for the first part of this chapter:

It comes as no surprise that there is little consensus among economists who study the prospects for the new European Central Bank (ECB). Some are overwhelmingly enthusiastic about the ECB's potential to eliminate
(5) exchange-rate currency fluctuations among its eleven member economies, while others are convinced that cultural differences and inevitable squabbles over monetary policy doom the central bank to failure.

The pessimists have a valid point. The ECB's primary
(10) goal, as specified by the Maastricht treaty, is to bring about price stability within its area of sovereignty. This stability, however, is predicated on reducing the current incongruity of prices throughout the region. Currently, though, there are too many cultural and financial
(15) variables that prevent prices from coming into alignment anytime soon.

For a start, the prices of many products sold in Europe already vary from country to country by large margins. The average cost of a pair of blue jeans is 34 percent
(20) higher in Germany than it is in Italy. Some reasons for this can be remedied through legislation. If Germany were to repeal its law prohibiting supermarkets from stocking aspirin on their shelves, for example, aspirin prices might come in line with the rest of the European
(25) Union. But most price differentials derive from seemingly immutable standards of living. Personal incomes in Spain and Portugal are well below the European average, as they have been for decades. Thus, prices stay lower to accommodate weaker buying power. And since
(30) Scandinavian countries show no sign of adopting the high demand for coffee products that exists in France and Italy, coffee prices will remain much higher in southern Europe than in the north.

Until now, Europe's different currencies have done well
(35) to divert consumers' attention from these price differentials. But now that Europe has adopted its one currency, the euro, Europeans are more likely to seek out the best price regardless of geography. This could mean

depressed localized economies of scale. Many countries
(40) will not recover from this situation in the short term.
　　　Fortunately for the ECB's architects, there are two
extraordinary financial models to study and replicate: the
German Bundesbank and America's Federal Reserve
Board. Each country within the European Union,
(45) regardless of its population or the size of its gross
domestic product, will be represented equally in the
ECB's governing council, which will dictate the policies
that the various national central banks will implement. As
long as the lines of communication remain open and
(50) country representatives keep an open mind toward what
may become a radical overhaul within European
commerce, the euro and the ECB have a fighting chance
to survive.

This baby has five longish paragraphs. Use your summarizing skills from the previous chapter to write a brief (two sentences max) summary of each. Reread the passage if you have to, but don't turn the page until you have something written down in all five blanks.

Paragraph 1:

Paragraph 2:

Paragraph 3:

Paragraph 4:

Paragraph 5:

Overall Main Idea:

Now, turn the page and compare your summaries to the ones provided.

Did your summaries look something like this?

Paragraph 1: Intro. There are two sides to the story of whether the ECB will survive. It could be great, or it could flop.

Paragraph 2: It'll probably flop because it will be impossible to keep prices the same throughout Europe. The countries are too different.

Paragraph 3: Lots of examples of how the countries are different—supporting points for paragraph 2.

Paragraph 4: More problems, this time about the new money.

Paragraph 5: There are a few positive comments about the ECB. It will be a long, hard fight, but there could be success.

Overall Main Idea: The ECB and the new currency face many diverse challenges before they succeed, but success is not out of the question.

There. You now have a general idea of the passage's content and a map of what is discussed in each of the five paragraphs. Now it's time to go after the questions.

QUESTION TYPES

ETS likes to ask two broad types of questions: (1) general questions that usually concern the passage's main idea, overall structure, or tone, and (2) specific questions that refer to a localized portion of the passage.

General Questions

If you practice, you can learn to determine the main idea of a passage without having to familiarize yourself with every painstaking detail. This is a wonderful time-saver, and it takes some time to get used to.

Each of these is a general Reading Comp question, and you should count on seeing at least one of these for every passage you read:

The primary purpose of the passage is to . . .

Which of the following best states the central idea of the passage?

The author's tone can best be described as . . .

Which of the following would be the best title of the passage?

The structure/organization of the passage can best be described as . . .

> If you've summarized each paragraph well and made accurate notes, you should be able to answer a general question without returning to the passage.

Answering a Reading Comp question with only a thumbnail sketch of the passage's content can seem like you're walking a high-wire without a net. When you first try this, you're going to want to reread the passage. Resist! Try to summarize the main idea *on your own* and look for a match among the answer choices. Of course, you can make your job easier by using the good old Process of Elimination:

> Although verbal questions can seem far less clear-cut than math questions do, each of the wrong answer choices to a verbal question *must be wrong for a reason*.

The Decoys
Wrong answers to general Reading Comprehension questions are usually:

- too specific, referring to a specific portion of the passage rather than to the passage as a whole

- too broad, mentioning a broad topic but neglecting to focus on the passage's specific subject matter

- too extreme, asserting that the passage has accomplished more than it possibly could (avoid words like *prove* and *resolve*, because it's very difficult to prove anything conclusively in four paragraphs)

- just plain not mentioned

The Main Idea
Each Reading Comp passage you'll see on the GMAT will probably have a main idea question. On more difficult passages, the main idea question might appear first because ETS thinks it's harder to answer a question about the entire passage first. Ha! The joke's on them.

Let's look at a sample general question about the passage you just summarized:

1. The primary purpose of the passage is to
   - ○ compare the ECB to other financial governing bodies
   - ○ assert that the European countries that have not yet embraced the euro are destined to so do before too long
   - ○ provide support for the theory that Europe's transition to a central bank will have many obstacles
   - ○ enumerate several examples of the constantly changing global financial climate
   - ○ prove that the ECB will never bring about the price stability on which its survival so dearly depends

Refer to the passage summary you made, then assess the answer choices one at a time. Which ones can you get rid of right away? You can start with (B), because there's no mention in your summary about whether other countries should accept the euro. (A) is mentioned, but only briefly in the fifth paragraph. It's too specific to be the primary purpose, so kill it. (D) is too broad, because the passage is clearly about Europe, not the globe as a whole.

Remember: Ask NOT which of the remaining two choices looks more appealing. Ask yourself which one looks *worse*. Both express the skepticism in the passage, but (E) is too extremely negative, especially because the last paragraph expresses some reasons for optimism. (C) is the best answer because it's more even-handed.

Sometimes, the main idea question doesn't directly concern the subject matter and instead is a bit more vague:

2. In the passage, the author is primarily concerned with which of the following?
   ○ comparing two different approaches to resolving a conflict
   ○ expressing dismay over a poorly reasoned conclusion
   ○ presenting information and offering different ways to interpret it
   ○ describing a problem that will not be solved easily
   ○ defending an established policy

Which is the best choice? You can use POE if you want to, but it isn't always necessary. There's no conflict to solve, so (A) is out. (B) doesn't account for the optimism in the last paragraph. The passage does present information, but there's only one interpretation of it; kill (C). And where's the "policy" to which (E) refers? The best choice is (D).

The important thing to note here is that you didn't need to reread anything in the passage to get either of these two questions right. If you've summarized the passage well, a basic understanding of the main idea (without a strong grasp of the actual points made) is all you should need.

Structure
Let's look at a sample general question pertaining to the structure of the passage. Again, your summary should be sufficient to answer the question.

3. Which of the following best describes the organization of the passage?
   ○ Two historical backgrounds are compared and contrasted.
   ○ A problem is identified, discussed, and resolved.
   ○ A theory is discussed, and evidence is introduced to condemn it.
   ○ A paradox is described, and one side is shown to be more dominant than the other.
   ○ A debate is introduced, and supporting evidence for both sides is presented.

Refer to your summary. You can forget about (A) and (D) right away, because there are no historical backgrounds mentioned, nor is there a paradox. (B) and (C) are incomplete, because they neglect the supportive comments in the final paragraph. You're left with (E), which provides the best overall description of the passage.

Some questions will dwell on the use of individual paragraphs and how they fit into the passage's overall structure:

4. Which of the following best describes the relation of the last paragraph to the passage as a whole?

   ○ It advances an argument to be debated further.
   ○ It outlines a process to be reexamined.
   ○ It adds some positive points to an otherwise negative outlook.
   ○ It reinforces a theory that is not easily disproved.
   ○ It poses a question that as yet has no answer.

You're well acquainted with the main idea of the passage by now, so you shouldn't be in much of a quandary here. POE is helpful as always, but the best answer to this question is clearly (C).

Tone

Tone questions are just as straightforward. Either they're right on, or they're way off:

5. The author's attitude toward the success of the ECB can best be described as

   ○ indifference
   ○ hostility
   ○ skepticism
   ○ amusement
   ○ admiration

You're not going to find many tone questions anymore because they're just so insultingly easy. In order for there to be no confusion, the four wrong answers must be *really* wrong. First, you can bounce (A) because authors are *never* indifferent about what they write. (Otherwise, why would they write about it?) The author is also clearly not hostile, amused, or admiring. Most of the evidence in the passage steers the reader to think that the ECB won't make it, so (C) is the best choice by a long shot.

Most of the general questions you'll see on the GMAT will fall into the above categories, and none of them requires a lot of hardcore reading. Leave that for the questions that refer to a specific portion of the passage.

Specific Questions

Now it's time to play search-and-destroy. As was said earlier, the three to four questions that pertain to each passage cover only a small portion of the text. Therefore, it's not very time-efficient to read the entire passage because you probably won't need all the information that you'll gather.

Specific questions take on many forms, and they each refer to a specific point made within the Reading Comp passage. Your quick summary won't be enough to answer them, because you'll need to read more carefully. But if you pick the right spot, you can minimize the reading you have to do in order to find the answers.

Most specific questions begin with "According to the passage," or they refer to a point made somewhere in the word pile. You'll get better at answering specific questions once you learn how to find information as fast as possible, which we discuss in more detail below.

> Once you recognize a specific question, the first thing to ask yourself is: *Where did I read that?*

The Decoys

Wrong answers to specific Reading Comprehension questions usually do the following:

- Refer to the wrong part of the passage. ETS likes to refer to something that you've already read even though it doesn't pertain to the current question.

- Make good common sense but are not mentioned. These are known as "heartstring" answer choices because they appeal to your heart but not to the passage.

- Refute the passage directly. ETS knows that it's very easy to misread text. You can miss just one word (such as "Magellan did sail around the world" instead of "Magellan did not sail around the world") and come away with the opposite meaning.

- Stray away from the passage.

Let's look at the most common types of specific questions you'll encounter.

Line Reference

Some questions are nice enough to give you a hint where to look:

> The author mentions the researchers' experiment in lines 26–33 for which of the following reasons?

Once you're given the lines to read, go read 'em and answer the question. You'll get the best results (and minimize rereading) if you put the reference point in the context of the whole passage by reading the whole paragraph (of course, adjust this strategy if the paragraph in question is thirty lines long).

Lead Words

Of course, questions don't always include references, but that isn't necessarily a bad thing. Suppose a question looked like this:

The passage suggests that the author has which of the following opinions toward underwater basket weaving?

There's no line reference, but the question does give you the next best thing: lead words. The question clearly centers around *underwater basket weaving*, so it makes sense to scan the passage for those words, then look for your answer. Try this technique on Sample Passage A above:

6. The author most probably mentions the Bundesbank in order to
   - ○ suggest an alternate composition of the ECB's governing council
   - ○ compare its fiscal policies to those of the Federal Reserve Bank
   - ○ provide an example of a financial institution to which the ECB will never measure up
   - ○ indicate that there are other established fiscal entities for the ECB to emulate
   - ○ urge the German government to ease its restrictions on supermarkets

The lead word in the question is *Bundesbank*, so skim the passage until you find the term. (Don't read, just skim. This one's an easier example because *Bundesbank* is a proper noun with a big fat capital letter—they're easier to find.) Once you find *Bundesbank* (in the first sentence of the last paragraph), start reading. The first couple of sentences should be enough for you to select (D) as the best answer.

Lead Word Drill
Circle the lead words in each of the following questions. The answers are in chapter 8.

1. Which of the following is an assumption underlying the author's conclusion regarding Beethoven's collection of rare Belgian tapestries?

2. According to the passage, which of the following is an accurate statement concerning Indian rope tricks?

3. The passage suggests that software bundling is the biggest threat to which of the following networking strategies?

4. It can be inferred from the passage that which of the following social programs was defunct by 1964?

5. According to the passage, a patient suffering from angina can collapse into complete cardiac arrest after each of the following happens EXCEPT:

When you work on specific questions like these, practice skimming the passage looking for the lead words. It all goes toward improving your ability to find what you want as quickly as possible.

THE OTHER QUESTION TYPES

The majority of the Reading Comprehension questions ask for general information about the text or begin with "According to the passage. . . ." There are a few other questions that ETS has worked into Reading Comp over the past few years, and you should be ready for them. Some of these, as a matter of fact, resemble Argument questions rather closely.

Inference Questions

The most common type of "other" question is the inference question, which works just like the inference questions we discussed back in the Critical Reasoning chapter. Rather than find information that appears explicitly in the passage, you have to determine what the passage *suggests* or *implies*. To determine an inference question, look for the three main verbs:

◆ Which of the following can be **inferred** from the passage about the author's opinion of genetic splicing?

◆ The author **implies** that one method Amway distributors hope to use in order to take over the galaxy is . . .

◆ The passage **suggests** that the Continental Congress did which of the following before they finally convened in Philadelphia?

You crack these the same way that you crack Argument inferences.

> Ask yourself: Which one do *I know* has to be true?

7. The passage most clearly implies which of the following?

○ Countries whose economies are depressed by the price wars following the arrival of the euro will eventually rebound and prosper.

○ The average German or Italian has more disposable income than does the average Portuguese or Spaniard.

○ Were it not for the Maastricht treaty, the ECB would never have come about.

○ The arrival of the euro has not solved the problem of price disparity in Europe.

○ The governing council may have to alter its plan of equal representation to account for the contributions of each country to Europe's overall gross domestic product.

Consider each answer choice individually and decide if you can tangibly prove that it's true. Otherwise, get rid of it. You'll find information pertaining to answer choice (A) at the end of the fourth paragraph. It says that "many countries will not recover in the short term," but you don't know what will happen eventually. (B) is a shameless attempt to relate different bits of data that the passage reveals. You're told that "personal incomes in Spain and Portugal are well below the European average," but you don't know if Germans and Italians are above average. This is one of those choices that seems to make sense but is not definitively supported by the passage. Kill it.

(C) is equally flawed. The second sentence of the second paragraph tells you that the ECB and the Maastricht treaty are related, but you can't infer that one wouldn't have happened without the other. And (E) is just plain wrong because it's never mentioned. The last paragraph talks about the current representative system, but there's no allusion to what future plans may be.

That leaves you with (D), which you know to be true from the evidence given in lines 36–38 in the fourth paragraph: "But now that Europe has adopted its one currency, the euro, Europeans are more likely to seek out the best price regardless of geography." That tells you that the euro has arrived, but pricing problems persist. (D) is the best answer.

Does the Author Agree?

Another form of inference question involves statements with which the author might agree. You reference the author's passage to determine his viewpoint and infer what other statements might be in line with the author's thinking. This question can be a hybrid between an inference and a main idea.

8. The passage suggests that the author believes which of the following?
   ○ Stabilizing the euro within global currency markets is the first step toward its legitimacy as a viable saving vehicle.
   ○ The cultures of the various European countries will begin to grow together soon after the euro completely supplants all the separate currencies that are now in use.
   ○ Multiple factors will prevent price stability from happening anytime soon, and it probably won't happen at all.
   ○ The Bundesbank should assume all financial responsibilities for the European Union until the ECB becomes fully operational.
   ○ The gross domestic product of a nation should determine the number of delegates that nation sends to the ECB's governing council.

Again, we shoot 'em down one by one. The global currency markets in (A) are never mentioned, nor is the prospect of European cultures growing together. Get rid of (B). You might be attracted to (D) at first because the author mentions the Bundesbank as a good thing to copy, but the author never asserts that it should completely take over. And lastly, the author does not indicate whether he has an opinion of the ECB's current policy.

The author's skepticism is evident throughout the passage, given that he spent four paragraphs tearing down the ECB and only one building it up. Therefore, (C) is the best choice.

Weakening and Strengthening

Within the past few years, ETS has developed a taste for adding weaken and strengthen questions to Reading Comprehension passages. Treat them just like the Arguments we discussed at great length in chapter 4, and look out for the distractor choices.

The Decoys

Wrong answers on weaken and strengthen Reading Comp questions most commonly make the following mistakes:

- ◆ Are out of the scope.

- ◆ Weaken instead of strengthen, or vice versa.

- ◆ Are heartstring choices that the passage doesn't mention or support.

9. Which of the following, if true, would most clearly weaken the chances of the ECB's survival?

○ Federal Reserve Board governors have no experience with having to reconcile various languages and cultures into their financial policies.

○ The prices for most cosmetics in Belgium and The Netherlands are virtually identical.

○ Some of the legislation that is necessary for price reform will take years to put into effect.

○ As prices fall in Russia, which is not part of the European Union, commercial entities in Europe will buy Russian raw materials in larger quantities.

○ The term of service for each member of the ECB's governing board is only three years.

Attack this one as you would any argument; get rid of the stuff that is outside the scope. (C) is wrong because the issue is whether the legislation will succeed, not how long it will take. (D) is irrelevant, because the ECB wants to stabilize prices within the European Union, and Russia is beyond its jurisdiction. (E) might seem like a negative because of the word *only*, but how are we to assume that longer terms for the ECB governors will help?

(B) has the most egregious problem of all. We're looking for a negative point, and (B) provides the positive idea that comparable prices in separate countries do exist. It's only a small example, but it supports the idea that the ECB will survive.

That leaves us with (A). Remember that talk we had in the Critical Reasoning chapter about weakening? When you compare two items, you must be sure that the two items are comparable. In lines 42–43, the passage states that the ECB's architects will "study and replicate" the Federal Reserve Board. If the Fed has no experience dealing with many cultures and languages (and the ECB most certainly will), then the Fed isn't exactly the best model to replicate after all. The best answer is (A).

Most of the questions that fall into the Argument category will be weaken and strengthen questions. If you can handle weaken and strengthen Arguments, then these Reading Comp questions shouldn't give you much trouble.

The Horror of EXCEPT Questions

You used to be able to save these for last on the P&P format, but you don't have that option now. Purely and simply, these stink. You have to know a lot about the passage to answer these, and you usually can't localize your aggressive reading technique on one portion of the text.

The news isn't all bad. ETS only attaches EXCEPT questions to its hardest passages, so if you see one—and they're hard to miss because EXCEPT always appears in ALL CAPS—either you're doing very well on the exam so far or the passage is experimental.

When you see an EXCEPT question, recognize that you've got a little more work ahead of you. Most of the work will entail skimming the passage looking for stuff. Here's one last question for Sample Passage A about the European Central Bank:

10. According to the passage, price stability within the European Union is affected on all of the following EXCEPT

- ⬭ regional tastes
- ⬭ currency exchange rates
- ⬭ consumer bargain-hunting
- ⬭ legislation
- ⬭ consumer wealth

By now, you should be familiar enough with this passage to recognize topics that have been mentioned. The last sentence in the third paragraph (about coffee) takes care of (A). (C) is a nice paraphrase of the fourth paragraph, in which "Europeans are more likely to seek out the best price." The word *legislation* appears in line 21, so (D) is out. And (E) refers to the lower buying power of Portuguese and Spaniards mentioned in paragraph 3.

(B) is a tricky one, because *currency exchange rates* are mentioned in the first paragraph. However, they are not referred to as a direct influence on price stability. The point is underscored in the fourth paragraph, which says that the different currencies have been replaced by the euro. The best choice is (B).

You've just answered ten questions about a passage. On the real exam, you'll see three or four. Before you move on to the practice exercises, here are a few finer points to keep in the back of your mind as you work.

HOW TO SPOT A GOOD ANSWER CHOICE

Although ETS tries to disguise correct answers, the best answer choices are fated to have certain revealing characteristics. Knowing about these will help you develop hunches you can depend on when you're eliminating choices and making an educated guess.

Paraphraseology

ETS knows that Reading Comprehension questions can be interpreted in many ways, so it likes to create questions whose correct answers are indisputable. One of the best ways to avoid arguments with students is to make right answers paraphrases of the text. The last question had a few good examples of this.

The text said:

Europeans are more likely to seek out the best price . . .

The answer choice said:

bargain-hunting

Paraphrasing is closely related to the practice of summarizing passages using the three Cs we discussed in chapter 3. See if you can match up each sentence with its paraphrased counterpart. (Yep, this is one of those annoying match-up games in which *not all* the items are linked.)

1. Left unprotected from foreign attack

2. Runs in a circle

3. Mates infrequently

4. A stalwart proponent of fiscal conservatism

5. Stands out for its modesty

6. Establishes a manufacturing presence overseas

7. Randomly distributed throughout the system

8. Inhibits any further lateral growth of root systems

9. Demonstrates extraordinary tactile sensitivity

10. Compromises the secrecy of England's intelligence ring

A. Has a highly developed sense of touch

B. Not exhibiting any recognizable pattern

C. Keeps plants from growing sideways

D. Not inclined toward funding excessive government programs

E. Shows movement in a counter-clockwise motion

F. Vulnerable to assaults from abroad

G. Spies on the British

H. Constructs a plant on foreign soil

I. Exemplary in its understatement

Be Nice . . .

The passages that ETS selects for Reading Comp rarely take potshots at America or at any "respected" professions: business, law, medicine, drama, etc. Any time you come across an answer choice that sends a negative vibe about any of these things, you can eliminate it. The same is true for any race of people who are not white males. ETS is sensitive to the accusations that its tests discriminate against minorities, so you won't see any text that denigrates anyone who uses an "American" suffix (African Americans, Latino Americans, and so forth).

. . . And Not Too Extreme

Compare these two sentences. Which one can you argue with more assuredly?

> Many people admired Picasso's artistic work.

> No one disliked Picasso's artistic work.

The second sentence makes an extreme conclusion and is therefore easier to disprove. All you need is one Picasso hater to blow the doors off it. But the first sentence is harder to dispute because it's not as extreme. It's nice and mushy.

If you've narrowed your choices down to two, and one question is more extreme than the other, pick the mushy one. Any answer choice that presumes to assert something unequivocally is disputable. Thus, it's also probably incorrect.

Look for These...	Avoid These
some, many	all
often	always
sometimes, rarely, usually	never
can, could, may, might	will
some people	everyone, everybody
few people	no one, nobody
more, less (or any word ending in *er*)	most, least (or any word ending in *est*)
likely, possibly	absolutely
doubtful, unlikely	impossible

PRACTICE READING COMP PASSAGES

As you work though these next three passages, try to use all the information we've discussed in this voluminous chapter. Make a summary for each passage, then attack each question as you would on a real exam. The answers and explanations are in chapter 8.

Also, you might want to develop your timing by doing each passage a little faster than the one before. Try to complete the first passage in fifteen minutes, the second in twelve minutes, and the third in ten minutes. If you have purchased other test-prep materials, work with them in the same way, each time finishing just a little bit sooner.

Sample Passage 1

Within most animal species, the males must do their best to attract females by showing off—by attempting either to demonstrate sexual prowess or to intimidate rivals. A new study, however, suggests that males are
(5) actually submitting to a more genetic imperative. By displaying their most prized attributes or talents, hopeful males do the best they can to show off superior genetic qualities that lesser males cannot mimic.

Biologists at the University of Missouri conducted this
(10) new study by analyzing the mating calls of the gray tree frog. Females have been shown to gravitate toward males whose calls last longest, and it has long been theorized that a male's lengthy mating call is linked to superior fitness and energy.

(15) Tree frogs were chosen for the experiment for two very important reasons. Since frogs fertilize their eggs externally, it is easy to trace the genealogy of each tadpole. Secondly, male frogs are utterly uninvolved with raising their offspring. This allows the scientists to
(20) address the "nature vs. nurture" conundrum directly by removing any chance that the tadpoles are "learning" anything from their fathers. Whatever strength or weakness the offspring displays, that characteristic must have been passed down through the father's genes.

(25) To start the experiment, eggs were harvested from several females and then split into two groups. The first cluster was fertilized with the sperm of a long-calling male, the second with that of a male whose call was demonstrably shorter. The scientists compared the
(30) progress of all tadpoles with different fathers but the same mother. Mating calls are strictly a male trait, so the biologists later planned to compare the mating calls of certain males with those of their male offspring.

The results were astounding. The physical
(35) characteristics of all the male tadpoles were virtually identical at first, but within weeks the children of long-calling males grew into faster and stronger tadpoles who eventually would metamorphose into frogs much sooner than the offspring of short-calling males. Such a finding
(40) lends credence to the theory that calling is an honest and reliable indicator of genetic quality.

1. The primary focus of the passage is on which of the following?
   - ○ supporting a new theory by providing a new explanation for an accepted mode of behavior
   - ○ evaluating the results of two separate experiments and contrasting the relative merits of each one
   - ○ pursuing evidence in the "nature vs. nurture" debate
   - ○ dismissing a current phenomenon as inconsistent with common trends
   - ○ embracing a new system of analysis that is likely to overturn much of today's accepted knowledge

2. According to the passage, which of the following is an accurate statement about the gray tree frog?
   - ○ Females teach their offspring to fend for themselves in the wild.
   - ○ Males are more energetic and physically fit than are females.
   - ○ Mating calls are restricted to the males of the species.
   - ○ Offspring acquire more of their genetic information from their mothers than from their fathers.
   - ○ The mating call of the female is hardly distinguishable from that of the male.

3. The passage suggests which of the following about the male tree frog?
   - ○ It is now no longer prudent to assume that the length of a frog's mating call is linked to its sexual prowess.
   - ○ Some females are attracted to long-calling males because of the quality of "parenting" that these males can provide.
   - ○ A male that exhibits a demonstrably shorter mating call is probably also betraying its physical inadequacy.
   - ○ A study comparing tadpoles with the same father but different mothers would yield similar results.
   - ○ A frog that is unable to sound a mating call will never reproduce.

Sample Passage 2

Most Americans are fascinated with their own history, particularly that of the colonial era. Whenever a crisis affects the current government, pundits and plebeians alike invoke the writings and teachings of the eighteenth
(5) century in order to support or denounce modern viewpoints. Many citizens wax nostalgic for the glorious times of their nascent union, when some of the most shrewd and free-thinking minds came together to construct "a more perfect Union." A new book by Nathan
(10) Parker, however, suggests that colonial New England was never the egalitarian Eden that modern Americans make it out to be.

Popular imagination holds that the Puritans were a virtuous group determined to create a new government
(15) through direct democracy. Communities convened town-hall meetings, at which policies were debated and decisions were made by the will of the people. Many renowned international thinkers, such as France's Alexis de Tocqueville and Hector St. John Crevecoeur, praised
(20) this new American commitment to the voice of the common man.

According to Parker, admiration for New England's first settlers is profoundly misplaced. In a typical show of their historical revisionism, Americans have mythologized
(25) these town meetings to the point of embarrassment. Parker asserts that town-hall meetings were open only to a select few male property owners who wielded a strong financial influence on the community. Thus, the laws that were put into effect as a result of these meetings hardly
(30) reflected the "consent of the governed." Therefore, there is vast evidence of voter apathy among the colonists. Citing the disparity between the roll calls of several meetings and the voter registries of the towns in which they took place, Parker demonstrates that attendance at
(35) town-hall meetings rarely exceeded 30 percent of all registered voters.

In making these points, Parker hopes to lie to rest the notion that simple, family-oriented colonial New England was far preferable to the modern America that many
(40) perceive has outgrown pure democracy. His objective is to lay bare the true nature of eighteenth-century governance and thus assure Americans that progress can't kill an equality that never was.

4. The primary purpose of the passage as a whole is to
   - ○ critique a system of logic
   - ○ clarify an ambiguity
   - ○ contrast two diverse notions
   - ○ discredit a commonly held perception
   - ○ question a dubious explanation

5. Which of the following best describes the purpose of the second paragraph?
   - ○ It extols the virtue of the first American settlers who were not daunted by the prospect of creating an egalitarian society.
   - ○ It first introduces de Tocqueville and Crevecoeur, by whom Parker was first inspired to write.
   - ○ It lists several perceptions about the early American colonies that Parker believes to be more myth than fact.
   - ○ It serves to emphasize the massive impact that French thinking had on New England's first settlers.
   - ○ It provides evidence that the Puritans were not nearly as virtuous as they asserted themselves to be.

6. According to the passage, it is common practice to refer to the colonial era in order to
   - ○ advocate the importance of pure democracy to a fledgling capitalist nation
   - ○ illustrate how American society has always depended upon the family unit that was so highly esteemed in the eighteenth century
   - ○ establish a historical context for the celebrated writings of de Tocqueville and Crevecoeur
   - ○ praise the perseverance of the Puritans, who never receive the recognition they so richly deserve
   - ○ indicate that the country's rampant growth since its creation has caused it to stray from its original path toward absolute democracy

7. According to the passage, Parker asserts which of the following about early colonial town meetings?
   - ○ Those who owned property in the area served as representatives for everyone in the community.
   - ○ Attendance at these meetings was restricted to wealthy landowners.
   - ○ All registered voters were permitted to attend, but fewer than one-third of them actually did.
   - ○ They became the inspiration for what is known today as direct democracy.
   - ○ They were looked upon as models by the framers of the Constitution.

Sample Passage 3

Anyone who thinks that rabbits make cute and cuddly pets has never owned one, and has most definitely never worked as a farmer or gardener. To people whose livelihood depends on agribusiness, rabbits are nothing
(5) more than ravenous vermin that inflict millions of dollars in damage to crops meant for both animal and human consumption. Until now, no one had undertaken to quantify the annual cost to a farmer's output for which a single rabbit is accountable. Great Britain's Ministry of
(10) Agriculture, however, has shown itself to be up to the challenge. Gordon McKillop, a biologist at the Central Science Laboratory in York, England, just finished a study that monitored the appetites of rabbits let loose to graze on several crops. As a result, farmers can gauge rabbit
(15) damage more effectively, allowing them to anticipate the crops they will lose and make necessary compensation.

During his three-year study, McKillop released a set number of rabbits into several enclosed regions, each containing one type of vegetation on which the rabbits
(20) subsisted. To keep numbers constant, each enclosure was surrounded by fence that was entrenched ten feet into the ground, and all rabbits released in a certain area were of the same sex.

The rabbits did the least damage in the pens
(25) containing grass, which many farmers cultivate as grazing land for their livestock. The average rabbit ate almost 300 pounds of grass in one year, which reduced the yield of one hectare (about two and a half acres) by half a percent. This translates to more than $3 worth of damage
(30) per rabbit per year—a seemingly nominal sum until one considers that most grasslands are home to as many as forty rabbits per acre. The rabbits' taste for barley was about the same as that for grass in terms of percentage, but the cost was calculated to be almost $7 per rabbit.
(35) By far, the most endangered crop was wheat, which rabbits munch at a rate that depleted normal yields by more than 1 percent of the maximum. Since wheat is also the most expensive on the open market, McKillop's group calculated that one rabbit can eat almost $1 worth
(40) of the crop in one month. This can mean financial ruin for wheat farmers in areas with abnormally high rabbit populations.

Farmers may now be able to attach a dollar value to the crops that rabbits feed on, but they still lack the most
(45) important piece of information that Dr. McKillop's study did not reveal: how to stop them. Shooting and trapping rabbits is too time-consuming and inefficient to keep up with the approximate 2 percent increase in rabbit

populations every year, and most rabbits have developed
(50) resistance to viral diseases such as myxomatosis and
viral hemorrhagic fever that have been introduced to curb
reproduction. Even the age-old remedy of releasing foxes
on the property has been blocked by chicken farmers,
whose commodity, according to the Ministry, contributes
(55) almost 14 percent of Britain's gross domestic product.

8. Which of the following statements best sums up the purpose of McKillop's experiment?

   ○ He contrasted several methods for establishing more
     credible methods for controlling rabbit populations.
   ○ He set out to express the damage inflicted by rabbits
     on farmers' crops in a more tangible, monetary
     sense.
   ○ He endeavored to prove that rabbits are more destruc-
     tive than most people perceive them to be.
   ○ He hoped to determine the crop for which rabbits
     showed the most ardent appetite.
   ○ He wanted to portray the rabbit in a less flattering
     manner.

9. The passage supplies information about each of the following EXCEPT

   ○ the population density of rabbits
   ○ the best way to prevent rabbits from decimating a
     certain crop
   ○ the duration of McKillop's study
   ○ the rate at which rabbits normally reproduce
   ○ the amount of grass usually grown annually upon a
     hectare of land

10. Each of the following can be inferred from the passage
    EXCEPT

    ○ in the agricultural marketplace, barley is at least twice
      as expensive as grass
    ○ at one point, myxomatosis and viral hemorrhagic fever
      were more effective than they are now
    ○ the power wielded by a certain type of farmer is at
      least partly influenced by financial impact of that
      farmer's product
    ○ the cost incurred by farmers to rid themselves of large
      rabbit populations far exceeds the monetary dam-
      age done to the farmers' crops
    ○ rabbits are unable to tunnel through the ground at a
      depth that is greater than ten feet

11. Which of the following hypothetical situations best exemplifies a potential problem that would most seriously undermine the merit of McKillop's study?

○ Several rabbits develop a new strain of myxomatosis that renders each completely sterile.

○ Due to a decrease in supply, the price of barley suddenly doubles.

○ It is determined that younger, more energetic rabbits consume almost double the food that an older rabbit does.

○ A rare drought inhibits plant growth in the enclosures for several months.

○ Soon after the experiment begins, a predatory animal finds its way into some of the rabbit enclosures.

12. In the last paragraph, the author is primarily concerned with

○ exposing a problem to which McKillop's study has failed to supply a solution

○ suggesting that rabbit farmers and chicken farmers are often at odds when it comes to agricultural legislation

○ citing evidence that McKillop's study is woefully incomplete

○ comparing the various methods that farmers have used in order to keep rabbit populations under control

○ establishing that foxes have an equal appetite for rabbits as they do for chickens

6

BE A BETTER WRITER

SWEET REVENGE?

We've spent five chapters talking about how to read all the diverse and convoluted verbal material that ETS shoves in your face on the GMAT. Now it's time to turn the tables.

Unfortunately, it's not in your best interest to force ETS to read the same dense, uninteresting dreck that you have to read on the GMAT. (As Paul Newman said in *The Sting*, "Revenge is for suckers.") Your writing needs to be all that ETS' is not: interesting, concise, and enjoyable to read.

This chapter is dedicated to helping you take on that sense of clarity, but let's not kid ourselves. Reading this book over a three-week period isn't going to turn you into a Vladimir Nabokov. What you can learn, however, is how to make your writing more pleasant for the many essay graders and admissions officers who will be grading it later.

What was said in chapter 1 about timing still applies; you should always learn something new without the added pressure of a time limit. These next two chapters will start with the basics of better writing; after a lot of practice, you'll be better acquainted with your new skills and you'll use them better in a more improvisational manner. (In other words, you'll do better on those AWA essays.)

Read More!

Writing better comes from a better appreciation of the process and from better acquaintance with the best writing you can find. If you're a native English speaker, you learned to speak English not by reading a textbook, but by mimicking whoever raised you. Mimicry is still the best way to learn any new language (to which anyone who has spent any time as an exchange student will attest) as well as to improve your grasp on the language you currently speak.

So as you prepare to tell the world about yourself, spend as much extra time as you can reading the work of professional writers. Sources of the best reading material include:

- **Newspapers:** You'll want what you write on your applications to have the same formal character that most daily newspapers project. Granted, you'll want your writing style to have a bit more flair than the choppy, no-nonsense style of basic print journalism, but it's still an excellent example of writing that states its case once and moves on. (More on that later.)

- **Magazines:** You probably have a few favorite weeklies and monthlies, so be sure to read them before you bundle them all up for the recycler. If you're feeling ambitious, buy a few copies of the more eggheady periodicals, such as *The Economist* (which, despite its misleading title, is not just about the economy).

- **Books:** If you're one of the lucky ones who have enough time to read books for pleasure (or you've just got enough self-discipline to turn off the TV), both fiction and non-fiction are wonderful ways to absorb various writing styles. Bear in mind, though, that some fiction can be wacky; your application writing should take on a more straightforward demeanor.

If you make the time to read more, you don't have to keep telling yourself, "Absorb the style. Absorb the style. Must learn to write better. Absorb. Absorb." At the risk of sounding new-age, your own writing style will evolve organically as long as you keep practicing.

YOUR APPROACH TO WRITING

If you're like most people about to embark on the GMAT/M.B.A. experience, then:

- You haven't written much of anything since you graduated from college.

- The prospect of having to do all that writing on your applications either annoys or petrifies you. These are normal emotions, especially if you don't consider yourself much of a writer and are especially intimidated by the tyranny of the blank computer screen.

> You can begin to derive a little comfort from writing if you start to think of it as less of a burden and more of an opportunity to tell your readers about who you are and how you think.

Once you can adopt a more optimistic attitude toward arranging words on the page, you'll be surprised how your whole viewpoint will change for the better. Writing will become less work and more interesting. Of course, any several-step program worth a plugged nickel needs to have some sort of catchy mnemonic title for maximum effect. With that in mind, we give you . . .

THE FIVE F's

Here's a basic five-step approach to formulating your thoughts and getting them on paper. No one expects you to get it all right the first time; the best essays, in fact, are the result of many drafts and rewrites. So find yourself a desk in a quiet, well-lit space, and get started.

Step One: Free-Think

Once you have your topic, start brainstorming. Let your mind generate ideas that you might want to incorporate into your essay, write them all down, and *don't censor anything*. You'll have plenty of time later to decide which ideas will fit into your overall theme and which ones are irrelevant.

Step Two: Form an Outline

To keep your essay from reading like a transcript of your stream of consciousness, you have to create an outline of what you're about to say. Organized essays are infinitely more pleasant to read, and essay readers will pick up on your sense of structure right away.

Now is your chance to choose among your brainstormed ideas. Organize them with some sense of order, and discard any of those that don't seem to fit in. This seems like an abstract practice, but you'll develop a feel for it.

Step Three: Flesh It Out

Most of us think in conversational English, not formal English. So why make it harder for yourself? Once you've got your outline, start writing as if you're explaining your thesis to a friend. You might even find that speaking into a tape machine is helpful; you can transcribe it later. Expressing your thoughts informally speeds the creative process and keeps your ideas more genuine.

Step Four: Formalize It

In chapter 3, we talked about turning formal English into conversational English as you read. As you write, you should follow the same process, but in reverse. When you feel as though your essay's content is complete, let your formal style take over and turn your thoughts into a more polished piece of writing.

Step Five: Fine-Tune It

This is where the reviews and rewrites figure in. After you've written your first draft, enlist the opinions of people you trust. These people don't necessarily have to be superstar writers; in fact, the opinion of an average person is a better indicator of how well you expressed your points.

As you revise your essay, you should also keep an eye out for these basic style points that form the backbone of competent writing. They're not that complicated, and they'll go far to help you turn a mediocre piece into a solid effort.

STYLE POINTS

No person has the right to tell you which writing style to develop, because how you write derives from who you are. The term *style* is hard to define; it could involve all of the points we're about to discuss, or none of them. Style is the difference between "It was the best of times, it was the worst of times" and "Times were great, but they were bad, too."

Your own style will evolve as you practice, but there are a few basic do's and don'ts that will increase an essay's value in the eyes of the reader. Before you write a thing, get a copy of Strunk & White's *The Elements of Style*. *White* is E. B. White, who authored such children's books as *Charlotte's Web* and *Stuart Little*, and edited *The New Yorker* for some fifty years. *Strunk* is Will Strunk Jr., White's English professor at Cornell. This little book is a brilliant source of information about proper grammar and word usage, and it extols above all else the virtue of brevity.

Let Every Word Tell

No primer on the virtues of writing is complete without some pompous Shakespearean quote, so here's one that's especially relevant. As Polonius told Claudius in *Hamlet*, "brevity is the soul of wit."

Pointless repetition drags too many essays into the morass of mediocrity. If you've made your point, don't linger on it. You'll be tempted to make it again, and you'll weaken your message. Many students make this mistake, especially during the AWA, if they can't think of anything else to say. If this happens, challenge yourself to come up with another supporting point. In his little book, Will Strunk voiced it this way:

> Vigorous writing is concise. A sentence should contain no unnecessary words, a paragraph no unnecessary sentences, for the same reason that a drawing should have no unnecessary lines and a machine no unnecessary parts. This requires not that the writer make all his sentences short, or that he avoid all detail and treat his subjects only in outline, but that every word tell.

Economic use of words is also important on your application essays if you've typed more than 1,000 words and you've been limited to 500. (B-schools are sticklers for word limits; it's okay to come in under the wire, but going over the limit is a surefire way to tick them off.) Should this happen, look for ideas that can be expressed in fewer words and eliminate the stuff that you don't need.

Word Variety

You don't have to have an encyclopedic vocabulary to vary your choice of words. And no one's asking you to study a thesaurus (although it's a good writing tool to have on hand). But adding a synonym now and then will help you avoid paragraphs like this:

Communication is as important as creativity, because no idea is worth anything unless it can be communicated to someone else. Communication starts at an early age, when we first learn to communicate with our parents. And let us not forget the quality of communication; an idea that is poorly communicated is not worth much more than one that is not communicated at all.

Without being too florid in your word choice, you can make a few strategic substitutions and turn that paragraph into this one:

Communication is as important as creativity, because no idea is worth anything unless **someone can convey it** to someone else. Communication starts at an early age, when we first learn to **talk** with our parents. And let us not forget the quality of communication; an idea that is poorly **expressed** is not worth much more than one that is not **expressed** at all.

It's okay to repeat a word once or twice within the same paragraph, especially a word like *communication* that has few appropriate synonyms. And it's also a good idea to use it twice in the same sentence (like *expressed* in the last sentence) for the sake of parallelism. But if you use the same word over and over and over and over and over (like now, for instance), your reader will likely be unimpressed.

Sentence Variety

As you write more, you'll also develop an appreciation for good rhythm. A paragraph that contains only identically constructed sentences sounds monotonous:

The North Atlantic Treaty Organization's days are numbered. None of the group's sixteen members can agree on the alliance's purpose. They also don't know how much power they have. NATO has been effective in the past. People are not convinced that previous triumphs merit more money.

See how dull and robotic that sounds? With some more descriptive words and a few connectors here and there, though, you can construct a paragraph with sentences that have different constructions and thus are more pleasant to read:

The days of the North Atlantic Treaty Organization are numbered, because none of the group's sixteen members can agree on the alliance's purpose or the degree of power it can wield over transgressors. No matter how effective NATO has been in the past, few people (especially Americans) are convinced that previous successes merit further financing.

No matter how sophisticated the sentence structure is, you can always overdo a good thing:

> Although the general public fears genetically modified organisms, they serve a great purpose. Some scientists assert that these organisms are dangerous, but there is no tangible proof of this. Despite urgings that such organisms require less in terms of pesticides and herbicides to survive, newspapers print stories that scare readers . . .

Each sentence has a nice complex rhythm to it, but the rhythm of sentences is very similar. Therefore, you're not going to score too many style points here.

Distinguish Yourself

You may have heard stories about people who submit outlandish essays and are accepted to all the schools they want. One of the most circulated stories involves an essay question like this: "If you could conjure anyone, living or dead, real or fictional, to sit next to you on a first-class, non-stop flight from New York to Tokyo, who would it be and why?" One waggish applicant apparently answered that he'd prefer the seat to be left empty so that he could get some sleep and not feel compelled to chat the whole time.

Whether this actually happened is the subject of passionate debate, but there is truth to the idea that you don't always have to color within the lines. Remember the plight of the AWA readers: eight-hour shifts, three minutes per essay. And b-school admissions people don't have it much better. If you can make your essays stand out (in a positive way, that is) from the thousands that are written each year, you'll definitely benefit.

There is a terribly insidious viewpoint among M.B.A. applicants that you have to write what the readers want to hear. Too many students do just that, resulting in thousands and thousands of carbon copies of platitudes. Essays are your opportunity to advertise who you are; if you've got a sense of humor, show it off!

> When writing your essay, concentrate on what you want to say, not on what you think the reader wants to read.

Feel the Burn!

Your writing ability is a lot like a muscle. If you use it often and keep in shape, your ability and endurance will improve, but in disuse it will atrophy and wither. If you're preparing to take the GMAT on your own, make sure you write at least two essays a week. (ETS' *Official Guide to the GMAT* is jammed with essay topics, so you can spread them out over as long a period as you would like.) After a month or so, compare your most recent essays to the ones from the beginning. If you've kept up a brisk writing regimen, you should see improvements that you didn't even know were happening.

7 | ESSAYS

A LITTLE HISTORY

The Analytical Writing Assessment (AWA) first appeared on the GMAT on the October 1994 exam, because business schools felt that applications didn't always afford them the best opportunity to judge applicants' verbal skills. In other words, the folks who read all the application essays were not convinced that the writing was, in fact, the work of the applicant. They decided to ask ETS to incorporate an extemporaneous writing exercise as a better gauge of how each applicant writes under pressure.

The essays are the last part of the verbal GMAT that we discuss in this book because the AWA is least likely to affect your chances of admission. After all, a person who scores a 700 on the GMAT but only a 3.5 on the essay has a much better chance of admission than someone who aces the AWA and gets a 450. On the GMAT, the AWA appears first for a reason. ETS knows that taking a four-hour standardized exam can turn your brain to oatmeal. Therefore, it wants to give you the chance to write your essays when you're at your freshest.

HOW THE AWA WORKS

The word processing program that ETS has created for the AWA is a bare-bones version of any program with which you may be familiar. It's basic, but it does have the only three functions you'll need: cut, paste, and undo. If you haven't had too much experience with a word processor, the tutorial will help you learn all you need to know. If you're very concerned about your word-processing prowess, you might also want to shell out the extra $60 for a practice GMAT (which is comprised of questions from the *Official Guide*) so you can hone your skills.

The screen you'll see on your monitor looks like this:

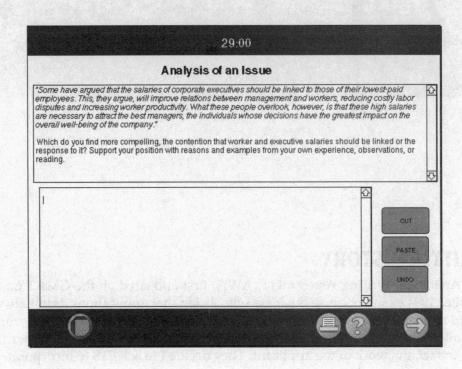

The statement for you to assess will appear at the top of the screen, followed by the instructions. Just type in your response and submit it within the thirty-minute time limit you have for each essay.

Two Types of Essays

During the AWA portion of the GMAT, you'll write two essays, and you'll have 30 minutes to write each one. One essay will be titled "Analysis of an Issue," and the other "Analysis of an Argument." Both essays rely on your ability to write well, but each one also has its own set of criteria by which it is measured. We'll discuss these differences in greater detail later in the chapter; right now, it's time to talk about the grading process.

The New Technology: The E-Rater

Hold onto your hats, folks, because the future is now. Throughout the history of the AWA, two readers graded each essay and ETS gave you the average of their two scores. Well, as of February 1999, one of the humans will be replaced by a new grading machine called the "E-rater." Believe it or not, the E-rater is a computer that can supposedly "read" an essay and assess the essay's organization, clarity, supporting examples, and grammar. It scans the essay looking for various words and phrases that indicate structure and also checks for spelling and grammar errors.

Take a moment to reread that last paragraph if you need to. It is not a misprint.

ETS' official take on this new E-rater will probably be something to the effect of "embracing the future of technology, blah blah blah," but it's just a way for them to reduce costs and increase their profit margin. ETS has said that the E-rater will save the company about $50 per test, but there have been no indications as of this writing that the price of the exam will come down. ETS administers 11 million tests a year and took in $417 million in 1998. Not bad for a non-profit organization.

Before you cry foul (or you go out and rent *2001: A Space Odyssey* again), GMAT administrators have claimed that the E-rater gives the same score as a human reader 91 percent of the time. Plus, the person and the computer are supposed to cancel out each other's weaknesses: The human has a greater appreciation for style and content, while the computer doesn't let fatigue or other distractions alter its perceptions.

All these new developments might make interesting patter at cocktail parties, but it should have no affect on your approach to the AWA. If anything, the arrival of the E-rater confirms that ETS has little time for creativity and whimsy.

How the AWA Is Graded

A human and the E-rater grade your Issue essay on a scale of 0 to 6, and the two scores are averaged. The Argument essay is scored the same way. Finally, the two averaged scores are themselves averaged and rounded off to the nearest tenth. This is your final AWA score, which has nothing to do with your three-digit GMAT score. A sample AWA score might be calculated like this:

AWA Issue: Human: 4 Score: 4.5
      E-rater: 5
Final score: 4.75, rounded to **4.8**
AWA Argument: Human: 5 Score: 5.0
       E-rater: 5

Although the official scale is 0 to 6, some 90 percent of all essays fall within the 3–5 range. If you receive a 6, the reader thought your essay was truly exceptional; if you receive a 2, the reader probably wondered if you have an opposable thumb. About the only way you can get a 0 is to leave the screen blank or just type gibberish for half an hour.

In the unlikely event that the two scores for one essay differ by more than a point, a second human is brought in to read the essay and determine the final score.

What Graders Are Looking For
According to its *Official Guide*, ETS officially looks for the following qualities in an exemplary essay response:

- a fully developed position based on insightful reasons and/or persuasive examples

- well-organized ideas

- superior control of language, diction, and syntactic variety

No big surprise. ETS would have you believe, however, that it employs legions of gifted professionals who carefully pore over all the AWA essays. After all, only the most educated palate can distinguish fine wine from jug wine, and only a seasoned veteran wordsmith can appreciate the subtleties and nuances of fine prose.

Yeah, right.

What Graders Are *Really* Looking For

The vast majority of essay graders are part-time workers whose careers are at least indirectly involved in the field of writing. Most of them are college teaching assistants and the like who could use the extra money. And you know how much time they spend on each essay? Two minutes.

Yup. That's it. Graders have to read some thirty essays per hour, and they work in eight-hour shifts. Even if you assume that your reader isn't a bleary-eyed mess who has been reading for five hours straight, she will still have only two minutes to give your essay a quick skim to determine your writing style and organizational skills.

As a matter of fact, a few essay readers have admitted that they formulate assumptions about an essay after reading the first paragraph. According to some, most essays display a mediocrity that they have termed "four-ness." If it looks like it gets the job done and isn't too badly written, your essay is bound to receive a score between 4 and 5. If the essay makes a wonderful first impression, the grader will consider giving it a 5 or higher; if it's incomprehensible or it looks as though it may have been written by a monkey, you'll get a 2 or worse.

Because of the short time-span for review, readers are really looking for an essay that:

- is long enough to look thorough
- doesn't ramble aimlessly
- addresses the question and supplies good supporting points
- is easy and interesting to read quickly

As you might imagine, there are ways to make sure your readers see what they're looking for right away.

OVERALL TIPS

There are many secrets for success on the AWA regardless of the subject matter. The purposes of the two essays, though, are very different, so we'll discuss each essay individually. But first we will go over some overall tips for how to get a high score on both essays and show how similar the AWA essays can be.

1. Brush Up on Your Typing.

Before the CAT, all AWA essays were handwritten in pencil, and business schools received reduced-size photocopies of every essay. Needless to say, reading these was a real hassle—especially when you consider the limited time graders have to make heads or tails of what you're trying to say. In fact, some graders have admitted that GMAT takers could score points just by making their essays neat enough to be read easily.

All essays are now composed at the keyboard, so handwriting is no longer an issue. (This makes the AWA readers very, very happy.) If you can't type well on a standard QWERTY keyboard, now is the time to learn. Writing under pressure is tense enough; you don't want to add to the headache by hunting and pecking around for the right letter. And remember that the E-rater will check for spelling mistakes (which doesn't seem fair, since the writing software doesn't have spellcheck). These mistakes are not supposed to affect your grade, but you will be penalized if your misspellings are so numerous as to make your essay too difficult to read.

If you can type the following in about fifteen seconds without looking at your keyboard, you'll do just fine:

> The quick brown fox jumps over the lazy dog.

This sentence is well known to anyone who has taken a touch-typing class, because it contains all twenty-six letters in the alphabet. If you have access to a computer, use it when you practice writing essays. You'll be better prepared for the real thing.

2. Follow the First Two F's.

You don't have time for a lot of revision and polishing, but the first two Fs from the previous chapter are still important on the AWA because your organization is so crucial. You get thirty minutes to write the essay; spend the first ten minutes or so thinking about what you'll say and how you're going to say it. Read the essay topic once or twice and start thinking of pertinent thoughts. No matter how stupid they might seem at first glance, *don't censor anything*.

Brainstorming is also helpful if you read the topic and have absolutely no idea how you feel about it. Given the stress of the process, it's rather common for a student to draw a complete blank and have a panic attack. If this happens, get a hold of yourself. (Sure, that's easy to say now.) Once you get a few ideas out of your head and onto your scratch paper, you'll have a better chance of formulating an opinion that you can discuss in a few paragraphs.

Then comes the outline, which is the most significant element in an essay's creation. If you spend the time to stitch all the elements into a viable structure, the essay will be much easier to compose. And since graders love organization and have so little time to look for it, make life easy for them. Every introduction you write should contain a sentence that looks something like this:

> I believe that [insert thesis here] for the following [insert number here] reasons.

Once your reader sees that, she knows you took the time to organize your thoughts before you started typing. This structure jumps out at the reader right away, and it makes a good impression. You can make your outline even easier to follow by numbering your supporting points paragraph by paragraph, like this:

> Last sentence of intro paragraph:
>
> *Pittsburgh, Pennsylvania, is the best place in the world to live for the following three reasons.*

First sentence of paragraph 2:

First, Pittsburgh boasts the cultural opportunities of a big city like Chicago or New York, but it maintains the charm of a much smaller community.

First sentence of paragraph 3:

Second, Pittsburgh's climate features the variety of all four seasons, but its unique geographical position helps temper the Midwest's bitter winters and keeps it mild in the summer.

First sentence of paragraph 4:

And finally, Pittsburgh's small market keeps its sports teams from signing obnoxious, overpriced athletes who favor wealth over the game they play.

3. Go for the Bookends First.

The paragraphs that will make the biggest impression on your AWA reader are the first and last—affectionately known as the bookends. Since you have to use a word processor on the CAT, why not use it to its greatest advantage? Most students start out okay on essays, but they tend to finish hurriedly when they see the time dwindling. Starting out with the bookends ensures that your essay will finish strong (especially if you take the time to read the whole thing at the end—see tip 10). If you can knock your reader's socks off with a strong introduction and conclusion, these paragraphs will stick in the reader's mind as she calculates your grade.

There is a saying that the easiest way to walk a straight line is to keep your eyes fixed on a faraway object on the horizon and walk toward it. That's the case with essays as well. If you know what you're going to conclude before you start typing, your essay will be much more cohesive. You would be surprised at the percentage of writers who just start typing and rambling when the timer for the AWA starts, hoping that their thesis will make more sense as time elapses.

4. Acknowledge the Other Side.

Your stance on a particular subject becomes much more compelling if you show an understanding for how supporters of the other side of the subject feel. This illustrates that you've considered both approaches to an issue (whether or not you actually have) and can talk about the subject in an informed matter.

Use of this technique will involve some contrary trigger words, like the following:

*Macro-Pute should be congratulated for the overwhelming success that its operating system enjoys, **but** there are four reasons why its monopolistic practices should be curbed.*

***Although** the Spice Girls have millions of devoted fans worldwide, I believe that their music heralds the end of Western civilization as we know it for the following ten reasons.*

> **While** many analysts blame North Korea for the current stand-off with its neighbor to the south, people should not be so quick to exculpate South Korea.

Once you have referred to those who don't share your opinion, however, don't spend any more time defending them. Your primary goal is to support your opinion and time is limited.

5. Refer to Books and/or Current Events.

As we mentioned in chapter 6, reading a lot is a great way to help you write better. But keeping up with your reading has a dual purpose. If you use current events or literary references in your writing, (1) you have many new premises on which to rely, and (2) your readers will value your opinions all the more because you'll appear well read.

Remember: The directions ask you to support your conclusion based on experience, observations, or *reading*. Note, though, that these references are more useful on your Issue essay than they are on your Argument essay. The Argument essay is more concerned with how students analyze the information they have been given. The Issue relies a lot more on outside information (in whatever form) to back up the writer's conclusion. Here are some examples:

Issue Topic 1: The astonishing rise in the number of patients suffering from mental illness has overwhelmed the resources of psychiatric hospitals, resulting in a much more diluted quality of care.

Response: Although the quality of many mental institutions is under fire, we must also be thankful for any hospital that doesn't emulate the one featured in *One Flew Over the Cuckoo's Nest* . . .

Issue Topic 2: The Food and Drug Administration has become more of a nuisance than a benefit lately, because its collectively cautious nature merely precludes effective, useful drugs from penetrating the American market.

Response A: The FDA has definitely not overstayed its welcome as a federal watchdog, because the motives of the giant pharmaceutical companies cannot be trusted. If the FDA can green-light a drug such as thalidomide, which caused horrible birth defects to newborns in the late 1950s, imagine what other drugs would get through without the FDA's watchful eye . . .

Response B: I agree that the FDA is no longer useful to the American public. Europeans are very familiar with RU-482, the morning-after abortion pill, but the FDA refuses to sanction its use in the United States . . .

6. Aim for Length.

Readers can't help themselves. If they look at an essay that's only half a page long, they will assume (subconsciously or otherwise) that the thesis is inadequately developed. Right away, your ceiling will be lowered to a maximum score of 4. On the other hand, if you go on and on with no concern for brevity or conciseness, your essay will appear verbose and rambling. Neither too short nor too long is what will get you a high score. Your goal should be to write at least one page of text. This roughly translates to about one-half to three-fourths of a page, single-spaced, using the Times New Roman font in twelve-point size. With practice this one-page target will become easier to achieve.

7. Cater to a Short Attention Span.

If you've had any experience writing essays in high school and college, you know that one of the best ways to make an essay look longer is to use lots of paragraphs. Padding your essay's length has a dual effect, though—it also makes the essay easier to read. Think of Reading Comprehension passages; each new paragraph offers you a chance to rest before you begin reading again. Look at these two short passages:

To the north of Massachusetts, most of what is now New Hampshire and Maine was granted in 1622 by the Council for New England to Sir Ferdinando Gorges and Captain John Mason and their associates. In 1629, Gorges and Mason divided their territory at the Piscataqua River; Mason took the southern side, which he named New Hampshire. The first settlement appeared at Rye in 1623, the same year as the genesis of what would become the Massachusetts Bay Colony. It remains uncertain whether Rye was deserted or merged into another colony founded at nearby Strawberry Bank, which was later renamed Portsmouth. In the 1630s, Puritan immigrants began filtering in, and in 1638 the Rev. John Wheelwright founded Exeter. Maine consisted of a few scattered and small settlements. Most of these were fishing villages centered around the main commercial hub of York. Like each of the other offshoots of Massachusetts, the Maine territory lacked a charter and maintained its autocracy until 1691, when Maine was officially incorporated into Massachusetts.

To the north of Massachusetts, most of what is now New Hampshire and Maine was granted in 1622 by the Council for New England to Sir Ferdinando Gorges and Captain John Mason and their associates. In 1629, Gorges and Mason divided their territory at the Piscataqua River; Mason took the southern side, which he named New Hampshire.

The first settlement in New Hampshire appeared at Rye in 1623, the same year as the genesis of what would become the Massachusetts Bay Colony. It remains uncertain whether Rye was deserted or merged into another colony founded at nearby Strawberry Bank, which was later renamed Portsmouth. In the 1630s, Puritan immigrants began filtering in, and in 1638 the Rev. John Wheelwright founded Exeter.

Maine consisted of a few scattered and small settlements. Most of these were fishing villages centered around the main commercial hub of York. Like each of the other offshoots of Massachusetts, the Maine territory lacked a charter and maintained its autocracy until 1691, when Maine was officially incorporated into Massachusetts.

Which one was easier to read?

Indentations in the passage make the text look less immense and ponderous. They also make the very important impression that you're not likely to repeat yourself as you make your points.

8. Say It Once and Move On.

The most common trap into which the average essay writer falls is repetition. It may be because you could only think of one pertinent thought and figured you'd do your best to string it out until it looked long enough. This is akin to adding water to soup so that it will feed more people. All you have is just a big vat of watery soup.

More often, repetition comes from the stress of the time limit. Once you decide that you have a good point to make, you want to emphasize it by saying it again, only in different words. (Some writers don't even bother to change the words, and that's an even worse transgression.) Don't do this.

9. Be Resolute.

Your job as a writer is to compel your reader to share your beliefs. Therefore, it's very important not to use wishy-washy words. If you don't seem convinced of your viewpoint, how can you convince others?

The best examples of well-written, compelling essays are in your local paper's opinion page. Each of the writers who appear there is a professional writer whose job it is to sway you to his or her way of thinking. A lead editorial in a newspaper might read something like this:

> The Pentagon can no longer plausibly suggest that daily air attacks on Iraq are solely in response to Iraqi efforts to shoot down its enemies. True, Iraq has enjoined British and American fighter planes, but only because NATO's expanded rules of engagement have been made decidedly less strict in the past six months. The White House must answer reports that fighter planes, under the auspices of self-defense, have mercilessly pounded an assortment of targets of dubious military significance.

After you've read this paragraph, there's no doubt of the author's viewpoint. Your writing should be just as sure of itself. Therefore, minimize the use of words such as *would*, *might*, and *possibly*, and replace them with stronger words such as *is* and *will*. Don't worry; you won't lose points for sounding too liberal or too conservative.

WRONG

This *would be* a major problem . . .

Single mothers *might* benefit from lower taxes . . .

Stock prices *are possibly* too overvalued . . .

RIGHT

This *is* a major problem . . .

Single mothers *will* benefit from lower taxes . . .

Stock prices *are* too overvalued . . .

10. Save Time for a Final Read.

Finally, even though the computer gives you thirty minutes to create literary magic, you really should use only twenty-eight or so. As you practice these essays, you may notice that you lose flow if you work on different parts of your essay at different times. Ideally, you should save a couple of minutes to give your essay a final read-through looking for typos, grammatical glitches, and any other stuff that doesn't make any sense.

Feel the Burn (Again)!

There is some practice material in this chapter, but it's also helpful to go right to the source for sample essay topics. In the back of ETS's *Official Guide* you will find about 100 Issue and 100 Argument topics. If you want to keep up steady improvement, make yourself write at least two essays a week. To keep things as spontaneous as possible, open up to a page of topics, close your eyes, and point to one. Then, set the timer for thirty minutes and start typing.

The best way to gauge your improvement is to pair up with another student. Write your essays and then swap them with your partner's, and give each other frank criticism (positive and negative).

And by all means, be patient! If you're not used to writing very often, it might take a while before your essays show a lot of improvement. If you keep practicing and you have a friend or colleague who is willing to work with you, you will get better. If you feel as though you're not making much progress, go back and read chapter 6's suggestions for becoming a better writer and try to find some inspiration there.

If All Else Fails

As was mentioned at the top of this chapter, the AWA is not going to keep you out of business school. The AWA essays are indeed another tool to help b-schools evaluate your verbal skills, but no admissions officer will look at a GMAT report sheet and think: "Hmm. This applicant looks perfect for our program. Too bad about that 3.5 on the AWA."

The AWA is not worth fretting over. Just take your time, do the best you can, and use the first hour of the GMAT to get ready for the rest of the exam (which is much more important). With that in mind, let's look at some techniques that are specific to each essay.

ANALYSIS OF AN ISSUE

When it's time to analyze an Issue, the computer will give you a statement and ask you for your opinion. The directions will vary based on the question, but they usually read something like this:

> Discuss the extent to which you agree or disagree with the opinion stated above. Support your point of view with reasons and/or examples from your own experience, observations, or reading.

Pick a Side

The simple translation of this is "State how you feel and why." The types of questions you'll see on the AWA Issue fall into two very broad categories: The first question type refers to both sides of a debate and asks you to choose a side and defend it. Here's a sample opinion that falls in this first category:

> Some people believe that one of the most important decisions that the owners of a new business can make is the location of their headquarters. Others, citing the rise of the Internet, e-mail, and telecommuting, argue that location has become virtually irrelevant.

It's a rather straightforward exercise. You decide which group has the more compelling case, then you write why you feel that way. Because of the opinion's narrow focus, though, ETS realized that the writer's job is easier if there are only two sides from which to choose. Further, ETS' graders found that they had to read virtually the same essay over and over again. This made the review process even more boring than it had to be.

More Ways to Go

Therefore, ETS soon introduced a second type of question that has a broader range of answers:

> You can determine a lot about a nation from its advertise-ments.

ETS likes questions like this because the writer is provided with several options, such as:

- comparing America's ads to those in Sweden

- contrasting the average ad in 1999 from one in 1959 (like those "retromercials" on *Nick at Nite*)

- discussing the different media (radio ads, print ads, billboards, etc.) and how technology has changed them

Essay graders love to read the answers to essays like this one because there's a greater chance that some of the reading might actually be interesting (and much less tediously repetitive).

Practice AWA Issue Questions

Below are five sample topics that are similar to those that appear on the Analysis of an Issue essay. Find a computer in a quiet place and practice writing answers to each of them. (If you want, write two, three, or seventeen answers for each one and compare them.) As you write, try to keep all that we've talked about in chapters 6 and 7 in the back of your mind. Try not to revert to any previous bad habits.

As we've mentioned before, the best place to look for extra essay questions is the *Official Guide*, which has more than a hundred of them.

A. Standardized tests are a tremendous burden on all prospective graduate students, but they are a necessary control by which all candidates are judged equally.

B. The study of how a company's stock has performed in the past is an utterly useless exercise, because previous performance has no bearing on future success or failure.

C. Tourism is a blight on peaceful seaside villages because wealthy summer residents cannot help but overwhelm the local residents.

D. In any situation, a good follower is more important than a good leader.

E. Computer users should not concern themselves over a new computer chip that lets companies determine the e-mail addresses of everyone who visits their sites.

The Good, The Bad, and The Ugly

Let's look at a few sample responses to Essay Topic A above. We'll assess each essay and spotlight the good qualities that you may try to emulate (and the bad qualities you should try to avoid). Here's that question again:

> "Standardized tests are a tremendous burden on all prospective graduate students, but they are a necessary control by which all candidates are judged equally."

Response 1:

> I disagree with the notion that standardized tests are a necessary control for applicants to college and graduate schools.
>
> First, standardized tests are a poor indicator of the quality of work of which a person is capable. My sister, for example, was valedictorian of her high school class. She compiled a 4.0 grade point average, was captain of the field hockey team, and was active in the school theater. She took the SAT three times, and despite her academic track record, she never

scored higher than the 70th percentile. Clearly, this shows that a person who is a poor test taker can be far more qualified than a standardized test might indicate.

Second, the content of the exams that schools use as admissions criteria is also questionable. The most egregious example of this are Sentence Correction questions on the GMAT. I can appreciate that business schools want to know that I have command of the English language, but they can determine that from the essays I write, both here and on my applications. Why test arcane grammar rules as well? Success in the business world certainly does not rely on an exhaustive knowledge of modifying clauses and such.

Lastly, the standardized tests are unreliable because wealthier people can pay for expensive preparation courses that others cannot afford. Most test-preparation companies guarantee an 80-point score improvement on the GMAT. So when an applicant submits a 700 GMAT score, is that score a genuine measure of that person's "intelligence"? Or has that score merely been artificially inflated by ten weeks of guided preparation?

As I have indicated above, standardized tests do not serve the purpose for which they were created. They don't show a person's ability to handle graduate studies. Rather, a standardized test score is an arbitrary piece of information that merely serves as an excuse for schools to accept or deny the applications of those who wish to attend.

Assessment: This student has a strong vocabulary, and she develops her points well. She makes a brief introduction, then creates three short supportive paragraphs, each of which has some sort of tangible example to solidify her point. She's also remarkably resolute; there's no question about her opinion on the subject. (And some might find her downright angry.) The only real problem with this essay is that it's a little off point. The issue is not whether standardized tests are flawed; the real point of discussion is whether they're necessary despite their "tremendous burden." An essay reader is inclined to forgive this, though, because of the overall quality of the writing. This writer would get a 5.5 or a 6.

Response 2:

Standardized tests are an important issue because so many people take them nowadays in order to get into schools. These tests are a tremendous burden, but you have to have them. Otherwise, applications to business schools would be much more arbitary.

If you're going to have a school that many people are going to apply to, you have to have some way to measure their abilities. You can't just have a subjective system like the one Harvard Business School had, where Harvard didn't take the GMAT and everyone was interviewed. Harvard became a very popular school, and too many people applied there. They're job was too hard, so they began to take GMAT scores on applications. With this action, Harvard learned a very important lesson.

Another important point is that business school should be hard to apply to. You shouldn't make it easy to apply to school, because if it was easy, everyone would do it. Students shoud realize that applying to graduate is a serious exercise and that you shouldn't do it unless you have a serious idea of what your going to do after school is over. A difficult test like the GMAT makes a potential student reflect on their situation and makes them be sure that business school is where they want to go.

In conclusion, standardized tests are difficult because graduate school is difficult. I think most students would vote to get rid of them, but I would not because they're a necessary evil.

Assessment: This example helps illustrate that there's more to an essay than just an appealing structure. This writer makes his point at the beginning and sticks to it throughout, but the writing style is overly simplistic and the grammar errors are too frequent. For example, *They're job* should have been written as *Their job* in the second paragraph, and *your* in the third paragraph should be *you're*. There's also a lot of pronoun trouble, because Harvard is a school, so it takes the pronoun *it*, not *they*. The spelling errors like *arbitary* and *shoud* are also embarrassing. They might just be typos, but they stand out. Therefore, readers are likely to remember them and lower your score because of them. This essay would be lucky to receive a 3.5.

Response 3:

In the wake of America's robust economy and booming stock market, thousands and thousands of working people have suddenly found it possible to realize their dreams of attending graduate school. And one of the major hurdles in the way of each American who plans to go back to school is the standardized test. These tests require a lot of time and money in order to prepare for them properly, and they aren't a real indicator of how well you'll do in school. But schools want to have a numerical score for each student so that they can compare applicants in an objective manner. Whether these standardized tests should be discontinued is a controversial topic that will not be decided any time soon.

Acceptance to graduate school is a subjective process, and applicants come from countless backgrounds. Many of us have excelled in business, either by working for a large company or by starting up our own successful ventures. We've had careers in college, and we've submitted our transcripts and lists of our widely diverse extracurricular activities. On top of all that, we've all written as many as 10 personal statement essays to accompany our applications, and many of us request interviews. It's a lot of work for an admissions professional to digest, especially at prestigious schools that attract a lot of interest. Some people feel that the GMAT is that necessary bit of information that allows admissions representatives to compare all applicants to each other directly, based on a universal standard. But how adequate is that universal standard, and how representative is it? Can you really tell how smart a person is just because of some verbal and math skills that are tested? And do people excel on these tests because they are smart, or because they spent a lot of money to be trained for the specific questions that the tests ask? When you think about all the money that ETS, a monopoly, receives from students who want to realize their dreams (not to mention the test preparation companies that also charge a lot of money), it all seems like a tragic waste of time, money, and energy.

In conclusion, therefore, I believe that standardized tests should be eliminated.

Assessment: Here's a classic example of a student who just started typing without a clue about how the essay would turn out. There's no indication in the first paragraph about the writer's opinion, and that's probably because he hasn't yet figured it out for himself. Instead, he uses one of those "funnel introductions" that start out very broad and gradually narrow their focus until the final sentence.

The problem is that there is no focus. The writing skills are rather good (and voluminous—there are 370 words), but they're not serving any purpose because nothing is being said. We don't even know the writer's opinion until the very last sentence, which seems tacked on at the last minute because he ran out of time. In sum, the essay reader had to slog through a lot of disorganized platitudes, and there wasn't much of a payoff. This essay would probably get a 4.

ANALYSIS OF AN ARGUMENT

Analyzing Arguments on the AWA is a much different exercise that is closely related to answering the multiple-choice Critical Reasoning questions. (If you haven't yet read chapter 4 on Arguments, you might want to do that now. Many of the terms we'll refer to here are discussed there in much greater detail.)

For your Argument essay, you'll be shown an author's conclusion and one or two premises on which the conclusion is based. Unlike the Issue essay instructions, which will vary slightly depending on the question, the instructions for the Argument essay will always look like this:

> Discuss how well reasoned you find this argument. In your discussion, be sure to analyze the line of reasoning and the use of evidence in the argument. For example, you may need to consider what questionable assumptions underline the thinking and what alternative explanations or counterexamples might weaken the conclusion. You can also discuss what sort of evidence would strengthen or refute the argument, what changes in the argument would make it more logically sound, and what, if anything, would help you better evaluate its conclusion.

Now that you've read these once, don't bother ever reading them again. You'll waste valuable time.

WHAT THE DIRECTIONS MEAN

Your job is to assess whether the logic the author uses to arrive at his conclusion is valid based on the following criteria:

- ◆ Do the premises he cites support the conclusion adequately?

- ◆ Are the assumptions he relies on valid?

- ◆ Is it possible to interpret the premises a different way and arrive at a different conclusion?

- ◆ What other information is missing?

That's it. It's just like using the CPA Model we discussed in chapter 4. And there's one very important thing to remember about the Argument essay: *Your opinion of the author's conclusion is utterly irrelevant*. It's not so much what he says; it's how he says it. For example, here is a stripped-down version of a student essay for an AWA Argument:

> The superintendent of a large residential property indicated that the termite problem has been brought under control because he has sprayed the basement.

WRONG	*RIGHT*
The author is correct to condemn the increase in the termite population of most American urban centers. These vermin have plagued humans for centuries, spreading disease and making the world we leave for our children into a dirty, disgusting ball of filth. Traps should be set in every square foot of every building on the planet in order to stem the tide of this reign of terror . . .	The superintendent's conclusion that he has solved the termite problem in his building is flawed because it relies on the dubious assumption that all the termites in the building are in the basement. Further, the super assumes that the termites will not somehow recognize the spray and avoid it. And we also don't know whether the spray will always work properly . . .

The essay on the left is an Issue essay, and it's inappropriate here. Your reader doesn't care what you think about termite control. He wants you to assess the way in which the author arrives at the conclusion. The passage on the right fits the bill; the writer asserts that the author's concluding statement is not defensible because the assumptions are dubious.

There's Always Something Wrong

Regardless of what the Argument says, your essay can *never* begin like this:

> The author's conclusion is completely valid in every way. I came away from her argument completely convinced of its authenticity as a piece of rock-solid logic . . .

The AWA Arguments are terse little statements with at most two or three supporting points. There's no way that anyone could come to an unassailable conclusion with so few premises. In fact, you can start out every Argument essay you ever write with a sentence along these lines:

> The author has come to a faulty conclusion that **[insert conclusion here]** because she relies on X premises that are insufficient and Y assumptions that are dubious at best. [Note the use of numbers in the intro to show how organized you are.]

Some arguments will seem very plausible at first, and you will be tempted to agree with the author at some point. It's still okay to acknowledge whatever good points the author makes, but look hard for the holes in the logic. The author always misses something, and your overall tone should be negative. Let's look at a few sample topics:

ARGUMENT 1: The following appeared in a newspaper editorial.

> The global entertainment company Zipney has signed an agreement with the government of the eastern European county of Magdania to build a Zipneyland theme park there within the next five years. Since Zipneyland parks in Los Angeles and London attract between three and six million tourists per year, the years of waning tourism in Magdania are clearly over.

Problems: Here's a classic "argument by analogy" in which the items being compared are not necessarily comparable. The author assumes that the Magdanian Zipneyland will attract the same number of tourists as those in London and Los Angeles, but that's not necessarily true. London and L.A. are big tourist hubs already; what if Magdania doesn't have the same appeal? Magdania is in eastern Europe, an area that might not espouse Western culture as well as the other two cities do.

There's also the issue of the quality of the park. Will it be exactly the same as the other two? Have Zipney's revenues stayed strong, or has a backlash against the Zipney-fication of society pared profits enough so that Zipney will cut a few corners here and there?

ARGUMENT 2: The following appeared in a campus newsletter.

> For years, student activists have been campaigning for a two-day fall break in October to give students a chance to relax and catch up with their studies. This year, the administration will institute such a break for the first time, occurring on the Thursday and Friday before Halloween. Given the activists' success, their desire to have fall break extended to a full week will certainly be fulfilled.

Problems: The author assumes that the fall break was instituted because of the activism, but we don't know if that's true. To weaken a causal argument, suggest an alternate cause: Maybe the fall break was a monetary decision, or perhaps the faculty finally decided that they wanted the break as well. If the students didn't bring about the break in the first place, they probably won't be able to extend it.

Even if the causal relationship does exist, the author also assumes that you can get whatever you want as long as you push for it. The administration might feel as though two days is fine, but that a week is too long an interruption. Is there a spring break? There might be some provision in the school's charter that prohibits more than one week-long break per year.

ARGUMENT 3: The following appeared in a finance magazine.

> At the annual SpoonCorp shareholders' meeting in Alaska this year, several shareholders expressed their objection to the company's imminent merger with archrival LadleWorks. Since these individuals own only a collective 15 percent of the company's stock, SpoonCorp's board of directors should go ahead with the merger as planned.

Problems: Here's where ETS likes to sway us with numbers. The author assumes that the other 85 percent of the shareholders support this merger. We don't know if that's true. The other shareholders might not have been able to come to the meeting; the Alaskan site might have been too remote. It's also possible that the objectors may have been sent as representatives of those people who couldn't come. Thus, the 15 percent figure is misleading.

It Is the Author's Fault

Notice that in the analysis of all three Arguments above, the problem was the author and his logic, not his conclusion. Your job is to tear the author apart. Problems the author will usually display include the following:

- insufficient premises
- missing premises
- wrong assumptions
- supporting data that need to be clarified

Making the author the culpable party keeps your attention on his logic and prevents you from addressing the conclusion itself.

And Don't Forget the Context Line!

The first line you read when your Argument essay begins is a reference to the publication in which the argument appeared:

- The following appeared as part of a memorandum to all members of an exclusive club.

- The following is an excerpt from the promotional literature for a new video game.

- The following appeared in the editorial section of an entertainment magazine.

Most people gloss right over this piece of information and jump right into the question, and that's a mistake. ETS likes to disguise this line as a throwaway introduction, but the source of the argument can often be as important as the argument itself. You might find an author's statement that predicts the outcome of an election very persuasive until you look up and realize that the writer is marketing director at a dog food company. What evidence is there that someone who hawks Rover's dinner knows anything about politics? That's the sort of thing you want to address in your essay.

Practice AWA Argument Essays

Try writing answers to each of these five Argument essays. There are no "right" answers obviously. Show your responses to someone whose opinion you respect. (Or if you want some real fun, show them to a person who you think is a complete idiot.) By following the tips we've outlined in this chapter, you are sure to do well.

A. The following appeared in an American medical journal.

A new study has shown that cardiac patients can reduce their chances of a heart attack by taking a reduced-potency aspirin pill once a day. Therefore, now would be a good time to invest in Malatet Pharmaceutical Corp., which happens to be Europe's largest producer of reduced-potency aspirin.

Discuss how well reasoned you find this argument. In your discussion, be sure to analyze the line of reasoning and the use of evidence in the argument. For example, you may need to consider what questionable assumptions underline the thinking and what alternative explanations or counterexamples might weaken the conclusion. You can also discuss what sort of evidence would strengthen or refute the argument, what changes in the argument would make it more logically sound, and what, if anything, would help you better evaluate its conclusion.

B. The following appeared in a media trade paper.

The average person who is fifty-four years of age or older watches about thirty-eight hours of TV per week, while people between the ages of eighteen and fifty-four watch only twenty-one hours per week. Since the American population is aging rapidly, advertisers would be better served to target their marketing to an older audience.

Discuss how well reasoned . . .

C. The following appeared in a promotional flyer.

In the three years since President Bilkus has been in office, the number of violent crimes in urban areas has decreased by 35 percent. During the administration of President Bilkus' predecessor, crime rose at an average rate of 10 percent per year. Thus, Americans who want to see crime reduced even further should vote to reelect President Bilkus this fall.

Discuss how well reasoned . . .

D. The following appeared in an internal memo of a small Internet company.

When Alice's Restaurant started making its waiters and busboys wear uniforms, employee tardiness decreased and tips increased. Thus, our productivity will rise if we impose a dress code on our employees.

Discuss how well reasoned . . .

E. The following appeared in a shareholder's prospectus of a large, manufacturing conglomerate:

Since 1980, golf courses have provided land developers with the most consistent source of revenue. Therefore, our company should transform the 200 acres of lakeside wilderness into a golf course.

Discuss how well reasoned . . .

The Good, The Bad, and The Ugly, Redux

Once again, let's revisit the first argument topic and assess some sample responses. Here's the argument again:

The following appeared in an American medical journal.

"A new study has shown that cardiac patients can reduce their chance of a heart attack by taking a reduced-potency aspirin pill once a day. Therefore, now would be a good time to invest in Malatet Pharmaceutical Corp., which happens to be Europe's largest producer of reduced-potency aspirin."

Discuss how well-reasoned . . .

Response 1:

> This argument is poorly arranged. It uses assumptions and premises that are not useful and is therefore not very strong.
>
> For example, how do we know that this study is a good one? Maybe the scientists didn't know what they were doing and their information is incorrect. After all, people are capable of making mistakes and experimenting is always subject to margins of error. It's not a good idea to believe this argument until you get to know more about the scientists and the other work that they have done. It is important to know that they have a history of excellence in their field and are able to determine when the tests they have performed are accurate. There have been many examples in the past of scientific failures, and this could be another one.

Also, it is important to know about "reduced-potency" aspirin. We need to know how "reduced" the potency is and test it with aspirin that is more potent. Is it possible for a "high-potency" aspirin to have an even better effect? Because if the company makes "reduced potency" aspirin but not "high-potency" aspirin, the company could be introuble.

In conclusion, this argument cant be a good one because we don't know if the study was propery conducted and that "high-potency" aspirn isn't betterfor you.

Assessment: Frankly, this person didn't have much to say, and it shows. From the get-go, it's clear that this writer was floundering around looking for a point to make. It happens sometimes. You read a topic, think to yourself that you have no idea what to write, and panic quickly sets in. Unfortunately, essay readers can detect this a mile away, and they don't have to read much to know that there isn't much content here. The lack of word variety is a problem (some form of the word *potent* appears six times in the third paragraph), and the misspellings toward the end make it obvious that the writer ran out of time. This one gets a 3 at best.

The best way to guard against brain power outages like this one is to practice as many essays as you can. You develop a way to get at least something interesting on the page in the half hour you've been given. Also, remember that a half hour is a long time. (If you're unconvinced, sit on the floor and do absolutely nothing for a half an hour.) If at first you draw a blank, be patient with yourself and try not to freak out. If you relax, something will probably come to you, and you'll be able to salvage your efforts.

Response 2:

Human behavior tells us that this argument is flawed on many levels because it relies so much on assumptions about how people will react to the news of this new study. There is an announcement that a weaker form of aspirin can guard against heart disease, and right away we are to believe that Malatet Pharmaceuticals will make a lot of money. This author forgets that reduced-potency aspirin won't be successful unless people trust the product and buy it over and over again. We humans are suspicious by nature, and it takes a lot to win over our trust when it comes to what we put in our bodies. What do we know about this Malatet company? It obviously chose a clever name because *mal a la tete* means "headache" in French, but that isn't enough. Humans need and appreciate humor in life, but we need more than just whimsy from drug companies because our health is serious business. First, Malatet has to convince us to buy its products, and then to buy its stock. Both are a tall order by themselves; together, it is an even more formidable challenge. The author also assumes that when we buy the aspirin, we will actually have the self-discipline to take it regularly. Humans can be lazy and forgetful, and this aspirin is unlikely to have the effect it portrays itself to have if no one bothers to take it. It's impossible to trust this argument. The fact that Malatet is a European company is also especially deceptive, because Americans often associate Europe with cutting-edge medicinal professionals, especially for its prowess among Swiss neurosurgeons. It is tempting to group this company with the many other fine European institutions, but sometimes the exception does not prove the rule. We humans must be alert and not jump to any unlikely conclusions.

Assessment: Well, now. This person clearly has a few mistrust issues. The subject matter that this writer has chosen might seem a little weird, but there are a few grains of sense within. For example, it is true that people might not be inclined to start taking aspirin as a preventative medicine just because of a new study. The word has to get out that it's safe, and then people have to decide that it's an important thing to do.

The main problem with this essay is that it's all one paragraph, and it falls at the feet of the reader with a large, ponderous thud. If this writer had chosen to break the essay up into smaller paragraphs, he might have scored a few points for originality. But most of the essay is off on its own tangent, it doesn't appear very organized, and the reader will resent the lack of paragraph structure. Depending on the reader's mood, the score will fall somewhere between 3 and 4.

Response 3:

This argument urging investors to start buying shares of Malatet Pharmaceutical is unconvincing because it relies on too many assumptions that aren't necessarily true. There are three areas that merit further explanation before this author should receive any degree of credibility.

My first problem with this argument is the author's enthusiasm for the company just because it's the market leader in one product. Is it ahead of the game because it's the best, or are its competitors likely to overtake it once they hear about this new study? The author could enhance his position by showing that the company is managed well and will stay on top if the market for reduced-potency aspirin grows.

This brings me to my second point: the market itself. The author says that Malatet is the largest maker of reduced potency aspirin in Europe, but we know nothing about Europe's relationship with the global market. Before we can send Malatet any money, we need to know if its business extends to larger markets in North America or Asia. If there are competitors in these areas with whom Malatet cannot compete, then it's unlikely that Malatet will enjoy any long-term growth. I would also like to know how big the European market is and how many European competitors there are. If Malatet is virtually unchallenged in its field, I'll invest; if there's another company breathing down Malatet's neck, then I'll probably pass.

Lastly, I take issue with the source of this article, which appeared in a medical journal. I can see how this publication would know about medicine, but do its editors know anything about investing? Any evidence that this journal has shown some financial acumen in the past would strengthen this argument greatly.

There are just too many holes in this argument, so it is difficult to take the author seriously. Unless some further evidence surfaces in each of the three areas described above, the premises that are presented are insufficient proof that the conclusion is viable.

Assessment: This is the argument you want to write. It is organized well, it describes three problems the argument has and describes them in detail, and it suggests ways to make the argument more sound. The grammar is good, the word choice is variant and expressive, and the tone is firm and resolute. This writer also makes good use of the context line by asserting that medical journalism and stock-picking aren't related.

There are a few minor points to add, because no essay is perfect. There are some people who will tell you not to write in the first person as this person did, and he mixes up his *I*'s and his *we*'s. But if you can crank out an argument essay like this, you won't have much of a problem getting a 5.5 or a 6.

All right, folks. That's the end of the pre-test prep work. The next chapter contains a complete practice verbal section. Be sure to try and work through it soon, and try to remember all that you've read.

8 | ANSWERS TO EXERCISES

Chapter 2: Sentence Correction

Modifiers, p. 17

1. Incorrect. Crazed with hunger, the stray coyote was finally subdued by the park ranger.

2. Incorrect. Using several manuscripts that date back to the Middle Ages, historians believe that Charlemagne first rose to power as a mere teenager.

3. Correct.

4. Incorrect. Unlike executive skills, which most people can learn at any qualified business school, a sense of leadership is usually derived from a person's social relationships.

5. Incorrect. Though usually a calm person, Arthur had his patience tried more than once by his son's destructive behavior.

6. Correct.

Pronouns, p. 19

1. Incorrect. As the melon farmers drove their crops to market, they were dismayed to find that the melons were infested with fruit flies.

2. Incorrect. The Commerce Department, which usually doesn't make any fiscal announcements until after the budget is ratified, announced that its accounting practices would be overhauled next year.

3. Correct.

4. Correct.

5. Incorrect. Neither Alice nor Beatrix could figure out why she failed the math exam. (Neither is a singular pronoun, so you have to use the singular pronoun she.)

6. Incorrect. Every employee brought his or her softball mitt to the game. (For more about the insidious use of they in conversation, refer to the Insidious "They" section of the Grammar Odds and Ends.)

Verb Tense, p. 21

1. Incorrect. Before the new library was built, children played around in the vacant lot.

2. Incorrect. A recent study has found that within the past decade, many lawyers not considered for partnership have chosen to quit rather than wait until the following year. (Since there's no other past tense event in the sentence, the simple past is the proper tense.)

3. Correct.

4. Correct.

5. Never before had my parents been more surprised as they were when my sister brought home her new fiancé. (Same reason as number 2.)

6. Correct.

Parallel Construction, p. 23

1. Correct. The structure of the two prepositional phrases within a strictly monitored regimen and at random times is parallel.

2. Incorrect. When he reached the age of sixty-one, my father chose retirement over the search for another job. OR When he reached the age of sixty-one, my father chose to retire rather than to search for another job.

3. Incorrect. Evaluating Internet stocks using antiquated valuation models is like competing in the Indianapolis 500 with a horse and buggy.

4. Incorrect. Even the most experienced teen counselor can find it difficult to distinguish attention deficit disorder, which results when a student is chemically unable to process information, from boredom.

5. Correct.

6. Incorrect. The first task to accomplish when writing an application essay is the formulation of an outline that lists all the things you want to say. (Task is a noun and formulation is a noun. You can't use to formulate because parallel construction requires that you use the same word form.)

Comparisons, p. 24

1. Incorrect. The population of Asian Americans in California is almost twice as big as that in Missouri.

2. Correct.

3. Incorrect. In New Zealand, the average sheep eats almost ten more pounds of grass annually than its Australian counterpart does.

4. Correct.

5. Correct. You're not comparing Rupert's tomatoes to a baby's tomatoes.

6. Incorrect. The New York Public Library's main branch, located on the southwest corner of Fifth Avenue and 42nd Street, is larger than any other branch in Manhattan. (You have to place other in there because the main branch is a branch in Manhattan. Without other, the sentence says that the main branch is bigger than itself.)

Subject-Verb Agreement, p. 26

1. Correct. Neither my pet monkey nor my sister's pet rabbit is able [to drive a car].

2. Incorrect. All [of the major food groups], including proteins, fruits and vegetables, and candy, are crucial for optimal health.

3. Correct. Of all its sea-faring relatives, the California gray seal stands out [because of its winsome demeanor and shiny coat].

4. Correct. A small number [of buildings] that were damaged [in the Great Fire] [of 1909] are finally about to be rebuilt with the cash of an anonymous benefactor.

5. Incorrect. Each [of Liz Taylor's husbands]—including actor Burt Lancaster, Virginia senator John Warner, and construction worker Larry Fortensky—has described her [as a rare beauty] [both in body and in mind].

6. Incorrect. A secret cache [of personal journals] that were the property [of Finnbar Brenneisen], the renowned and reclusive billionaire known as much [for his eccentric behavior] as [for his extraordinary philanthropy], is about to be published.

Sample Questions, p. 27

1. (E)

    The two/three split is about as obvious as possible—right at the beginning of the answer choices. Since the enthusiasts are predicting what will happen in the future, it makes sense to use the future tense: will. Eliminate (A) and (B). (C) unnecessarily used the future perfect tense with *will have subsided*. You might be inclined to keep it until you reach (E), which is better because it uses the present tense *is*, and the sentence is less verbose than (C). (D) uses the subjunctive tense.

    Note: About the subjunctive tense: You might be inclined to like (B) because it uses would and were, but (B) has a problem because random modifies the wrong word. Random should modify testing, not animals.

2. (C)

    The first idiom to recognize is *find that*. Since (A) and (B) don't contain *that*, you can eliminate them. The key to the rest of the question is parallel construction. (C) is correct because it describes people with three parallel adjectives: agitated, defensive, and suspicious. (D) is wrong because it used *mostly* to describe *willing*. Also, the two descriptions (willing to cooperate and agitated, etc.) are contrary thoughts; therefore, you should use yet, not and. (E) does not use parallel construction—there's no need to use *are becoming*.

3. (B)

    Here's a subtle example of parallelism, and it relates to the word *either*. The drug companies obtain records either to contact or to estimate. Therefore, (B) is the only parallel choice. Also, (E) has pronoun trouble, because the drug companies are doing the estimating. The plural noun takes *they*, not *it*.

4. (A)

    The first idiom to consider is not (this) but (that). (B) uses not . . . and, so get rid of it. (C), (D), and (E) are not parallel like (A) is; the proper construction is not be judged by (this) but by (that).

5. **(B)**

Note the two/three split once again. The three airlines are separate businesses that are being combined, so you can eliminate (A), (D), and (E). This is an example when the majority doesn't always rule on a two/three split. (B) is better because of the comma it uses. The construction in (C), *merger of their businesses that*, suggests that the businesses created the alliance, but it was the airlines who did the creating. Also, the use of *would control* here is better because the actual control hasn't happened yet.

6. **(E)**

Here's a stellar example of the old subject-verb sucker punch. Many students are inclined to pick (A) because *adults carry* makes sense to the ear. But the subject of this latter thought is *one*, which needs to be paired up with the verb *carries*. Use the two/three split and cross off (A) and (B). The rest comes down to the proper use of the statistics cited in the sentence. (C) and (D) are incorrect because they use *every* and *each*, which suggest that if you take fifty people off the street and put them in a room, exactly one will be carrying a handgun. But the point of the sentence is to establish a more general ratio: for every forty-nine people who don't pack heat, there is one person who does.

7. **(D)**

The sentence is wrong as written because *more* needs *than*. Since it uses *as* instead, you can get rid of (A). (B) changes the tense to the past tense, but the present tense *is* remains later on. There's also an improper tense shift, so it's gone as well. (C) isn't parallel, because *destruction* and *making* aren't in the same format. It might have a chance if it used *destroying* instead. And (E) is a verbose mess; there's no need to use *the making of* when *making* is just fine by itself.

8. **(D)**

Here's one of those obscure idioms: liken . . . to. (In case you're worried, this idiom appears in the Idiom List appendix in the back of the book.) Note that *liken to* is correct, but *liken to be* is wrong. Also, there is a construction issue here. The use of *which* in (A) suggests that the fortune tellers likened themselves to prognosticators. (See the Grammar Odds and Ends appendix for clarification of the use of which.) Since the Supreme Court did the likening, (D) is best because it is in the active voice. (B), (C), and (E) are passive.

9. (C)

    These total-sentence questions can be either a real pain in the neck, or the answers can come to you right away. In the past, The Princeton Review used to counsel people to avoid these types of Sentence Correction questions, but the CAT has made that a moot point. When you see one of these, just scan each one individually and look for boo-boos. (A) is out because it contains *being*; (B) compares Wichterle to the developments of the other inventors; and (D) compares the contact lens to the other inventors. Both are apples-and-oranges mistakes, and both must go. (E) is also screwy because it suggests that the inventors had been inspired by necessity instead of by their developments. (C) is correct because its modifiers all match and are in the right place.

10. (E)

    Don't get these two idioms confused: intend . . . to and intent . . . on. Each is correct as is, but many students confuse the prepositions. The use of *who* in answer choices (A), (B), and (C) is fine, but (E) is better because *who* is not necessary; in this case, shortest is sweetest. (D) is wrong because it should read intending to run.

    Note: This question does a good job of illustrating that it's better to decide among the choices rather than cook up your own answer. Many students who see this question think the right answer should be *who intends to run*. That's a correct answer, but it's not among the choices.

11. (A)

    Be sure to line up your subjects and verbs! The subject of the sentence is *attempts*, so the verb needs to be *have*. (B) and (D) use has, so they're gone. (E) has a different verb problem, because there's no reason to use the past perfect form of *had*. Therefore, you can knock that off as well. Once you're down to (A) and (C), the only difference is the placement of the word political, which should modify resistance. (C) is wrong because it turns *political* into the adverb *politically* and makes it modify *encountered*.

12. (D)

The subject of the sentence is the noun result. For the sake of parallelism, then, *discover* should also be in noun form (result . . . has been the discovery). Remember that basic noun forms are usually preferable to -ing words, unless the words all end in -ing for the sake of parallelism. The best choices left are (B) and (D), and (D) is better because it uses the simple past tense *ruled* instead of *had ruled*, which is unnecessary. Also, (D) has an important distinction from (B) because it uses the word *were*. The best parallel tense should appear like this: Pharaohs were buried with fewer artifacts than their successors were. The *were* can also appear in the middle of the sentence: Pharaohs were buried with fewer artifacts than were their successors.

13. (C)

Process of Elimination is the only way to go here, because it's hard to express grammatically why (C) is superior. However, it's much easier to kill off the other choices because of their flaws. (A) and (B) contain *being*, so they can go. (D) is a wordy mess that contains that most odious phrase *the fact that* and also needlessly uses the past perfect tense *had been fueled*, and (E) suggests that Stanley Kubrick had his temperament fueled on purpose, as if he pulled into a gas station. That point is clearly not what the author wanted to get across.

14. (D)

Time to weed out the misplaced modifiers. The beginning of the nonunderlined portion of the sentence begins with each room, so if the sentence wants to compare anything by using the word *Unlike*, the underlined portion should also be about rooms. (A) compares smaller buildings to rooms, and so do (B) and (C), even though they replace *Unlike* with *Apart from* and *In contrast to*, respectively. A lemon painted blue is still a lemon. (E) survives the first cut because it doesn't commit this error, although its construction is still awkward because it suggests that each room is *Excluding* those apartment buildings. Given the choice of (D) or (E), though, (D) is much more concise.

15. (B)

Be sure you know the idiom *so . . . as to . . . .* It's an idiom that ETS loves because it doesn't make its way into basic conversation much, so most people are probably unfamiliar with it. It's questions like this that make you wonder why all the grammar nonsense isn't just a complete waste of time.

16. **(B)**

Again, the simple noun form *use* is better than the gerund *the using*; (A) is history. There's also a two/three split on the end of each answer choice; (B) and (D) use *have*, and (A), (C), and (E) do not. Because the sentence begins with *Since*, you need to use *have*. The construction is similar to this one: "I have eaten three dozen Oreos since breakfast." (C) and (E) can join (A) on the sidelines. (D) has another one of those subtle modifier problems, because *public* should modify *money*, not *use*. The taxpayers aren't actually using the money; they're paying and it will be used by someone else.

17. **(E)**

Before you give yourself migraines trying to figure out the proper use of *extent*, look instead at the need for parallelism. Since *how* appears in the nonunderlined portion at the end of the sentence, it should also appear at the beginning of the underlined portion (affected *by how . . . and how*). Eliminate all but (C) and (E), and then compare the remaining choices to each other. The only difference is that (E) uses *been*. Those who argue that shortest is sweetest might pick (C) at this point, but (E) is actually correct because the property hasn't developed, it has been developed by others.

Note: Here's a good example that although "vigorous writing is concise," the shortest answer isn't automatically correct. A short answer choice could omit something very important.

18. **(A)**

This is another toughie that is best attacked using POE. (B) is long and redundant, because you don't need to say *and it was also*. (C) tries to combine the two thoughts, but they're better off left apart (and there's no need to say *was* twice). (D) wants to use that highfalutin idiom *so . . . as to*, but it suggests that baseball and the weather were actually compared to each other. (E) is awkward because it suggests that the weather is sometimes not present.

19. **(D)**

Nothing like two consecutive baseball questions to get the blood pumping, eh? Well, this one may have been a little easier for you to solve. The idiom you're looking for is *as . . . as . . .* , and (B), (C), and (E) are unidiomatic. (A) is wrong because you don't need to use the past perfect tense *had*, although you do need to add the verb *did* at the end. Also, (C) and (E) change the meaning slightly; *collective* should be an adjective and modify *grief*.

20. **(A)**

Here's another full-sentence question, and it also needs to have all of its descriptive words and phrases placed in the proper order. (B) and (E) are wrong because they change the meaning; *declining minorities are enrolling* does not mean the same thing as *minority enrollment is declining*. The former suggests that minorities themselves are declining, when in fact it is their numbers that are declining. (C) has pronoun problems (support its cause?) and (D) has a subject-verb flaw. Since enrollment is the subject, the verb should be *is*, not *are*.

21. **(C)**

There is a straightforward comparison going on here; Atlanta is like other cities, so *like* is all you need. *Just like* is redundant, so (D) is out. The *have* in (B) and the *with* in (E) are not parallel with the rest of the sentence (and (E) is not idiomatic), so they can go, too. The use of *as* in (A), (B), and (E) is also incorrect because you use *as* to indicate that the processes are the same. Therefore, you would use *as* here only if you knew that Atlanta had expanded in exactly the same way as the other cities had. Since you don't know that for sure, like is the better choice.

22. **(B)**

The verb tense should remain constant throughout a sentence unless there's a tangible reason to do otherwise. (B) is the best choice because its verbs *are not required* and *do so* are both in the present tense. The verb tenses in (A) don't match, because *were* is in the past tense. (D) also uses the past tense *were* and complicates things further by using *had been doing so*, which is completely unnecessary. The same is true for (E)'s *had not had* the requirement. (C) is close, but *do so* is better than *do it* because it is an ambiguous pronoun. (Remember, you can't assume anything when it comes to pronouns.)

Chapter 3: Be A Better Reader

Paraphrasing Passages, p. 39

There's no "correct" answer to these questions, of course, but these are approximations of the length of your synopses and the type of language you should use.

1. Two groups who study history view it in different ways; one group likes to study the more famous people that shaped world events, while others prefer to study the little people who get lost in the shuffle.

2. Hong Kong lost a lot of trees during World War II, and a lot of other environmental damage has resulted. So, scientists are trying to replant all the trees and bring things back to normal.

3. Two Japanese banks are trying to copy the way that American banks do business by helping individual people, as well as big businesses, spend their money.

4. Tchaikovsky got a lot of money from this rich German lady, but he loved and respected her so much that he was too chicken to ever meet her in person.

5. The FeRAM chip is better than the normal RAM chip because it's safer and faster, but it's also much too expensive for ordinary people to afford it.

6. Lots of Koreans can't send their kids to the same snooty private schools that they went to because the stock market is tanking and lots of adults are looking for work.

7. The goal of a new web site is to help people understand that investing isn't that hard, and they'll show this by buying a bunch of stocks showing how they grow.

8. State fairs are full of people trying to sell stuff, win stuff, or talk about stuff, and three times as many people attend state fairs now as did ten years ago.

9. The IMF won't shell out any more dough to this new country until the country's government shapes up and becomes capitalist. The country will repay everything in five years.

10. After a year in space, satellites get crusted up with a bunch of gunk that causes them to sink a little off course. This is called orbital decay.

Dead Giveaways, p. 44

1. It is no longer possible for an individual to wield such power today, because most corporate stock is owned by large institutions. Dead giveaway: were once run.

2. If provoked, however, they'll rise up and rip your throat out. Dead giveaway: Normally.

3. But further research shows that the rebellion revealed how close the new country was to absolute chaos. Dead giveaway: At first glance.

4. In today's market, stocks are more valued for their potential for growth. Dead giveaway: Traditionally.

5. After the ascension of Thomas Jefferson to the White House in 1801, the Republicans ran the show. Dead giveaway: Until the end of the eighteenth century.

Paraphrasing Arguments, p. 45

Below are examples of how the arguments could be translated, but remember there is no absolute correct answer.

1. People who live in farm country might actually be better consumers to target than city folk, because farmers' costs are a lot less and have a lot of extra money to throw around.

2. The city has suggested selling off some of its rebuilding projects to raise cash, but some people don't like the idea because London did it and their commuter trains stink as a result.

3. Don't trust the big banks when they rate an investment opportunity, because they might just be trying to boost their own stock holdings.

4. Buying ads during the Super Bowl is no longer worth it, because the teams with the most fans (and the most viewers) currently stink and fewer people are watching.

5. During economic booms, the number of kids who want to go to college goes up. The number applying to graduate programs goes down, though, because adults want to work during the best economic times.

6. This company has gotten rich off a certain product it makes, and it wants to make more of them so it can make more money.

7. Viruses that people get are becoming too strong to be killed off by usual drugs, so drug companies have to spend a lot of dough developing new drugs to kill off the new bugs.

8. Avoiding paying your taxes is dumb, because the government will only raise taxes so that you'll have to pay more later. Also, the government will be really upset when it finds you.

9. Lots of people think that ads for alcohol make kids drink too much and break the law. There are lots of booze ads in France, though, and they haven't got as many booze-related problems as the U.S. does.

10. This furniture collector and expert says a lot of old desks that are supposed to be antiques are actually all a bunch of fakes.

Chapter 4: Critical Reasoning

Sample Arguments, p. 75

1. (A)

   The author of the argument doesn't support the new football stadium because everyone will pay for it and only a few will reap the benefits. Therefore, you want to find an answer choice like (A), which shows the new stadium will actually benefit more people. (B) tugs at your heartstrings because it seems like a good reason to build a new stadium, but it doesn't address the issue of benefits to the few rather than to everyone. Neither does (C), (D), or (E); if anything, (C) is another reason not to build the stadium, and (D) and (E) are irrelevant.

2. (C)

   The company hopes to keep its clients from leaving by giving them money to stay. If this money, however, is earmarked for solving the problem at its source by fixing the satellites (as answer choice (C) stipulates), then the satellites will never be repaired, clients will keep complaining, and the company will keep paying them off. The cycle is doomed to continue indefinitely. (A) and (D) might have a negative impact on sales, but neither addresses the premise that the company is paying the customers to stay loyal. It's difficult to determine (B)'s effect on the argument, because we don't know if the company's problems are normal or worse than normal. And since the company might not need to launch any more satellites, (E) is irrelevant.

3. **(B)**

Among the answer choices, you're looking for the best reason for Farmer to abandon its new ideas and keep making personal computers. The company's premise is a year-long downward trend in global sales, but (B) says that Farmer is doing well despite the global downward shift. Therefore, it should keep doing what it does well. (A) is a compelling choice, but the analysts could be wrong. (C) also appears negative, but you can cut prices and still make profits. (D) is irrelevant because we don't know if Farmer has anything to do with cell phones. The merger mentioned in (E) wouldn't be worth much if the PC market were declining; in order for the merger to be worthwhile, we'd need to know that global PC sales will rebound.

4. **(C)**

You're looking for the best reason why Ms. S should not be worried, and (C) provides it. The new policy that the adoption agency has put into place requires that all adoptions be approved by the birth father, so he has signed away his right to sue for custody. If (A) and (B) are true, then the father could still sue if he wanted. (D) and (E) are irrelevant, because age was never mentioned as an issue, and neither was the number of children that Ms. S has adopted.

5. **(D)**

This argument relies on a causal assumption that her fits of depression cause her to receive horrible news. She assumes that this causal link is the work of someone up there, but it's possible that there is an alternate cause: her own perceptions. Her depression might make her believe that any new problems are worse than they actually are. (A) is not helpful because the degree of her emotional vulnerability isn't at issue. (B) and (E) don't address the causal link either. (C) is way beyond the scope because it's too general.

6. **(A)**

The consultants think that the company's employees lose productivity between 2:00 p.m. and 4:00 p.m., so that is the best time for them to eat lunch. The consultants assume, therefore, that lunch and the "slump" are unrelated. If (A) were false, and eating lunch caused this "slump," then it wouldn't matter when the employees ate lunch, and the conclusion would be worthless. Breakfast is irrelevant, so (B) is out. (C) is a heartstring choice that argues by analogy, but we don't know how different (or similar) Companies X and P are. You can also eliminate (D) and (E) because the employees' preferences and any other suggestions are out of the scope.

7. **(E)**

As in any inference question, your job is to ask yourself, "What do I absolutely know is true?" The data suggest that a family history of schizophrenia greatly increased the chance that a child will have the disease, so it makes sense that heredity is at least partially determined by genetic factors. (E) is a nice choice because it's so weak. It doesn't say much at all, so it's hard to argue against. (A) might seem attractive, but it says a grandparent with no diagnosed mental disease; what about the other three grandparents? (B) is a heartstring choice because it makes sense in our minds, but it's never mentioned in the argument. (C) is also out of the scope. We know nothing about medical advances, so (D) is out.

8. **(E)**

This is a paradox question; you have to figure out why people want prisons to be built but don't want them near their homes. Once you boil the question down like this, you'll probably realize that the people of Essex County are suffering from a classic case of NIMBY (Not In My Back Yard). Answer choice (E) expresses this best; prisons help the whole state, but they threaten the people who live near them. (A) explains why they like prisons, but we don't know why the referendum was defeated. (B) explains why the prison was voted down, but it doesn't address why the folks like prisons. (C) is in the right ballpark, but we don't know whether the people who voted are representative of the whole. (D) doesn't help to explain anything, because the cost of the prison is not at issue.

9. **(B)**

The conclusion of this weaken argument is that baldness is caused by external factors (and not internal ones), and it states that there are more bald guys in big cities. (B) turns this premise on its head by saying that many bald guys in cities are related to other bald guys in the same city, so the cause might be heredity after all. Treating baldness is utterly irrelevant, so you can get rid of (A). (C) is too general, because it talks about all men rather than just those who live in big cities. (D) strengthens the argument by saying that guys who don't live in cities don't go bald. (E) also lessens the chance that baldness is hereditary.

10. (C)

The governor says that the kids are the difference because only kids can talk to kids. Therefore, the best way to determine if the ad campaigns written by kids were successful is to compare State F to other states that didn't hire kids to write the campaigns. If kids' work has had a greater impact than adults' work has, then the kids should continue to get funding. (A) and (B) are wrong because they don't address whether kids should write the ad campaigns. (D) has no impact on the creative aspect of the campaigns, so it's out of the scope. And (E) isn't helpful because the campaign was set up to reduce teen smoking, not all smoking. Adult smokers may have been unaffected.

11. (D)

Before we discuss the answer to this strengthen EXCEPT question, it's important to make a point: Four of the answer choices strengthen the argument, and one does not. That doesn't necessarily mean that this fifth choice weakens the argument. It just means that it doesn't strengthen it (it could be out of the scope). The argument says that people who drive SUVs are more likely to be injured in a car wreck, and (B), (C), and (E) strengthen the idea by asserting either that cars are safer or that SUVs are more dangerous. (D) is irrelevant (and therefore the best answer) because we don't know if a lack of acceleration makes a car any less safe to drive. (A) strengthens because the argument says that SUVs don't have as many safety standards; thus, SUV designers will cut corners if they can.

12. (D)

You want to support the idea that scorpion venom isn't any more dangerous than it was in 1984, and there is some tricky math involved. The percent of scorpion bite victims who go to the hospital and then die is increasing, but it's possible that people have learned to treat the bites at home and that hospitals receive only the most severe cases. Let's plug in some numbers: In 1984, 100 people came to the hospital with scorpion bites, and two died. In 1994, let's say that 100 people were stung, but fifty of the victims treated their wounds at home and the other fifty came to the hospital (two of whom died). The statistics are the same, but the percent of hospital cases who die increases because there were fewer hospital cases in the first place. Each of the other answer choices is irrelevant.

13. (C)

This is a well-disguised assumption question, because the conclusion that prices of new computers will go up relies on answer choice (C). In order for new computers to increase in price as much as used computers, it must be true that new computers are being bought at about the same rate as used computers. (C) fills the gap in the argument's logic. (A) and (B) might help explain why the market for used computers has gotten larger, but they don't address the commensurate rise in new computer prices. At first glance, (E) looks as though it might help; however, it doesn't link used computers to new computers like (C) does. (D) is too general, and the issue is whether seniors will buy new computers, not how long they'll wait to buy them.

14. (A)

Watch out for the convoluted nature of this question: You want to support the critics, so you want to weaken the physician's claim and find evidence that injecting lipazine is dangerous. The physician says that no animal will be injected with a harmful dose of lipazine, and he assumes that there isn't any lipazine already present in animals. If (A) is true, then the lipazine injections can be harmful. Warning labels don't affect the health value of lipazine, so (B) is out. (C) might help build muscle in humans, but we don't know if it's harmful. If (D) is true, then people are less likely to eat the meat that is injected with lipazine; that doesn't address whether the meat is safe. (E) is irrelevant.

15. (E)

Let's paraphrase the three points of this inference question: (1) conjunctivitis (or pinkeye, for those of you who want to know) was more common than glaucoma; (2) glaucoma affects older people, but conjunctivitis affects everyone; and (3) people are getting older. From this information, we know that since the average age of Americans will rise, then the average age of pinkeye sufferers will also rise; (E) is the best choice. People have better success on this problem by ruling out the alternatives. (A) and (B) are opposites of each other. We don't know which disease will be more common, so they're both out. (C) is also tempting, but we don't know if it will be the case. What if some new wonder drug is invented? And we most certainly know nothing about (D); *most Americans* is awfully extreme.

16. **(B)**

The words *previously believed* indicate that the first phrase is an old theory that is about to be supplanted by new information. The second phrase provides a piece of evidence that the first theory is wrong (in other words, a counterexample).

17. **(D)**

Malcolm states that he doesn't feel guilty about cheating on his income taxes because everybody does it. Luka says that his rationalization doesn't cut it; a crime is a crime is a crime (that's not a typo—it's just in there for emphasis), and it doesn't matter how many people commit that crime. (D) captures this idea best. She never assails Malcolm's credibility or his perception of the crime (he knows it's bad); eliminate (A) and (B). She also doesn't say that Malcolm didn't talk to enough people, so you can cross off (C). (E) might be true in general (watch out for those heartstrings!), but it's not what Luka says.

18. **(C)**

The senior partner has a bad track record with mergers, but her colleagues still believe that she's a real whiz. If (C) is true, then it makes sense that many of the deals the senior partner worked on were doomed to fail, regardless of who worked on them. Therefore, it's still possible that the senior partner is a good negotiator. (A) is wrong because her predecessor's work is not relevant to the discussion. (B) might explain why the junior partners respect her, but we don't know that for sure. They may have disliked her teaching technique. (D) is also irrelevant, because the issue revolves around percentages, not actual numbers. The best chance that (E) has is that the board of directors doesn't know much about investment banking and thus promoted someone who is incompetent. Then why do the junior partners like her so much?

Chapter 5: Reading Comprehension

Lead Words, p. 97

1. Beethoven, rare Belgian tapestries

2. Indian rope tricks

3. software bundling, networking strategies

4. social programs, 1964

5. cardiac arrest

Sample Passage 1, p. 104

1. **(A)**

The main idea of the passage is to establish that tree frogs exhibit their long calls to display their genetic superiority. The accepted mode of behavior is the calling, but the new study indicates a new theory about this behavior. (E) is along the same lines, but its assertion that it will overturn much of today's accepted knowledge is too extreme. There is only one experiment, so (B) is wrong. The "nature vs. nurture" debate is mentioned in line 21, but it's not the passage's chief concern. And there is no common trend with which this new theory is inconsistent, so eliminate (C). (D) might confuse you at first, but this passage shows the importance of the new findings; it doesn't dismiss them.

2. **(C)**

In line 32, the author asserts that mating calls are strictly a male trait, so it must be true that females do not have mating calls of their own. This excerpt also torpedoes (E) right away. We don't know that females teach their offspring anything; we only know that the males don't (lines 20–23). Eliminate (A). Some students might assume that males are more energetic and pick (B), but the passage never says anything about this. (D) is also never clarified.

3. **(C)**

The entire passage is devoted to establishing the link between a long mating call and genetic superiority. From this information, it's feasible to infer that a shorter mating call is tantamount to genetic (or physical) inferiority. (A) is too extreme, because the passage never asserts that old information is completely useless. (B) is false, because male frogs are utterly uninvolved with raising their offspring (lines 19–20). There's no information to support (D) or (E); they're both just assumptions that can't be clarified.

Sample Passage 2, p. 106

4. **(D)**

Nathan Parker has some really controversial thoughts to express, and he wants us all to know that modern technology hasn't destroyed the idyllic pure democracy of colonial times because the democracy was never as pure as we thought. That's why (D) is the best choice. There's no logic involved in the passage, so (A) is out. Further, the passage does not address an ambiguity or an explanation, so you can get rid of (B) and (E) . There is only one viewpoint that is discussed, so (C) is way off.

5. (C)

The author of the passage uses the second paragraph to indicate the inaccurate popular imagination that most Americans have about colonial New England. (A) traps people who don't pick up on this. The two writers are introduced, but there's no reference that Parker (or the first settlers) were inspired by them; scratch (B) and (D). And (E) takes too extreme a stab at the Puritans, because Parker never attacks their virtue.

6. (E)

In the first paragraph, the author refers to instances when a crisis affects the current government, people like to invoke the writings and teachings of the eighteenth century in order to support or denounce modern viewpoints (lines 2–6). Thus, (E) is the closest choice. None of the other answer choices is supported by the passage.

7. (B)

In lines 26–28, it says—"Parker asserts that town-hall meetings were open only to a select few male property owners who wielded a strong financial influence on the community." There's all the support you need for answer choice (B), which is a nice paraphrase. Get rid of (A), because there is no reference to representatives. (C) is also false, but it tries to lure you by referring to the 30 percent figure in line 35. The thoughts expressed in (D) and (E) run contrary to the passage.

Sample Passage 3, p. 108

8. (B)

McKillop's study is clearly based on the monetary damage inflicted by rabbits; the first sentence of the last paragraph indicates that farmers may now be able to attach a dollar value to the crops that rabbits feed on. Controlling rabbit populations is mentioned in the final paragraph, but it's not the main idea, so eliminate (A). (C) and (E) are related, but people's perceptions are mentioned only briefly in the first paragraph. (D) is out because although McKillop learned that rabbits like wheat best, this knowledge was not his initial objective.

9. (B)

As the last paragraph indicates, the only problem with this new study is that it quantifies the problem without providing a solution to it. Several methods are mentioned, but the best way is never identified. Population density is mentioned in the third paragraph (most grasslands are home to as many as forty rabbits per acre). The second paragraph mentions that the study lasted three years. The last paragraph asserts that rabbit populations increase by about 2 percent each year. The third paragraph also mentions that 300 pounds of grass translates to half a percent of the yield, so it's also possible to determine how many pounds of grass can be harvested from a hectare. (Don't bother with the math, though, because you don't need an actual answer.)

10. (D)

This question is a toughie, because you have to infer and it's an EXCEPT question. The easiest way to solve it is to work systematically: What do you know for a fact? You know that (A) is true, because the third paragraph says the rabbits' taste for barley was about the same as that for grass, but the cost of barley ($7) is more than double that of grass ($3). Lines 49–53 says that rabbits have developed resistance to . . . viral myxomatosis, so it must be true that the disease used to kill a lot more bunnies than it does now, as stated in (B). (C) is also true, because the passage's last sentence says that chicken farmers have strong influence in government because they contribute a lot to Britain's gross domestic product. (E) is defensible because the second paragraph says that all fences were entrenched ten feet into the ground in order to control populations. It must therefore be true that rabbits can't tunnel below that. The only answer choice that is not definitely true is (D).

11. (E)

McKillop's study relies heavily on population control, as is evidenced by the parameters of the experiment detailed in paragraph 2. McKillop takes the amount of damage done and divides by the number of rabbits in each enclosure. If some of the rabbits are missing (because they're eaten by a predator), then those data are unreliable; rabbits are actually doing a lot more damage. (A) isn't a problem, because McKillop doesn't want the rabbits to reproduce (that's why they're all the same sex). If the price of barley doubled, McKillop would still be able to calculate the financial cost of the rabbits' eating habits, so eliminate (B). (C) is close, but McKillop's data are based on the group in each enclosure, and it's impossible to predict if younger rabbits eat more. And a several-month drought wouldn't have much effect over a three-year period, so get rid of (D).

12. **(A)**

Again, the last paragraph talks about methods that people have used to control rabbit populations, yet none stands out as the best idea. (And they're not compared to each other, so you can cross (D) off.) McKillop's study has not provided any new information about population control, and this is the one problem to which the author refers. Chicken farmers are mentioned in the last paragraph, but they are not his primary focus; get rid of (B). (C) is wrong because *woefully incomplete* is far too extreme. We know nothing about (E).

SAMPLE GMAT VERBAL SECTION

Okay, folks. Here's your chance to shine. This chapter contains forty-one questions that you should sit down and answer as best you can in seventy-five minutes. It can't begin to match the experience of working at a computer because we haven't yet achieved the technology required for computer-adaptive books. But if you can answer each of these during a standard time limit, you're on your way to a good score.

Note: In order to treat this practice exam as a real GMAT CAT, do these questions in order. Do not skip a question and return to it later.

The answers and explanations are in the next chapter. Good luck.

Ready? You know what to do . . . now GO!

1. Equestrian enthusiasts predict that the alleged abuse of anabolic steroids among horse trainers <u>would subside if the testing of random animals is</u> more vigorously enforced.

    ○ would subside if the testing of random animals is
    ○ would subside as long as the testing of the animals is more random and
    ○ will subside if random testing of the animals is
    ○ will subside if the animals were tested more randomly and
    ○ will have subsided when testing of the animals is more randomly and

2. <u>Using steganography, the practice of hiding information in other information, encryption experts can conceal extensive messages in only a paragraph of ordinary text.</u>

○ Using steganography, the practice of hiding information in other information, encryption experts can conceal extensive messages in only a paragraph of ordinary text.

○ Using the practice of hiding information in other information, which is called steganography, extensive messages can be concealed in only a paragraph of ordinary text by encryption experts.

○ Extensive messages can be concealed by encryption experts who use steganography, the practice of hiding information in other information, in only a paragraph of ordinary text.

○ Concealed in only a paragraph of ordinary text, encryption experts can use the practice of hiding information in other information, which is called steganography, for extensive messages.

○ The concealing of extensive messages in only a paragraph of ordinary text using steganography, which is the practice of hiding information in other information, is possible by encryption experts.

3. A survey of 1,200 residents of a certain state revealed that 34 percent found hunting to be morally wrong. Of those same 1,200 respondents, 59 percent said that they had never hunted before. From this information, the surveyors concluded that . . .

Which of the following best completes the passage above?

○ some respondents expressed their moral convictions more strongly than others

○ the people who expressed an objection to hunting had never hunted before

○ moral objection is not the only reason why people do not hunt

○ the people who had hunted before but stopped because of a moral objection outnumbered those who had never hunted but didn't find it morally wrong

○ some people hunt even though they are morally opposed to it

4. Many historians who have analyzed the exceedingly profound events in American history assert <u>the electric light
bulb of Edison's</u> was the most groundbreaking invention of
this or any century.

   ⬭ the electric light bulb of Edison's
   ⬭ it was when Edison invented the electric light bulb that
   ⬭ that Edison's electric light bulb, which
   ⬭ that it was Edison's electric light bulb that
   ⬭ that it was Edison, who invented the light bulb, that

5. Dorsey received a dining room set from his grandmother,
who had stored the furniture in a storage facility for more
than a year. When he sat in one of the chairs, however, the
wicker seat buckled and split. Dorsey attributed the break to
the damp and musty conditions in the storage locker, which
had caused the seat to rot.

   Which of the following, if true, casts the most serious doubt
   on Dorsey's conclusion?

   ⬭ The table, which was not made of wicker, did not
   appear to sustain any substantive damage.
   ⬭ Dorsey broke through the seat of a brand-new identical
   chair that he bought to replace the broken one.
   ⬭ The storage company had never received any complaints about rotted furniture in the past.
   ⬭ Dorsey keeps a lot of his old furniture in his basement,
   which is also musty and damp.
   ⬭ The furniture manufacturer refused to honor the chair's
   warrantee because it felt the chair had been treated
   poorly.

Questions 6–9 refer to the following:

In her seminal work, *The Continuum Concept*, Jean Liedloff presents the controversial theory that Western methods of child rearing create the very problem these methods purport to eliminate—excessive dependency

(5) upon the caretaker. Liedloff contrasts her observations of modern American society with those of the Yequana tribe of the Amazon, with whom she lived on four separate occasions spanning several years.

Liedloff claims that all humans operate on a continuum

(10) and are genetically predisposed to thrive under certain conditions. We also compensate for treatment which does not coincide with these optimal conditions by adapting our behavior to stabilize our psyches. A baby who is in constant bodily contact with its caregiver

(15) receives physical stimulation that allows the child to feel secure and "right." In contrast, a child who is alone most of the time and left to "cry it out" does not receive the necessary physical contact. This creates a dependency in the child, who soon develops the grasping need for

(20) attention, even negative attention. Liedloff contends that some parents' fears that they will spoil their baby by holding it "too much" or by feeding it on demand are unreasonable and even detrimental to the child's mental health and social development.

(25) Adults who have been deprived of their continuum needs as children often seek to stabilize themselves by engaging in self-defeating or destructive behavior, which replicates the treatment to which they have become accustomed. Victims of emotionally barren parents may

(30) tend to seek mates who are domineering and cold, making true intimacy virtually impossible. Others may feel a lingering sense of guilt induced by a caregiver who never seemed to accept the child's existence. This guilt makes it difficult for an adult to feel peaceful or happy

(35) unless he is in crisis either physically or emotionally; the unresolved feelings of shame from childhood do not allow the adult to live a pain-free life.

Liedloff's critics argue that this form of "attachment parenting" does not enforce the natural hierarchy of

(40) parent over child in the family relationship. They stress that without a clear dominance of parent over child and discipline requiring the child to bend to the will of the parents from the moment of birth, the child does not develop a sense of right versus wrong. Many of these

(45) critics espouse more scientific methods of raising children that rely on regularly scheduled feedings in infancy and careful control of the child's environment as the child grows older. Liedloff's response is that tight

parental control over the child undermines its natural

(50) impulses toward socially acceptable behavior. Without
choice, the child will not gain experience in making
decisions and will be forced to look to an outside
authority rather than use his own judgment. Upsetting
the balance of the continuum by co-opting the child's

(55) natural ability to move toward independence and
decision-making skills, she asserts, ultimately results in a
lack of maturity and self-reliance in the adult.

6. The primary purpose of the passage as a whole is to

- ○ describe a strange phenomenon
- ○ clarify a vague notion
- ○ condemn an ill-informed opinion
- ○ refute a grievous misconception
- ○ support an alternative theory

7. According to the passage, Liedloff believes that adults
whose sense of continuum is denied to them as children

- ○ are unable or unwilling to have children of their own
- ○ develop a strong sense of discipline and familial
hierarchy
- ○ may suffer feelings of shame and inadequacy
- ○ seek mates whose strong sense of compassion can fill
the void
- ○ are too self-absorbed and domineering to become
adequate caregivers for their own children

8. Which of the following best describes the function of the
passage's fourth paragraph?

- ○ It provides the reader the opportunity to see how both
Liedloff and her critics rebut each other's opinions.
- ○ It resolves the argument between the two parenting
schools by calling for further testing and research.
- ○ It undermines the passage's overall conclusion by
suggesting that Liedloff's theories may be incomplete.
- ○ It stresses the need for all parents to establish their
familial authority over their children.
- ○ It suggests that Liedloff would be willing to modify her
theories and acknowledge the importance of more
scientific methods.

9. According to the passage, which of the following qualifies as an adult behavior that disturbs "the balance of the continuum" (line 54)?

  ○ Prematurely encouraging interaction with other children who are slightly older

  ○ Imposing a strict sleeping regimen, regardless of the child's expressed desire to sleep

  ○ Resolving not to have children in order to stop the cycle of inadequate parenting

  ○ Providing the child with his own room as soon as is financially possible

  ○ Punishing a child who deliberately disobeys an order

10. A small marketing consortium wanted to get more young people to take up chess. Since chess is most enjoyable when two people of equal ability play one another, the group believed that few people play chess because it is so hard to find a suitable opponent.

Which of the following statements would most seriously undermine the consortium's viewpoint?

  ○ On average, a set of chess pieces costs much more than most other board games.

  ○ The chess industry received a lot of favorable publicity last year when a computer defeated the world chess champion for the first time.

  ○ Tennis is most enjoyable when two equally matched opponents play each other, and the number of young tennis players has risen steadily.

  ○ Playing chess helps children develop analytical minds and learn to devise strategies to achieve long-term goals.

  ○ More than 50,000 chess sets were sold last year.

11. The transit authority of a certain city announced plans for a daily subway pass, which would cost $2.50 and afford a passenger unlimited access to the subway over a twenty-four-hour period. A consumer advocate was unimpressed with this offer because it benefited only tourists and did nothing for the average city commuter, who rides the subway only to and from work each business day.

If each of the statements above is true, which of the following conclusions can be drawn about the city's subway system?

○ The transit authority's special committee will weigh the merits of the day pass when it reconvenes.

○ The average commuter is dissatisfied with the price of the subway and is turning to other methods of transportation.

○ Discounting the day pass would put a strain on funds normally reserved for emergency measures.

○ The cost of one ride on the subway, regardless of the length of the ride or the time of day, is no more than $1.25.

○ A four-day pass at a cost of $10 would be equally useful to tourists.

12. The newest statistics released by the Labor Department indicate that jobless claims are down almost 1 percent, while real <u>wages, which had been expected to rise, have remained</u> steady.

○ wages, which had been expected to rise, have remained

○ wages, that had been expected to rise, remained

○ wages that were expected to rise, instead are remaining

○ wages, which did not rise expectedly, remained

○ wages, which it had been expected would rise, instead are remaining

13. South Korea and Japan, which have the two most robust capitalist economies in northeastern Asia, have clawed their way back from the brink of financial ruin and <u>now they take an active role in the success of both companies that are newer and smaller as well as</u> larger conglomerates.

○ now they take an active role in the success of both companies that are newer and smaller as well as

○ now take an active role in the success both of newer, smaller companies as well as that of

○ they take an active role now in the success both of newer, smaller companies, as well as those of

○ take an active role now in the successes of both companies that are newer and smaller as well as those of

○ take an active role now in both the success of newer, smaller companies as well as

Questions 14–16 refer to the following:

No other country on earth has more profound lingual diversity than China, whose 1.3 billion inhabitants fall within eight major linguistic groups. Mainland academics may argue that all Chinese people are linked by the
(5) universal characters of written Chinese, but this assertion fails to address the simple fact that the eight localized spoken dialects, though related, are mutually incomprehensible.

Efforts to standardize spoken Chinese date back to
(10) 1913, when the Qing dynasty collapsed and the first Chinese republic was created. The delegates of this new representative government regarded a common language, or *guoyu*, as an ideological imperative, but regional loyalties threatened to scuttle the attempt from the start.
(15) Southern Chinese resented the thought that Mandarin, the language of the north and east that was spoken by the vast majority of Chinese, would be adopted as the official tongue at the expense of much of their own Cantonese terminology. In fact, it was the dialectic
(20) subtleties that helped widen the rift between the north and south when the northern Mandarin leader, Wang Zhao, attacked southern delegate Wang Rangbao after Zhao mistook a mundane utterance for an insult.

Further attempts to establish *guoyu* were revisited with
(25) rare fervor in the 1930s under the rule of Chiang Kai-shek, who went so far as to order that all literature not written in *guoyu* be confiscated and burned. When the Communists seized power in 1949, a common language fit perfectly with the party's plans for universal ideology
(30) according to Stalin's teachings. And still, the mutual

enmity between the north and south persisted, as northerners rallied around the cry of "Force the south to follow the north!"

(35) Modern China's government has succeeded in bringing about a universal language, now referred to as *putonghua*, which is now the standardized version of modern Chinese language that is taught in universities and spoken by government members in official addresses. *Putonghua* has become the language of the

(40) urban and educated, but it has yet to permeate the more rural areas of the country, where local dialects predominate. Even those who can speak *putonghua* have such thick regional accents as to make it impossible for a Mandarin farmer in Beijing to understand his southern

(45) counterpart in Shanghai. Further, the Taiwanese and Cantonese languages have undergone a new resurgence as part of the counterculture at universities and along China's southern coastline. Chinese have made laudable inroads toward unifying their lingua franca, but China's

(50) size, coupled with its increasing growth rate, suggests that local tongues will persevere for a long time to come.

14. According to the passage, the most consistent obstacle that the prospect of a unified language has encountered is

○ political uncertainty
○ government censorship
○ widespread ignorance
○ regional pride
○ a lack of nationalized education

15. As a result of the events of the twentieth century in China as described in the second and third paragraphs of the passage, the author would probably agree with which of the following statements?

○ *Putonghua* will persist in Chinese culture because its characters are far more universal than those of *guoyu* ever were.
○ In very populous countries, government edict is not always strong enough to resist the will of the people.
○ The resurgence of counterculture is a constant phenomenon, but the individual events seldom have the staying power to become anything more than a passing fad.
○ Mandarin may yet become China's national language because most Chinese speak it already.
○ A government cannot call itself a representative democracy as long as it sanctions the destruction of literature.

16. According to the passage, each of the following has influenced the adoption of a universal language in China EXCEPT

- ⬭ Chiang Kai-shek
- ⬭ members of the Qing dynasty's royal family
- ⬭ Communists
- ⬭ resistance from Cantonese speakers
- ⬭ the modern Chinese government

17. In an exhaustive study that explains how humans distinguish different scents, Dr. Linda Quidd asserts that the nerve lining of a mouse's nose contains roughly the same number of olfactory receptors <u>that a human nose does</u>.

- ⬭ that a human nose does
- ⬭ that human noses do
- ⬭ as that of a human's nose
- ⬭ as those of a human
- ⬭ as human noses do

<u>Questions 18–19 are based on the following</u>.

Terry, a high school senior from State A, expressed an interest in attending Fullem State College, which was located in State B. After a little research, Terry's parents discovered that Fullem State College offered residents of State B a substantial discount from its normal tuition cost. Therefore, the parents decided to move to State B.

18. Which of the following, if true, is the most important reason why the parents might reconsider their decision?

- ⬭ Most scholarships are given to applicants who establish financial need.
- ⬭ To qualify for the lower tuition, applicants must prove that they have lived in State B for at least three years.
- ⬭ There are many colleges in State A that offer tuition discounts.
- ⬭ State B is several hundred miles from State A, and moving there would be difficult.
- ⬭ Regular tuition at Fullem State College is lower than that of most state colleges.

19. Which of the following, if true, would strengthen the parents' conclusion?

- ◯ State B offers a large tax credit to families who send their children to colleges within State B.
- ◯ Terry's sister, Leslie, graduated from Fullem State College five years ago.
- ◯ The housing market in State B is unpredictable.
- ◯ More than two-thirds of all students who attend Fullem State College do not need financial aid.
- ◯ If the lower-tuition plan at Fullem State College is successful this year, it is likely that the program will be expanded in subsequent years.

20. According to a survey by the American Council on Education, today's college students are inclined to involve themselves in political issues <u>only if they would be expecting to financially gain</u>.

- ◯ only if they would be expecting to financially gain
- ◯ if they would expect only to gain financially
- ◯ only if their expectations can be gained financially
- ◯ if financial gain could only be expected by them
- ◯ only if they can expect to gain financially

21. In most cases, the price of a commodity is directly proportionate to its scarcity in the marketplace; however, there is one notable exception. Worldwide diamond production tripled between 1986 and 1996; in that time, however, the average price of a diamond increased by more than 50 percent.

Which of the following, if true, would explain the diamond's rise in price despite its abundance?

- ◯ The price of precious gems such as sapphires and opals is at an all-time high.
- ◯ The number of contractors whose sole job is the cutting and polishing of raw diamond ore has doubled.
- ◯ Newly established stable governments in African nations have encouraged foreign investment and helped diamond mines flourish.
- ◯ Per capita diamond consumption is much higher in North America than it is in Asia.
- ◯ A powerful cartel that controls more than 90 percent of the world's diamonds releases them into the market depending on conditions in the world economy.

Questions 22–24 refer to the following:

Inspired by a wave of uncertainty about currencies in several emerging markets in recent years, many investment banks are beginning to market their versions of a new investment tool designed to predict when a
(5) currency's value will decline sharply. Many academics and economists have combined their efforts to create these "risk indicators" in order to predict when financial turmoil in a nascent capitalist market is forthcoming.

Creators of this new model define a currency crisis as
(10) a drop of at least 10 percent in a currency's real value. Working with a list of all of the currency crises that have occurred within the past ten years, researchers suggest a number of market or economic variables that may have helped bring the crash about. Such factors include a
(15) country's exchange-rate overvaluation, slowing economic growth, or a rising debt burden. Statisticians then use sophisticated econometrics to look for relationships between these factors and the currency dips they may have caused.
(20) Representatives of the International Monetary Fund (IMF) question whether these new models are any improvement over the techniques that are currently in place. The risk indicators, the IMF argues, are too dependent on the benefit of hindsight and cannot
(25) account for any new economic phenomena that may arise. The IMF has also accused some of the investment banks of "data mining," whereby analysts configure the information they cull from various sources until they finally verify the conclusion they have conditioned
(30) themselves to seek.

Further skepticism has been fueled by a comparison study of the risk indicator models, which was convened by Andrew Berg and Catherine Pattillo, a pair of IMF economists. After funneling economic data through each
(35) of the three most prominent models, Berg and Pattillo determined that none would have accurately predicted Asia's currency freefall that began when Thailand's baht was dislodged from its American dollar standard in July 1997. In fact, two models would have sounded a more
(40) severe alarm toward the Philippines, which has not undergone a currency crisis, than for either South Korea or Thailand, whose respective recoveries may never be complete.

22. The passage is chiefly concerned with

   ○ warning that attempting to predict currencies fluctuations is a useless enterprise

   ○ advocating the indispensable role of the IMF in stabilizing the currencies of countries to which capitalism is relatively new

   ○ expressing doubts as to the reliability of some new attempts to predict financial phenomena

   ○ contrasting new and sophisticated financial models with older methods that are more concerned with careful research

   ○ recommending that better investor models be created before one isolated contagion leads to worldwide recession

23. Which of the following does the passage suggest about South Korea?

   ○ It has received financial consultation and support from the IMF.

   ○ Its currency recently devalued by more than 10 percent.

   ○ Its economy is currently growing slower than that of the Philippines.

   ○ The new risk indicators would have detected its economic downturn had they been in place several years ago.

   ○ Its currency is closely tied to the American dollar.

24. Which of the following, if it happened soon after this article was published, would undermine the skepticism toward the viability of the "risk indicator" models?

   ○ The value of the Filipino peso plummeted.
   ○ Berg and Pattillo resigned from the IMF.
   ○ The South Korean economy showed signs of slowing down further.
   ○ Thailand restored its connection to the American dollar.
   ○ The IMF changed its definition of a currency crisis to an 8 percent drop in value.

25. Public safety activists, <u>being concerned about the rise in the number of car accidents and the average person's attention span being shrunk gradually</u>, feel that the introduction of the "netcar," a vehicle equipped with access to the Internet, is a terrible mistake.

   ○ being concerned about the rise in the number of car accidents and the average person's attention span being shrunk gradually

   ○ concerning themselves about rising car accidents and shrinking attention spans among average people

   ○ because they are concerned about the rising of the number of car accidents, also the shrinking of the attention span of the average person

   ○ concerned about the rise in the number of car accidents and the gradual shrinkage of the average person's attention span

   ○ given that they had been concerned about the rise in the number of car accidents and the gradual shrinkage of the average person's attention span as well

26. Antismoking lobbyists have tried to label smoking as a societal concern that must be curbed by government legislation. A problem can't be labeled a social problem, however, unless it harms others without their consent. Governments are powerless to regulate a harmful activity if those who do not indulge in that activity are not at risk.

   Which of the following strategies would most likely achieve the lobbyists' goal?

   ○ Quoting legislation that has been drafted to punish drunk drivers

   ○ Calling for higher "luxury taxes" on tobacco products

   ○ Citing the number of cancer-related deaths in the past ten years

   ○ Compiling statistics about the health hazard of second-hand smoke to non-smokers

   ○ Boycotting all items produced by tobacco companies and their wholly owned subsidiaries

27. Many of America's political allies have demanded that the United States repeal the <u>Helms-Burton law of 1996, tightening the embargo on all Cuban products and, according to opponents of it, violating</u> several international treaties.

○ Helms-Burton law of 1996, tightening the embargo on all Cuban products and, according to opponents of it, violating

○ Helms-Burton law of 1996, whose tightening of the embargo on all Cuban products violates, according to its opponents,

○ Helms-Burton law of 1996, which tightens the embargo on all Cuban products and which, according to its opponents, violates

○ embargo's tightening by the Helms-Burton law of 1996 on all Cuban products and the violating, according to opponents of it, of

○ tightening the embargo of the Helms-Burton law of 1996 on all Cuban products and, according to its opponents, violating

28. To encourage each student athlete to remain at one institution throughout his or her four years of eligibility, the intercollegiate rules committee drafted a new rule mandating that students who transfer to a different college wait a year before representing that new college in athletics. The mother of one such athlete thought the rule was unfair, because the time off would cause her son's skills to atrophy and thus damage his chance to pursue a professional career.

The mother assumes that

○ she would have advised her son not to transfer if she had known about the rule

○ all professional athletes owe their success to the playing experience they received in college

○ the rules committee is made up of former college athletes who understand how difficult it is to balance scholarship with athletics

○ it is uncommon for someone with no collegiate experience to thrive at the professional level

○ her son has no place else to play during his one-year suspension

29. To determine whether there are deposits of frozen water on the moon, research scientists at NASA launched two un-manned satellites that orbited the moon's atmosphere, <u>analyzing</u> radar echoes from the lunar surface.

   ○ analyzing
   ○ as an analysis technique of
   ○ to the analysis of
   ○ to analyze
   ○ a technique for analyzing

30. The new legislation governing presidential campaign contri-butions allows political parties to raise money only through a <u>process with high standards in contrast to</u> a group of fundraising events that are unregulated and unsanctioned.

   ○ process with high standards in contrast to
   ○ process that has been standardized highly and not within
   ○ highly standardized process rather than at
   ○ high process of standards instead of
   ○ process of high standards rather than that of

31. Interest in a 3,200-acre parcel of barren land in Welsh County has been virtually non-existent because it is not zoned for commercial use. A real estate developer, though, has created a business plan to convert the property into a low-grade airport that, when completed, would drive the value of the surrounding properties lower. Many local residents, therefore, are trying to pool their assets and buy the prop-erty outright.

   Last week, the Welsh County town council voted to repeal the restriction in the town charter that prohibits all commer-cial development on parcels of land smaller than 5,000 acres.

   The statements above, if true, best support which of the following conclusions?

   ○ The people who have property adjacent to the land in question will seek out other real estate developers who might want to use the land for other more aesthetically pleasing uses.
   ○ The Welsh County town council does not always act solely in the financial interest of town's residents.
   ○ Though short-term property values will probably drop, the community will ultimately benefit when young families arrive to take advantage of the bargains.
   ○ If residents can persuade the town council to recon-sider its decision, their property values will rise.
   ○ The original zoning laws in Welsh County were enacted because of pressure from the area's wealthiest residents.

32. The visual phenomenon known as refraction alters the appearance of objects as they are seen through water. All objects look larger than they actually are, but darker objects appear much more magnified than lighter objects. Hence, a darkly colored pebble on the floor of a swimming pool looks much larger than a white pebble, as long as the two are placed an equal distance from the eye of the viewer.

The conclusion above would be more properly drawn if it were made clear that the

- ⬭ darkly colored pebble is assumed to be greater in size than the white pebble
- ⬭ darkly colored pebble is assumed to be the same size as the white pebble
- ⬭ darkly colored pebble is assumed to be smaller in size than the white pebble
- ⬭ pool floor is light in color
- ⬭ pool floor is dark in color

33. The mass-marketing of companies that specialize in DNA testing has inspired fears that the DNA testing process will become too commonplace, resulting in emotional trauma to those who are ill equipped to cope with the results, and greatly increasing the number of lawsuits that are brought against hospitals and adoption agencies.

- ⬭ greatly increasing the number of lawsuits that are brought
- ⬭ greatly increase the number of lawsuits brought
- ⬭ it would greatly increase the number of lawsuits that would be brought
- ⬭ it would greatly increase the bringing of a number of lawsuits
- ⬭ greatly increasing the number of those who would bring lawsuits

34. During periods of extreme economic volatility, it is easy to mistake an increase in overall stock prices as the start of another bull market.

- ⬭ an increase in overall stock prices as the start of another bull market
- ⬭ the overall increasing of stock prices as the starting of another bull market
- ⬭ overall increasing stock prices for another bull market that is starting
- ⬭ an overall increase in stock prices for the start of another bull market
- ⬭ an increasing of stock prices as a starting bull market

Public health officials are becoming concerned about chlorine, a chemical that is added to many municipal water supplies to reduce bacterial growth. New evidence shows that the rate of first-trimester miscarriages is
(5) increased significantly when pregnant women drink five or more glasses of chlorinated water per day. When the chlorine in the water reacts with plant material acids the chemical trihalomethane is formed. Trihalomethane is believed to be the cause of the miscarriages, and it is
(10) also linked to increased cancer risk in animals. Lead, which has been shown to cause brain damage in small children, is another main contaminant of urban water systems, as it seeps from old pipes into the water flowing through them. Many water supplies are also
(15) contaminated with toxic bacteria, cysts, or algae. Increasing concerns about the effects of harmful contaminants have caused an increase in the number of alternate methods of water filtration that are available to the general public.
(20) There are six major systems, each with its advantages and considerable drawbacks. Steam distillation, in which water is boiled and the steam is collected and cooled, produces water without contaminants. However, energy must be used to heat the water, the resulting water
(25) tastes flat, and some organic compounds may boil with the steam and contaminate the water. Carbon filtration removes chlorine from water and leaves it with a better taste, but it cannot remove minerals or heavy metals. In addition, the filter is no longer effective if it becomes
(30) clogged, and the carbon can trap and breed harmful bacteria. The ion exchange method uses charged particles in a filter which are exchanged with charged particles in the water to remove minerals and toxic metals. This method has a very corrosive effect on pipes,
(35) and it does not remove organic molecules. It also increases the level of sodium, iron, and lead in the water. Ultraviolet light is simple and can kill microorganisms, but it has no effect on chemicals or minerals in the water. Reverse osmosis removes minerals, toxic heavy metals,
(40) and bacteria by forcing the water through a semipermeable membrane. This method is extremely slow, wastes large amounts of water, and corrodes the most durable of pipes.
Of the many different types of water filtration systems
(45) available, a combination KDF/carbon block system may be the most effective. The KDF system, which stands for kinetic degradation fluxion, forces water through a chamber containing a mixture of copper and zinc. In the

chamber, the copper becomes a cathode and zinc an
(50) anode; the electrochemical reaction that takes place
removes chlorine, chloramine, iron, hydrogen sulfide, and
many other harmful substances from the water. The
water is then forced through a solid carbon block filter,
which removes more impurities, such as bacteria and
(55) algae, from the water. Many KDF/carbon block filtration
systems also contain a ceramic pre-filter, which removes
other bacteria such as *Escherichia coli*, *Streptococcus sp.*,
and fecal coliform, as well as cysts such as
Cryptosporidium sp. and *Giardia sp*. As a by-product of
(60) filtration, the KDF/carbon block system puts small
amounts of copper and zinc into the water that are not
harmful to humans.

35. Which of the following best describes the organization of the
passage?

○ Several methods are described and ranked in terms of
    desirability.
○ A general theory is offered and refuted by several
    counterexamples.
○ A current process is assailed, and several alternatives
    are presented as possible replacements.
○ An old solution is revived as a possible remedy to a
    new problem.
○ A paradox is presented, and several examples are used
    to reconcile it.

36. Each of the following is a disadvantage of the ion exchange
method of water filtration EXCEPT:

○ higher sodium levels in the water
○ damaged pipes
○ unaffected contaminants of an organic nature
○ dangerous copper and zinc contamination
○ an increase of lead

37. According to the passage, which of the following can be inferred about the KDF system?

○ It prevents the formation of trihalomethane in the water supply.

○ It would work much better if used in concert with a semipermeable membrane.

○ The electrochemical reaction causes most of the copper and zinc that are originally introduced into the water to dissolve.

○ Without the additional ceramic pre-filter, it is no more effective than the combined effect of ion exchange and ultraviolet light.

○ Its ability to remove iron from water is superior to that of ion exchange.

38. According to the passage, the author's opinion of the best water filtration system would probably change if which of the following were true?

○ If the KDF system is used indefinitely, the levels of copper and zinc that it introduces into the water supply will eventually become toxic.

○ All new residential dwellings are fitted with pipes made of durable plastic that lead cannot seep through.

○ Ultraviolet light is one-tenth as expensive as each of the other techniques mentioned.

○ Subsequent studies have revealed that there is no relation between trihalomethane and cancer.

○ KDF is available only in urban areas with tax bases that withstand the cost of installing such a system.

39. Mesoporous metals are not indestructible, but their durability is such that they are able to withstand any delivered blow of a force of less than twelve newtons.

○ their durability is such that they are able to withstand any delivered blow of

○ they are of such durability, they have the ability to withstand any blow delivered with

○ there is so much durability that they can withstand any blow that is delivered by

○ they have such durability as to withstand any delivered blow of

○ they are so durable that they can withstand any blow delivered with

40. In each of the past four years, the percent increase of the profits of Japan's five largest semiconductor firms has been less than that of the year before. This trend marks a severe departure from the industry's peak in 1993, when revenues of each of these five firms grew at an average annual rate of 47 percent since the beginning of the decade. Clearly, the trade-deficit law enacted by the Japanese government in 1993 has had an adverse effect on the industry, which accounts for a large portion of the Japanese gross domestic product.

   The conclusion of the argument above cannot be true unless which of the following is true?

   ○ Japan's gross domestic product has also shrunk since 1993.
   ○ The original goal of most trade-deficit laws is to protect domestic products from cheaper imports, yet not every one achieves this goal.
   ○ The five companies mentioned have encountered new pressure from smaller companies that hold patents on newer semiconductor technology.
   ○ Profits of semiconductor companies would have kept climbing steadily if the government had not passed its 1993 trade-deficit bill.
   ○ Many other sectors of Japanese commerce, such as its auto industry, have also suffered declining profits since 1993.

41. Some State Department officials hope to end the border skirmish by bargaining with the new dictator, others <u>by proposing imposing stiff economic sanctions on the country's exports, and still others by demanding</u> that NATO launch a full-scale invasion.

   ○ by proposing imposing stiff economic sanctions on the country's exports, and still others by demanding
   ○ by proposing the imposition of stiff economic sanctions on the country's exports, and still others demand
   ○ propose imposing stiff economic sanctions on the country's exports, and still others are demanding
   ○ are proposing the stiff imposition of economic sanctions on the country's exports, and still others are demanding
   ○ propose the stiff imposition of economic sanctions on the country's exports, and still others demand

That's it. Pencils down, buttocks up. Go out and get a refreshing beverage, or take a nap. Then come back in a little while and see how you did. The answers and explanations for this section are all in the next chapter.

If you didn't do all these questions in the order they were given, you were a very naughty person.

1. **(C)**	8. **(A)**	15. **(B)**	22. **(C)**	29. **(A)**	36. **(D)**
2. **(A)**	9. **(B)**	16. **(B)**	23. **(B)**	30. **(C)**	37. **(A)**
3. **(C)**	10. **(C)**	17. **(C)**	24. **(A)**	31. **(B)**	38. **(A)**
4. **(D)**	11. **(D)**	18. **(B)**	25. **(D)**	32. **(B)**	39. **(E)**
5. **(B)**	12. **(A)**	19. **(A)**	26. **(D)**	33. **(B)**	40. **(D)**
6. **(E)**	13. **(B)**	20. **(E)**	27. **(C)**	34. **(D)**	41. **(E)**
7. **(C)**	14. **(D)**	21. **(E)**	28. **(E)**	35. **(C)**	

1. **(C)**

The sentence is incorrect as written because it misuses the subjunctive tense (the abuse *would* subside if testing *were enforced*). (B) also has this problem and is long and wordy. (D) brings in *were*, but forgets about the *would*; it also tries to sucker you because it looks parallel (*more randomly* and *more vigorously*). (E) unnecessarily introduces the future perfect tense (*will have subsided*) and is also very wordy.

2. **(A)**

This sentence is fine, because *Using stenography* correctly modifies *encryption experts*. Also, the phrase *in only a paragraph of ordinary text* should modify *extensive messages*. (B) has a misplaced modifier because it suggests that messages use steganography. In (C), the phrase *in only a paragraph of ordinary text* should modify where the messages are hidden, not steganography; it's also constructed passively. (D) has a misplaced modifier here, because the experts weren't concealed in the text. (E) is constructed passively, and *the concealing* is not the right subject of the sentence.

3. **(C)**

Inference question, involving fun with numbers. If 59 percent of the residents said they had never hunted before, and only 34 percent expressed a moral objection, at least 25 percent of the respondents had some other reason. (A) is wrong because we don't know how strongly the views were expressed; all we have is the numbers. It's possible that someone had tried hunting and later found it morally wrong, so (B) is out. As confusing as (D) is, it's actually false. Do a little math: 34 percent think hunting is wrong, and 59 percent said they had never hunted. (E) is also certainly possible, but we don't know if this is *definitely* true.

4. **(D)**

The idiom is *assert . . . that*, so you can eliminate (A) and (B). The idiom being tested here is *it was . . . that was*. Since the *was* part of *that was* is not underlined, you need *it was* in the underlined portion. (C) is a sentence fragment, and (E) incorrectly suggests that Edison was the invention, instead of his light bulb.

5. **(B)**

A weaken question. If Dorsey broke a brand-new chair as well, then it's possible that the chairs could support his grandmother but can't hold anyone who is heavier. (A) is out because the table and chairs aren't comparable—we don't know if Dorsey sat on the table as well. (C) might be true, but that doesn't mean there isn't a problem now (there's a first time for everything). (D) doesn't address whether the chair rotted in the storage facility, and neither does (E); his grandmother could have been at fault.

6. **(E)**

In line 2, the passage refers to Liedloff's theory as *controversial*, and it's also different from the Western methods that Liedloff asserts are causing more problems than they solve. The majority of the rest of the passage lists supporting points of Liedloff's thesis.

7. **(C)**

Begin reading at the beginning of the third paragraph, where the passage talks about *adults who have been deprived of their continuum.* Lines 31–32 mention that some of these adults *may feel a lingering sense of guilt*, and the use of the *shame* in the answer choice (C) is a nice paraphrase.

8. **(A)**

The beginning of the fourth and last paragraph begins with *Liedloff's critics*, and then we see a reference to *Liedloff's response* on line 48. Though most of the passage is devoted to examining Liedloff's ideas, the difference of opinion is never resolved. Nor do we get the impression that Liedloff's work is incorrect or incomplete; we just know that some people disagree with her.

9. **(B)**

Upsetting the balance of the continuum appears in the passage's last sentence, and it refers to *coopting the child's natural ability to move toward independence*. Thus, depriving a kid's continuum involves imposing your own schedule on him, and (B) is the best example of this.

10. **(C)**

Since tennis and chess both require a suitable opponent and tennis is flourishing, there must be some other reason why kids don't play chess. (A) is a knock against chess, but it doesn't address the premise about finding someone to play with; neither does (B). Whether chess is a useful activity is not relevant, so (D) is out. (E) is bad for two reasons: (1) we have no data to compare, so we don't know if the number is rising or falling, and (2) we don't know that all sets that were purchased are being used.

11. **(D)**

If the cost of one ride were more than $1.25, the day pass would benefit *anyone* who rode the subway at least twice a day. Since the pass does not benefit daily commuters, each trip must cost less than $1.25. (A) is completely irrelevant, so we can't infer it. We can't infer (B) either; just because this new pass offers no benefit doesn't mean that commuters are unhappy. (C) is wrong because we don't know how the transit authority allots its money. Many people fall for (E), but it's not necessarily true; a $10 pass benefits only those tourists who stay in town at least four days.

12. **(A)**

Don't get bogged down by the *that* vs. *which* conundrum. Instead, look at the verbs. The sentence is in the present tense (*jobless claims are down*), so *remain* must be in the present tense also. Eliminate (B) and (D), which are in the past tense. (A) uses *have remained*, which is consistent, and it properly sets off *which had been expected to rise* with commas; (C) doesn't do that. (E) has all sorts of problems, not the least of which is its excessive wordiness.

13. (B)

If you have another subject in the underlined portion of the sentence, it becomes a run-on sentence. Therefore, you don't want the pronoun *they* to appear in your final answer; eliminate (A) and (C). The key to the rest of this question is the placement of *both*. The construction in (D) is flawed because it's possible that there are only two newer and smaller companies and that the government supports *both* of them. *Both* is also misplaced in (E), making the construction not parallel. (B) sounds a bit awkward, but it is perfectly parallel (*the success of . . . as well as that of*); *that* is a pronoun for *success*.

14. (D)

The passage first mentions *localized spoken dialects* at the end of the first paragraph, and the theme persists throughout. *Regional loyalties* are mentioned in line 13, and *mutual enmity between the north and south* occurred after the Communists arrived.

15. (B)

The passage talks about several government plans to impose a universal language on its 1.3 billion people—the first republic in 1913, Chiang Kai-shek, and then the Commies. Even the modern government has tried (with a bit more success), but the new language hasn't reached the rural counties, and other languages have become part of the counterculture (line 47).

16. (B)

Read carefully here. The Qing dynasty is mentioned in the first paragraph, but the first attempts to create a universal language didn't happen until after the family had been overthrown. It's possible that the new language was a reaction against dynastic rule, but we don't know that for sure. Every other answer choice has had an influence, including (D); Cantonese speakers have kept both *guoyu* and *putonghua* from becoming universal.

17. (C)

The idiom is *same . . . as*, so eliminate (A) and (B). Now it gets a little tricky because you have to keep track of the things you're comparing. The sentence compares the nerve lining of a mouse's nose to the nerve lining of a human's nose. So you need the pronoun *that*. (D) is wrong because *those* is plural (a human only has one nerve lining), and (E) doesn't refer to the nerve lining.

18. **(B)**

If (B) were true, Terry's parents wouldn't be able to get the discount. Therefore, moving to State B wouldn't do them any good. (A) doesn't factor in because we don't know if Terry needs the money or not. (C) might be true, but Terry wants to go to Fullem State. (D) is an attractive choice, but even though it might be a real hassle to move to State B, the move might be worth it if the family can save substantial money on Terry's education. (E) might also be true, but out-of-state tuition might still be too high for Terry's family.

19. **(A)**

Getting a big tax credit is an excellent alternate reason to move to State B, especially if Terry wants to attend Fullem State. (B) doesn't address whether moving to State B is a good idea. Lots of people pick (C), but *unpredictable* doesn't necessarily mean *bad*; this is a common trick that ETS uses. A question will include a word that conjures a negative connotation when it isn't necessarily negative at all. *Unpredictable* means you don't know what will happen, but it could work out great. The housing market could skyrocket, for example. Get rid of (D), because the other students don't matter to Terry. He might still need the money. And (E) is out because an expanded program next year doesn't do Terry any good now.

20. **(E)**

To financially gain is a split infinitive, so eliminate (A). The first part of the sentence is in the present tense, so the rest should be as well. You can eliminate (B) because *would expect* doesn't agree. (C) and (D) are passively constructed, and *only* is misplaced in (D) as well. (E) is in the active tense, there's no split infinitive, and *only* is in the right place.

21. **(E)**

It doesn't matter how many diamonds are being produced if a cartel restricts their entry into the market. Keeping them scarce for consumers keeps the price up. The other gems in (A) are irrelevant, and (B) and (D) don't explain how diamonds defy economic principle. (C) doesn't explain why the price rose either.

22. **(C)**

The main idea of the passage is the discussion of these new "risk indicators" that can help people predict a fall in the value of a currency (or a *financial phenomenon*) and the author's overall opinion is that they aren't that reliable. (A) expresses a similar point, but it's too extreme (*a useless enterprise*?).

23. **(B)**

You have to look in two different places to answer this, but the logic follows. The last paragraph implies that South Korea has endured a currency crisis because it is in the process of recovery (line 42). Line 10 defines a currency crisis as a 10 percent dip in a currency's value.

24. **(A)**

We're still looking at the last paragraph, which talks about *further skepticism*. Berg and Pattillo found that two of the models predicted problems in the Philippines, yet there were no problems as of yet. If the Filipino peso were to plummet, the risk indicators would seem more accurate.

25. **(D)**

The underlined portion must describe the activists, who are *concerned*. The construction also needs to be parallel (concerned about the *rise* and the *shrinkage*). (A) contains *being*, so it's out right away. (B) is wrong because car accidents aren't rising; the *number* of accidents is rising. The use of *they* and *also* is awkward and unnecessary in (C). Apart from the wordiness of (E) and the unnecessary use of *had been*, the use of *as well* is awkward and redundant.

26. **(D)**

The argument's premise is that you can't penalize smokers unless they harm non-smokers. The lobbyists can make their point by attempting to prove that smokers do put non-smokers in danger. Lots of people like to choose (A), but we don't know if smokers and drunk drivers are comparable—that's what the lobbyists must establish. (B), (C), and (D) don't address the harm to those who don't smoke.

27. **(C)**

You can eliminate (D) and (E) right away, because people want to repeal the *law*, not the *tightening*. (C) is the best choice because it uses *which* properly, and it also uses parallel construction. (A) makes it look like the political allies are doing the tightening and violating. Also, the pronoun *it* is ambiguous. (B) is wrong because you should use *who* or *whose* only when you're referring to a person. *Whose* incorrectly refers to the law.

28. (E)

If it were possible for her son to play someplace else and keep his skills sharp, she wouldn't have to worry about her son losing his talent. (A) is wrong because what she *would have* done is not as important as what she *is* doing now—challenging the rule. (B) is too extreme, and (C) is wrong because the makeup of the rules committee is out of the scope. (D) may be true, but it's not impossible. This kid might be a star!

29. (A)

You should use *analyzing* at the beginning of the phrase, because that's what the satellites did. Because NASA launched two satellites, it's incorrect to refer to them as a *technique*; eliminate (B) and (E). (C) is incorrect because *to the analysis* is not idiomatic. And you can cross off (D) because *to analyze* is not complete. It would have been better if the sentence had said *used to analyze*.

30. (C)

This one is really tricky. (In fact, it just plain stinks.) The key is the word *at*, which is the preposition you need for parallel construction (*raise money **through** . . . rather than **at***). Also, *highly standardized* appropriately modifies the process.

31. (B)

Here's another inference question. The land in question is smaller than 5,000 acres, so it is about to become available for commercial use. Since this will hack off a lot of residents, it must be true that the town council has other motives in mind. (Note the nice wishy-washy tone: *does not always act*.) We don't know how the residents will respond, so (A) is out. (D) is also a popular wrong choice, but we can't assume that property values will rise. We can assume that they won't fall because of the new airport.

32. (B)

This is an obliquely worded assumption question. The conclusion is that a dark pebble will look larger than a white pebble, so it must be assumed that the two pebbles are the same size. (A) and (C) are eliminated because refraction would have nothing to do with the situation if the dark pebble actually were larger than the white pebble. (It would of course look bigger—it is bigger!) Conversely, a larger white pebble might counteract the illusion and make the two appear to be the same size. (D) and (E) are wrong because the color of the pool floor affects each pebble equally, so the color doesn't matter.

33. (B)

This question also revolves around parallel verb choice. If you focus your attention on the second half of the sentence, the secondary subject is *the DNA testing process*. The process will **become** *too commonplace . . . and greatly* **increase** *the number*. The verb *resulting* is a red herring, because it appears in the appositive clause between the commas and has no direct bearing on the parallel construction. Therefore, *increasing* is incorrect; eliminate (A) and (E). Also, the phrase *it would* is unnecessary and not parallel, so you can eliminate (C) and (D).

34. (D)

The proper idiom is *mistake . . . for*, and there's a subtle two/three split (*for* vs. *as*) among the answer choices. (A), (B), and (E) use *as*, so they're out. (C) has awkward, non-parallel construction, and *overall increasing stock prices* is not idiomatic.

35. (C)

The first paragraph discusses the new concerns about an established method of purifying water (chlorine). The remainder of the passage bombards us with many alternative ideas and the pros and cons of each. (A) is close, but the six new ideas are never actually ranked.

36. (D)

Go back and read all about ion exchange, which is first mentioned in line 31. Each of the answer choices is mentioned in the subsequent sentences except (D). Use of copper and zinc doesn't come up until the last paragraph, which is about the KDF process. It's a classic case of misdirection.

37. (A)

This one requires a little reading in two different places. The last paragraph (line 44) tells us that the KDF system *removes chlorine* from the water. Earlier in the passage, we learn that chlorine *reacts with plant material acids* and *trihalomethane is formed*. Since the KDF system gets rid of chlorine, trihalomethane can't be formed. Even though the passage's author asserts that KDF *may be the most effective* (line 45), we still don't know anything about direct comparisons with any of the other alternatives mentioned.

38. (A)

The author is clearly a big fan of the KDF system, which works by introducing *copper and zinc into the water* (line 61). The author states that these metals are *not harmful to humans*. If we later learned, though, that unlimited use of KDF creates toxic levels of copper and zinc, then the KDF system isn't nearly as effective as the author thinks. She might change her mind.

39. (E)

Look at the last word of each answer choice. The difference is between the prepositions *of*, *with*, and *by*. In this case, it is idiomatic to use *delivered **with** a force of less than twelve newtons*, so you can eliminate everything except (B) and (E). (E) uses the proper idiom *so durable that*, and (B) is wrong because the idiom it wants to use is *such . . . that*. Since *that* doesn't appear in the sentence, it's unidiomatic.

40. (D)

An assumption question. The author of this argument says that the semiconductor companies were doing just fine until the new law in 1993. Therefore, it must be assumed that without the law, these companies would have maintained growth. If the companies would have faltered anyway, then the law clearly isn't to blame. (A) and (C) follow this last line of reasoning; if the GDP is also shrinking or new companies are adding new pressure, then maybe the law didn't bring on the problems. Since this weakens the conclusion, it can't be an assumption. The original goal of the law in (B) is out of the scope.

41. (E)

Here's a great sample question about parallelism. The non-under-lined portion establishes the form that the rest of the sentence must take: (1) the sentence is in the present tense (*officials **hope** to end*), and (2) *by bargaining* indicates that we're going to use *-ing* words. The key is recognizing that *propose* needs to agree with *hope*, not *bargaining*. Therefore, (A) and (B) have to go. (C) is not parallel, because *propose* doesn't match *are demanding*. The words *are proposing* and *are demanding* are parallel in (D), but neither is parallel with the original verb, *hope*. (E) is parallel, and the three verbs—*hope*, *propose*, and *demand*—are all in the same form.

APPENDIX I
GRAMMAR ODDS AND ENDS

Well, here we are at the end of the book. (Sure was a page-turner, wasn't it?) Before you finally put this book down and move on with your life, here are some miscellaneous thoughts about proper grammar to look for on Sentence Correction questions and when you write your essays.

You won't get called on many of these in conversations with your friends (unless your friends are a bunch of pedantic know-it-alls), but they'll come in handy during the GMAT application process. Feel free to forget them all as soon as you receive your acceptance letter.

MORE OF ETS's HABITS

The following four items are common tricks ETS uses to create wrong answer choices. Once you're familiar with them, you'll see how often they show up on the GMAT.

Be Sure to Watch Your Order Word

This is a catch-all problem that ETS likes to create. It's mostly related to the rule for misplaced modifiers: A word that modifies another should be next to it. You can really mess up a sentence just by putting the same words in different places and creating awkward sentence construction.

> Based on accounts of **various** political theorists . . .

> Based on **various** accounts of political theorists . . .

The meaning of the sentence depends on the placement of *various*; in the first phrase, various modifies political theorists, and the second phrase suggests that the accounts vary.

ETS likes to change the word order around to create wrong answer choices, especially when the entire sentence is underlined. When you see a disparity like this one, compare the two answer choices to each other and decide which one best conveys the meaning of the original sentence.

Verbosity, Loquaciousness, Prolixity

As you've read in chapter 6 about being a better writer, the best writing conveys the most using the smallest number of words. Why say something in eight words when you can do it in four?

> Most of the time, the shorter answer choices are better than the longer ones. When in doubt, keep it short and sweet.

Here's a sample question in which the number of words in the answer choice is a compelling factor:

> Although he had decided to become an actor <u>while being very young</u>, Damon DiMarco didn't act in his first major motion picture until he reached the age of seventy-eight.
>
> ○ while being very young
> ○ while in his youth
> ○ at the time that he was being young
> ○ in the time of his youth
> ○ in his youth

You can eliminate (A) and (C) because they contain *being*, and you're left with (B), (D), and (E). Since (E) expresses the exact point that the other two do and uses fewer words, it's the best answer. Sometimes ETS just likes to test your proficiency with economy of words (and your essay readers will thank you for expressing your ideas as succinctly as possible).

Note: This is *not* an instruction to look at all five choices and pick the shortest one. There is absolutely no guarantee that the shortest answer is the best answer. It's more of a guideline than a rule. If you've narrowed your choices down to two and you have to make an educated guess before you move on to the next question, pick the shorter choice.

Being Repetitious and Redundant by Repeating Things Again

Redundancy is related to verbosity, and it's a sickness from which many average writers suffer. ETS' test-writers know this, and they like to write answer choices that don't seem redundant at first. Some examples of redundant phrases include:

Redundant	Remedied
free gift	gift (when is a gift not free?)
surrounded on all sides	surrounded
as many as six inches wide or wider	at least six inches wide
and my father was also there	and my father was there
the same exact thing	the same thing

whether or not	whether
used for mining purposes	used for mining
the reason why	the reason
demand that she should go	demand that she go

A question that contains redundant answer choices might look something like this:

> An individual investor must develop the discipline not to sell blue-chip stocks when plummeting prices <u>have fallen to reach</u> their short-term lows.
>
> ◯ have fallen to reach
> ◯ are falling to reach
> ◯ have fallen or reached
> ◯ have fallen or are reaching
> ◯ reach

The non-underlined portion of the sentence already contains *plummeting*, so there is no reason to use any form of the verb *fall* in the answer choices. Therefore, you can eliminate all of the choices but (E).

The Subjunctive Verb Tense

If you grew up in an English-speaking household and studied a foreign language in high school, you probably learned about the subjunctive verb tense in your second language before you acknowledged it in your first. The subjunctive tense has two purposes in English. The first is to express the conditional tense, and it usually involves *would* and *were*:

> I **would** not water-ski naked if I **were** you.
>
> If he **were** to grow another four inches, he **would** have to buy new pants.

Note that the verb is always *were*, regardless of the subject.

> **Wrong:** If I **was** a rich man . . .
>
> **Right:** If I **were** a rich man . . .

The second use of the subjunctive is to express a demand or request, and this construction follows two strict rules—*that* always comes right after the verb, and the second verb is always in the simple present tense:

> Her father demanded **that** she **return** home by 8 p.m.
>
> Grandma requested **that** the window **be** closed.

Wrong answers on questions that involve the subjunctive tense usually involve the word *should* (note the redundancy list above):

Despite the thousands of protests from devoted fans who
<u>demanded that he should</u> shave off his new moustache,
Freddie Mercury insisted on changing his visual image.

- ○ demanded that he should
- ○ were demanding him that he
- ○ demanded that he
- ○ had demanded him to
- ○ demanded for him to

If you follow the basic construction rules for this form of the subjunctive, you'll see that (C) is the best choice.

OTHER STUFF YOU SHOULD KNOW

These points don't appear as often on Sentence Correction questions, but you should keep them in mind as you write your essays. They're simple and rather obvious, but it never hurts to brush up on the little things.

Singular Pronouns

What's wrong with this sentence?

Each of the fifty states have an official flag, bird, and flower.

Some students think this sentence sounds fine because the plural noun *states* agrees with *have*. As we discussed in chapter 2, though, *of the fifty states* is a prepositional phrase. The subject is *Each*, which is a singular pronoun. The sentence should look like this:

Each [of the fifty states] **has** an official flag, bird, and flower.

To maintain a strong sense of subject-verb agreement, you should know that each of the following pronouns is singular:

another

any

anything

each

either

every

everybody

neither

no one

nobody

none (not one)

To make this easier to visualize, think of this:

> If you can place the word *one* after a pronoun, it's a singular pronoun that takes a singular verb tense.

Neither (one) of the astrophysicists **is** able to perfect time travel.

Also: *The number of* suggests a definite number of things, so it takes a singular verb. *A number of*, on the other hand, is less clear, so it takes a plural verb:

The number of people who can access the Internet at home **is** rising dramatically.

A number of people who have resisted using the Internet **are** finally caving in.

The Insidious "They"

Remember Sting's song lyrics at the beginning of chapter 2? In conversational English, it has become commonplace to use the pronoun *they* instead of *he* or *she*, because of basic convenience. Therefore, we end up saying things like this:

Before taking a test, it's important for every person to do **their** homework.

Yeesh. That's some really rotten grammar; *person* is a singular noun, and *their* is a plural pronoun. The sad truth about English is that there is no gender-neutral third-person pronoun that we can use in place of *he* or *she*.

ETS knows that we use *they* incorrectly all the time in our daily conversation, so it likes to set traps using *they*:

<u>Each American, regardless of their ethnic background, is</u> protected under the rights explicitly expressed in the Constitution.

- ○ Each American, regardless of their ethnic background, is
- ○ The ethnic backgrounds of each American is regarded as
- ○ All Americans, regardless of their ethnic background they have, are
- ○ Each American, regardless of his or her ethnic background, is
- ○ The ethnic background of all Americans is regarded to be

The correct answer is (D), because *each* is a singular pronoun that takes *is* as a verb. (A) might appear correct at first glance, but *their* doesn't agree with *each*. (E) has idiom trouble, because *regard to be* is not idiomatic. And (B) and (C) are incorrect because the subject and object don't agree; it's impossible for one American to have more than one ethnic background.

Make the Subjects and Objects Agree

That's the point of this next bit: Make sure the objects reflect their actual numbers. Okay, that didn't come out right. Let this sentence explain it better:

> Celia and Ella brought their husband to the wedding.

This sentence is incorrectly worded because it looks as though the two women have the same husband. It's unlikely that a GMAT sentence would advocate bigamy, so the correct sentence should be written like this:

> Celia and Ella brought their husbands to the wedding.

Subject and Object Pronouns

Pronouns that perform the action in a sentence (subject pronouns) are different from those that receive the action (object pronouns):

	Subject	Object
First person singular	I	me
Second person singular	you	you
Third person singular	he/she/it	him/her/it
First person plural	we	us
Second person plural	you	you
Third person plural	they	them

The pronoun you use depends on the word's role in the sentence. Most people have no problem with the singular pronouns; the problems arise when multiple nouns are used.

> Between you and I, my parents are starting to act very strangely.

Although the pronouns appear in the beginning of the sentence, they each receive action from the word *between*. If you separate the two, you'll realize that *between you* makes sense, but *between I* does not. Therefore, the correct sentence reads:

> Between you and **me**, my parents are starting to act very strangely.

In some conversations you're inclined to use the pronoun and the noun right next to each other. If you're ever unsure of which pronoun to use, take out the noun and see if it makes sense:

> We revolutionaries need to stick together.
>
> **We** [ ] need to stick together.
>
> There's nobody here but us bank robbers.
>
> There's nobody here but **us** [ ].

Also, when making comparisons, make sure the pronouns are in the same form as the nouns:

WRONG: He is taller than **me**.

RIGHT: He is taller than **I** [am].

And if your name is Sheila and someone calls asking for you, you should say "This is *she*" instead of "This is *her*."

The Unbearable Wrongness of "Being"

If there is one absolute certainty as far as Sentence Correction is concerned, it is this: If some answer choices contain the word *being* and others do not, then all the ones that contain *being* are wrong. There's usually a way to avoid using *being* in a sentence:

> **Wrong:** As a result of his being too short, Jerome was cut from the basketball team.

> **Better:** Because he was too short, Jerome was cut from the basketball team.

If you see *being* in an answer choice, make sure that other choices don't contain *being* and then cross out all the ones that do.

Semicolons

Those of you who frequent Internet chat rooms should know that the semicolon is used for more than just the winking eyes on your smiley-face. The only time to use a semicolon is when you want to link two complete sentences.

> Joan paused for a moment as she considered her options; it still wasn't too late to run back to her car and forget about the blind date.

Weird Plurals

As you match up your subjects and your verbs, be sure to remember that each of the following words, even though it sounds singular, is actually plural. We often misuse these words in conversation, but it's important to get them right in your writing.

Data is the plural form of *datum*:

> **Wrong:** The data is sufficient to answer the question.

> **Right:** The data **are** sufficient to answer the question.

Media is the plural form of *medium*:

> **Wrong:** The media has always portrayed the president too positively.

> **Right:** The media **have** always portrayed the president too positively.

Criteria is the plural form of *criterion*:

> **Wrong:** What is your criteria for the perfect date?

> **Right:** What **are** your criteria for the perfect date?

Alumni is the plural form of *alumnus* (a male graduate of a school); *Alumnae* is the plural of *alumna* (a female graduate of a school):

> **Wrong:** My brother is an alumni of Notre Dame.

> **Right:** My brother is an **alumnus** of Notre Dame.

WHEN TO USE WHICH WORD

Have you ever had a prolonged debate over the proper use of a word? Do you want to become more popular at your next cocktail party or family gathering? Then this section is for you. Below are a few words that are common on Sentence Correction questions.

Between vs. Among

If a sentence compares two items, use *between*. If you're dealing with three or more items, use *among*:

> In a presidential election, most Americans choose **between** the Democratic candidate and the Republican candidate.

> **Among** the five candidates at the New Hampshire primary, Senator Batard is clearly the front-runner.

Note: You'll see *among* on the GMAT, but you won't see *amongst*. The two words are absolutely interchangeable when you're writing a sentence, but *amongst* isn't used as much in normal discourse because it's antiquated. Avoid using it when you write your essays; stick with *among*.

-er vs. -est

When you're comparing two things, add *-er* to the end of the adjective to form the *comparative* degree:

> Texas is much larg**er** than Oklahoma.

If you're comparing three or more objects, add *-est* to the adjective to form the *superlative* degree:

> Maine is easily the larg**est** of all six New England states.

Further vs. Farther

Lots of people think these words are interchangeable, but there is a distinction. Use *farther* to indicate a greater tangible distance, and use *further* to indicate that intangible progress has been made:

> I don't intend to pursue this matter any **further**.

> Forrest Gump ran **farther** than any other man had ever run.

Fewer vs. Less

The use of either of these words depends on whether the nouns in the sentence are countable. If the nouns are countable (such as books, people, or kneecaps), use *fewer*:

> There are **fewer** people in the state of South Dakota than there are in New York City.

If you have an uncountable quantity (such as time, soup, or money), use *less*:

> When my wife had our first child, we found that we have a lot **less** time to ourselves.

All together, now:

> There is a lot **less** traffic during rush hour now, because **fewer** people drive their cars to work.

Note: The only time that *less* is involved with countable objects is when fractions, percents, or other numbers are involved. (It's an arcane rule and it doesn't come up on the GMAT very often, but it might if you get a really hard question.)

> **Less** than one-quarter of all high school students can find Argentina on a map.

> The production of East Timor amounts to **less** than 1 percent of the world's GDP.

Note the distinction between these two sentences:

> There are **fewer** than 1,000 species of frog left in the Amazon river basin.

> The number of species of frog left in the Amazon river basin is **less** than 1,000.

Its vs. It's

Never confuse these two, because their meanings are very different. *Its* is the possessive of *it*, and *it's* is the contracted form of *it is*:

> **It's** never too late to learn to play the piano.

> The baby elephant never strayed far from **its** mother.

Note: Words that sound the same but have different meanings are called homonyms. The most common examples of homonyms that are frequently confused are *your* vs. *you're* and *their* vs. *they're*. You won't have to distinguish these on Sentence Correction questions, but you'll lose your readers' respect if you mess them up on your essays.

> **Your** mother said that **you're** expected to be home by 7:30.

> **They're** too far away to hear what **their** mother wants.

Lie vs. Lay

One meaning of the word *lie* is straightforward; it means to say something that is false:

> The witness should never **lie** to the jury.

> The judge believed that Wu **lied** under oath.

The confusion arises when you consider the other meaning of *lie*, which is to recline. *Lay*, on the other hand, means to put something down. The confusion occurs because the past tense of *lie* is *lay*:

> **Present tense:** After church, my dad usually **lies** down on the couch.

> **Past tense:** After church, my dad **lay** down on the couch.

Many vs. Much

The rule here is just like the rule for fewer vs. less. If the nouns that are being compared are countable, use *many*; otherwise, use *much*:

> There is too **much** traffic on this highway because too **many** people drive to work.

More vs. Most

The rules for these words are just like those that pertain to *-er* vs. *-est*. *More* and *most* are just irregular forms of comparative words; use *more* for two items, and use *most* for three-plus items:

> Nicole has **more** stock options than Heather does.

> Of all the companies in the Fortune 500, Microsoft is worth the **most** money.

The same rule holds true for each of these adjectives that have irregular forms when used as comparative or superlatives:

Adjective	Comparative	Superlative
bad	worse	worst
good	better	best
little	less	least
far	farther, further	farthest, furthest

Note: There are also several words that have no comparative or superlative form, because the simple form of that word expresses the point to the highest possible degree. For example, it's impossible for something to be more unique than something else. Either it's unique (which means there's nothing else like it), or it's not. Words like this include perfect, fatal, empty, wrong, dead, blind, alone, and pregnant.

That vs. Which

You're not likely to be forced to make this distinction on the GMAT. If something is wrong with an answer choice, there will probably be a much more egregious flaw other than it used *that* instead of *which*. The rule is: *Which* refers to a group as a whole, and *that* refers to a specific subset of a group.

> Bananas, **which** are high in potassium, are considered an ideal food for dieting.

> The bananas **that** I left in the refrigerator have gone bad.

Also, the pronoun *which* always refers to the most recent noun in the sentence (usually the one right before the comma):

> **Wrong:** I bought a car and a dress, which had only 3,000 miles on it.

> **Right:** I bought a dress and a car, which had only 3,000 miles on it.

Who vs. Whom

> Lou: So I pick up the ball, and I throw it to who?

> Bud: Now that's the first thing you've said right.

> Lou: I don't even know what I'm talking about!

Lou was right; he doesn't know what he's talking about. You don't throw to *who*, you throw to *whom*!

Lots of people are unsure about when to use *who* or *whom*, but it's really very simple. *Who* is a subject pronoun that indicates that you don't know the person committing the action:

> **Who** left this empty milk carton in the refrigerator?

Whom is an object pronoun that receives action:

> To **whom** am I speaking?

Note that *whom* usually comes right after a preposition (*to* whom, *at* whom, etc.). The simplest way to remember which pronoun to use is this:

> If you answer the question with *he*, use *who*. If you answer the question with *him*, use *whom*.

Let's answer those two questions above as an example:

> Q: **Who** left this empty milk carton in the refrigerator?

> A: **He** did.

Q: To **whom** am I speaking?

A: You're speaking to **him**.

Get it? If you stick to that rule, you can't go wrong.

Lastly, here's a list of famous people whose names are complete sentences. Try to think of as many more of these as you can the next time you're having trouble sleeping.

Frank Burns

James Caan (if said with a British accent)

Cher (using the imperative tense)

Fred Couples

Norman Fell

Henry VIII (if pronounced "Henry ate")

Don Knotts

Lee Majors

Karl Marx (or any of the Marx Brothers)

Elaine May

Rosa Parks

Charlie Rose

Sting (see Cher)

Don Was

Natalie Wood

George Wendt

APPENDIX II
GRAMMAR GLOSSARY

Below are several grammar terms that you might come across either in this book or while on some other grammatical pursuit. This is by no means an exhaustive list, but it's all you need to know for the GMAT (and then some). Don't spend a lot of time memorizing these, because you won't be tested on the terms themselves on the GMAT. They will be helpful to know as you study, though.

active voice	A verb that represents the subject performing an action. In general, the active voice is usually better than the passive voice. (Example: The girl threw the Frisbee.)
adjective	A word used to modify (or describe) a noun or pronoun.
adverb	A word usually used to modify a verb, but also to modify an adjective or another adverb.
antecedent	The noun to which a pronoun refers.
apples to oranges	A term (related to parallel construction) that relates to the importance of comparing unlike things (nouns to verbs). Comparing like things would be apples to apples (noun to nouns).
appositive	A word or group of words (set apart by commas) that modifies another word or group of words.
article	The words *a*, *an*, and *the*. *A* and *an* are indefinite articles, and *the* is the definite article.
collective noun	The name given to a group or collection of objects.
complex sentence	A sentence that consists of one independent clause and one dependent clause.
compound sentence	A sentence that consists of two or more independent clauses.

conjugation	The systematic arrangement of all the forms of a verb.
conjunction	A word used to join other words or groups of words, such as *and, but,* and *so.*
dependent clause	A group of words that has a subject and verb but is not a complete sentence. It needs to be attached to an independent clause to be part of a sentence. (Also known as a *subordinate clause.*)
direct object	The noun in a sentence that receives the action.
future perfect tense	The verb tense that denotes action that will be completed at some definite time in the future. (Example: By the year 3000, the Red Sox *will have won* the World Series many times.)
future tense	The verb tense that denotes future time. (Example: The Red Sox *will win* the World Series next year.)
gerund	The result of adding *-ing* to a verb, thus creating a term used as a noun. (Example: *Winning* the World Series would be a great thing for the Red Sox to do.)
imperative	The verb tense that expresses a demand. This form doesn't include a subject because it's understood that the comment is directed at the person spoken to. (Example: Clean up your room!)
independent clause	A group of words that expresses a complete thought and thus can exist as a simple sentence.
indirect object	The object for which something else is done. (Example: Carlos gave the book to *me*. *Book* is the direct object, and *me* is the indirect object.)
infinitive tense	The verb form in which the verb is preceded by the preposition *to*. (Example: I want *to win* the Publisher's Clearinghouse Sweepstakes.)
interjection	An expression that shows excitement or emotion, usually set apart from a sentence by an exclamation point (or by a comma when the feeling is not as strong). (Example: Hey! I saw that on *Schoolhouse Rock*!)
misplaced modifier	A modifying word or phrase that is in the wrong place in a sentence and thus seems to modify the wrong word.
modifier	A word or group of words that limits or qualifies the meaning of another word.

noun	A person, place, or thing.
participle	A verb form that is used as an adjective. (Example: This book is *exciting*.)
parts of speech	Words that are classified depending on what they do in a sentence (nouns, verbs, adjectives, etc.)
passive voice	A verb that represents the subject receiving an action. In general, the active voice is usually better than the passive voice. (Example: The Frisbee was thrown by the girl.)
past perfect tense	The verb tense used to convey the thought that two events happened in the past and one happened before the other. Verbs are usually accompanied by *had*. (Example: Apes *had conquered* the world when the Red Sox finally won a World Series.)
past tense	The verb tense that denotes an event that happened before right now.
person	A reference to the speaker in a sentence. The first person is the person speaking (I); the second person is the person spoken to (you); and the third person is the person spoken of (he, she, it).
phrase	A group of words that lacks either a noun or a verb (and thus is not a clause nor a sentence).
possessive	The case that shows ownership, usually denoted by *'s* at the end of a noun.
preposition	A word that shows the relation between its object and some other word in the sentence. Many idiom questions involve using the proper preposition. (Example: Scholars attribute many clever quotations *to* Winston Churchill. *To* is the proper preposition.)
prepositional phrase	A modifying phrase containing a preposition and an object. (Example: The Red Sox ran *on the field*. The prepositional phrase *on the field* describes where the Red Sox ran; *on* is the preposition; and *field* is the object of the preposition.)
present perfect tense	The verb tense used to convey action that is completed before the sentence was said. Verbs are usually accompanied by *has* or *have*. (Example: This cable channel *has shown* the same awful movie fifteen times this week.)
present tense	The verb tense that denotes what is happening right now.

pronoun	A word used in place of a noun for the sake of brevity.
proper noun	A noun (like a name) that designates a particular person, place, or thing and is usually capitalized.
run-on sentence	A sentence in which two independent clauses are linked together without the use of a conjunction or semicolon between them. (Example: The candidate won the election, the students went crazy celebrating on campus.)
simple sentence	A group of words that expresses a complete thought and follows all the rules of sentence construction.
split infinitive	An improper verb usage in which the infinitive form is interrupted by another word. (Example: The female astronaut wanted *to* boldly *go* where no woman had gone before.)
subject	The part of a sentence that drives the action.
subjunctive mood	A verb tense used to express: (1) hypothetical situations that are contrary to fact (If the Red Sox *were* to win the World Series, Boston would burn down); and (2) wishes and demands (Tyrone demanded *that* the Red Sox *win* the World Series before he died).
subordinate clause	A clause (also known as a *dependent clause*) that cannot serve as a sentence all by itself and needs to be linked to a main clause (or *independent clause*).
superlative degree	A term used when more than two items are compared. This is usually denoted by the suffix *-est* after an adjective. (Example: Rosa scored the *highest* on the GMAT of anyone in her class because she did all of the practice questions and drills in the book.)
verb	A term that denotes the action in a sentence.

APPENDIX III
IDIOM LIST

Here's a list of some of the idioms that have appeared in Sentence Correction questions that have appeared on actual GMATs in recent years. Of course, this is not an exhaustive list of all the idioms you'll have to know; that's why there are a few empty sheets at the end of this list. Whenever you encounter an idiom that you've never seen before, add it to this list and memorize it.

A

able to, ability to

I am no longer able to run ten miles as fast as I used to.

Sloths have the ability to sleep while hanging from their toes.

accede to

Once defeated, the military dictator had to accede to NATO's demands.

access to

After the home team lost, reporters were not given access to the coach's office.

according to

According to the etiquette expert, it is very rude to stick out your pinkie as you drink tea.

account for

The Brazilian rain forest accounts for 40 percent of all species of tree frog.

accuse of

I accused my little brother of stealing my favorite football jersey.

acquaint with

When I moved to London, I had to acquaint myself with English social customs.

agree with

I don't agree with your viewpoint.

allow for

> When you budget your money, you should allow for emergency expenses.

amount to

> When the trial was canceled, all the lawyer's preparation amounted to nothing.

appear to

> The natives of this island don't appear to be very friendly.

apply to

> Traffic laws don't apply to international diplomats.

argue over

> The newly married couple didn't argue over money very often.

as [adjective] as

> Your cat isn't as friendly as my cat.

associate with

> My mommy told me never to associate with people I don't know.

assure that

> I assure you that my sister is the ideal person for this job.

at a disadvantage

> Our desperate financial situation put us at a disadvantage while we were negotiating.

attempt to

> I will attempt to write my b-school essays after I finish dinner.

attend to, attention to

> New parents must attend to their child's cries.

> The book editor was known for her attention to detail.

attest to

> I can attest to the fact that John has never been to Indonesia.

attribute to

> Many clever quotes are attributed to Oscar Wilde.

available to

> Before you make a decision, be sure you know all the options that are available to you.

B

based on

> The award-winning movie was based on a book that virtually no one read.

because of

> Because of her broken leg, she was unable to ski for two months.

believe to be

> These artifacts are believed to be remnants of the Ming dynasty.

between [A] and [B]

> There are fourteen rest stops on the highway between Baltimore and Washington, D.C.

C

call for

> Desperate times call for desperate measures.

choice of

> Given the choice of liver or ice cream, I would select the latter.

choose from [nouns]

> B-school candidates can choose from hundreds of accredited programs.

choose to [verb]

> Many people choose to attend business school after they have worked for only two years.

claim to

> My uncle claims to have eaten 200 hot dogs in half an hour.

collaborate with

> The actor collaborated with two ghost writers on his autobiography.

conclude that

> After years of research, the scientist concluded that baked beans do not cause baldness.

consequence of

> Bankruptcy is usually a consequence of poor money management.

consider

> Dr. Melnitz is considered the world's foremost authority on medieval manuscripts.

Note: Although ETS doesn't like you to use *consider to be*, it's perfectly fine to use it in ordinary English. This is just one of the ways in which ETS English differs from normal English.

consist of

> The heart consists of four chambers that pump blood throughout the body.

consistent with

> Her new findings are consistent with contemporary theories.

continue to

> If you continue to make noise back there, I'll turn this car around and we'll go home.

contrast with

> His low-key speaking style contrasted with his partner's more passionate oratory.

contribute to

> Would you care to contribute your time to the church's tutoring program?

convert to

> The alchemist Rumpelstiltskin can convert lead to gold.

cost of [something]

> The cost of sending your child to college has tripled in the last decade.

cost to [someone]

> After the war, the cost to the surviving inhabitants of the small village was devastating.

credit with

> Dr. Jonas Salk is credited with the discovery of the polio vaccine.

D

date from

> This ancient parchment dates from the Revolutionary War.

deal with

> I'll deal with that problem later.

debate over

> My parents always debate over which movie the family will see.

decide to (*not* decide on)

> After a lot of deep thought, Latisha decided to take the job offer in Moscow.

defend against

> The small startup defended itself against the hostile takeover.

define as

> Perjury is defined as the act of lying while under oath.

delighted by

> The woman was delighted by her daughter's impending solo flight.

demonstrate that

> This evidence will demonstrate that dogs can do algebra.

depend on

> Whether I go to the ball game depends on the weather.

depict as

> In recent textbooks, Columbus has been depicted as a genocidal maniac.

descend from

> On the Fourth of July, lots of firecrackers descend from the sky.

different from

> The customs of the countries of the Far East are different from ours.

difficult to

> It is difficult to determine whether mice can sing to each other.

distinguish [A] from [B]

> Can you distinguish indigo from violet?

draw on

> Surgeons draw on years of experience when they try new procedures.

due to

> The company's shortfall was due to lessening global demand for its products.

E

[in an] effort to

> In an effort to end the war, the general called for a cease-fire.

either . . . or

> I will either read the paper or go to the movies.

enamored with

> When my family met my new girlfriend, everyone was enamored with her.

encourage to

> Recent college graduates are encouraged to work for five years before applying to business school.

-er than

> My biceps are stronger than your biceps.

estimate to be

> The estate of Count von Hammerbanger is estimated to be in the billions.

expose to

Parents are worried that television exposed their children to too much violence.

extend to

I extended my arm to the dog and let it lick my palm.

extent of

No one knows the extent of the queen's fortune.

F

fear that

I fear that robots will take over the world in 2013.

fluctuations in

There have been many fluctuations in the new company's growth pattern.

forbid to (not forbid from)

Native South Koreans are forbidden to attend gambling casinos within Korea.

force to

My parents forced me to attend military school, even though I didn't want to go.

frequency of

The frequency of electrical fires on the subway is truly alarming.

from [A] to [B]

Every house from Allentown to Bethlehem lost power during the blackout.

H

hypothesize that

Some nutritionists hypothesize that too many dairy products can cause cancer.

I

in contrast to

In contrast to my opponent, I believe that town funds should be used to build a new library.

in danger of

People who ignore speed limits put themselves in danger of causing an accident.

in order to

> You have to break a few eggs in order to make an omelet.

in violation of

> By mistreating the prisoners, the general was in violation of the rules laid out by the Geneva Convention.

inclined to (also **disinclined to**)

> Young children who watch television are inclined to become very lazy adults.

infected with

> People who are infected with the Ebola virus must be isolated from other patients.

instead of

> Today I will eat a salad instead of my usual meal of meat and potatoes.

introduce to

> My mother almost fainted when she was introduced to Frank Sinatra.

isolate from

> People who are infected with the Ebola virus must be isolated from other patients.

J

just as . . . so too

> Just as I have crossed over to the Dark Side, so too will you, my son.

L

less than

> On average, college students have less money than their parents.

likely to (also **unlikely to**)

> Whenever I eat Brussels sprouts, I'm likely to throw up.

liken to

> The clerk likened the man's complaining to the barking of a small dog.

M

mistake for

> My brother is often mistaken for Robin Williams.

model after

> The Rotunda at the University of Virginia is modeled after the Pantheon in Rome.

more than

> The Chinese eat more rice than any other people do.

move away from

> The police officer told the intruder to move away from the door.

N

[a] native of

> The famous opera singer is a native of Italy.

native to

> Koala bears are native to Australia.

neither . . . nor

> Neither rain nor sleet shall keep me from the swift completion of my appointed rounds.

not [A] but [B]

> The opposite of love is not hate but indifference.

not only . . . but also

> My sister is not only brilliant but also quite charming.

not so much . . . as

> The reason for the soaring stock market is not so much ignorance as it is optimism.

O

on account of

> On account of the brutal winter, the farmer's corn production suffered greatly.

opportunity for [noun]

> Before I take this job, what is my opportunity for advancement?

opportunity to [verb]

> I'd like to take this opportunity to thank all the little people who made this award possible.

opposed to

> Pacifists are opposed to any form of fighting or aggression.

opposite of

> The opposite of love is not hate but indifference.

P

permit to

> Children are not permitted to attend an R-rated movie without their parents.

persuade to

> I finally persuaded my parents to let me attend the rock concert.

predisposed to

> Baby turtles are predisposed to fend for themselves early in life.

pressure to

> The United Nations was pressured to impose sanctions on the country.

prevent from

> Safety latches prevent small children from playing with cleaning products.

prized by

> Rhinoceros horn is prized by some cultures as a potent aphrodisiac.

prohibit from

> In New York City, smokers are prohibited from smoking inside any public building.

protect against

> Chemical treatment can help protect your car against rust and corrosion.

provide with

> The technical college provides each new student with a brand-new computer.

Q

question whether

> I'm beginning to question whether Saltines have any nutritional value.

R

range from [A] to [B]

> Scores on the GMAT range from 200 to 600.

rather than

> I'd rather swim in the ocean than sit on the beach.

regard as

> In Asian cities, waving crazily for a taxicab is regarded as a rude gesture.

replace with

The five-star restaurant replaced its homemade desserts with frozen ones.

require to

Grandma always requires us to remove our shoes before we come in the house.

required of

What exactly is required of the applicants for this job?

[the] responsibility to

I have the responsibility to care for my dog.

responsible for

I am responsible for my dog's welfare.

result from

Success usually results from hard work.

result in

Hard work usually results in success.

rule that (subjunctive)

The principal has ruled that all students can call her by her first name, Maria.

S

[the] same as

Your hat is the same as mine.

see as

The dictator saw the uprising as a threat to his authority.

send to

I sent a birthday card to my grandmother.

sense of

Dogs have an acute sense of smell.

so [adjective] as to [verb]

Her debts are so extreme as to threaten the future of the company.

so . . . that

His debts are so extreme that the company may soon go bankrupt.

spend on

I spend more than $10,000 a year on eating out.

subject to

Members of Congress are subject to the same laws as are ordinary Americans.

substitute [A] for [B]

In an effort to lower my cholesterol, I substituted margarine for butter in my diet.

suffer from

I suffer from the heartbreak of psoriasis.

superior to

My grandfather's spaghetti sauce is superior to that store-bought brand.

supplant by

After the massive cutbacks at the plant, my uncle was supplanted by a large robot.

suspicious of

I'm suspicious of people who don't shake hands firmly.

T

target at

The shoe company targeted its advertising at high school-age kids.

the -er . . . , the -er

The bigger they are, the harder they fall.

think of . . . as

I've grown to think of my best friend as the brother I never had.

threaten to

After ten hours of negotiations, both parties threatened to walk out of the room.

train to

I trained my puppy to bring me the newspaper every morning.

transmit to

The submarine transmitted the coded message to all the ships in the area.

try to (*not* try and)

If you try to hold your breath for more than a minute, your face will turn blue.

type of

This is the type of situation that I usually try to avoid.

U

use as

> My wife hates it when I use the lamp as a hat stand.

[the] use of

> The use of nuclear weapons in World War II was condemned by many nations.

V

view as

> The dictator viewed the uprising as a threat to his authority.

vote for

> Rather than vote for the Democrat or Republican, I voted for the Libertarian.

W

[the] way to [verb] is to [verb]

> The way to deal with my father-in-law is to nod enthusiastically at everything he says.

willing to (also **unwilling to**)

> Most teachers are willing to meet with their students after school and give extra help.

worry about

> Economists worry too much about America's trade deficit.

ABOUT THE AUTHOR

Doug French has been a GMAT instructor and course developer with The Princeton Review since 1992, and he has been training GMAT instructors since 1995. He has taught classes for the GMAT, SAT, LSAT, and GRE in the U.S., Europe, and Asia, and he can teach you any math topic from simple addition to BC calculus.

Doug also writes, draws cartoons, and does voice-overs. He and his wife live in New York City, which is known to be the best city in the world (except during the summer, when it becomes really pungent).

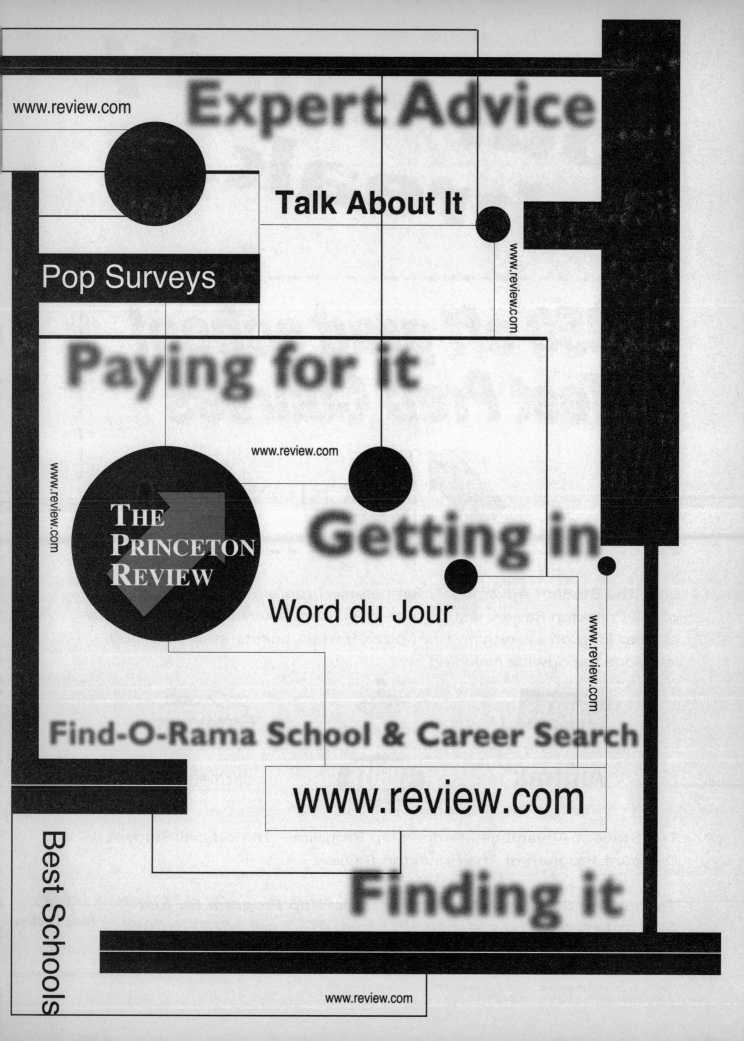

FIND US...

International

Hong Kong
4/F Sun Hung Kai Centre
30 Harbour Road, Wan Chai,
Hong Kong
Tel: (011)85-2-517-3016

Japan
Fuji Building 40, 15-14
Sakuragaokacho, Shibuya Ku,
Tokyo 150, Japan
Tel: (011)81-3-3463-1343

Korea
Tae Young Bldg, 944-24,
Daechi- Dong, Kangnam-Ku
The Princeton Review- ANC
Seoul, Korea 135-280,
South Korea
Tel: (011)82-2-554-7763

Mexico City
PR Mex S De RL De Cv
Guanajuato 228 Col. Roma
06700 Mexico D.F., Mexico
Tel: 525-564-9468

Montreal
666 Sherbrooke St.
West, Suite 202
Montreal, QC H3A 1E7 Canada
Tel: (514) 499-0870

Pakistan
1 Bawa Park - 90 Upper Mall
Lahore, Pakistan
Tel: (011)92-42-571-2315

Spain
Pza. Castilla, 3 - 5° A, 28046
Madrid, Spain
Tel: (011)341-323-4212

Taiwan
155 Chung Hsiao East Road
Section 4 - 4th Floor,
Taipei R.O.C., Taiwan
Tel: (011)886-2-751-1243

Thailand
Building One, 99 Wireless Road
Bangkok, Thailand 10330
Tel: (662) 256-7080

Toronto
1240 Bay Street, Suite 300
Toronto M5R 2A7 Canada
Tel: (800) 495-7737
Tel: (716) 839-4391

Vancouver
4212 University Way NE,
Suite 204
Seattle, WA 98105
Tel: (206) 548-1100

locations

National (U.S.)
We have over 60 offices around the U.S. and
run courses in over 400 sites. For courses and locations
within the U.S. call 1 (800) 2/Review and you will be
routed to the nearest office.